EMERGING CRIMINAL JUSTICE

Books Under the General Editorship of
DANIEL CURRAN

CRIME AS STRUCTURED ACTION
by James W. Messerschmidt

EMERGING CRIMINAL JUSTICE:
Three Pillars for a Proactive Justice System
by Paul H. Hahn

CRIME CONTROL AND WOMEN:
Implications of Criminal Justice Policy
edited by Susan L. Miller

PAUL H. HAHN

EMERGING CRIMINAL JUSTICE

Three Pillars for a Proactive Justice System

SAGE Publications
International Educational and Professional Publisher
Thousand Oaks London New Delhi

For information:

SAGE Publications, Inc.
2455 Teller Road
Thousand Oaks, California 91320
E-mail: order@sagepub.com

SAGE Publications Ltd.
6 Bonhill Street
London EC2A 4PU
United Kingdom

SAGE Publications India Pvt. Ltd.
M-32 Market
Greater Kailash I
New Delhi 110 048 India

Printed in the United States of America

Library of Congress Cataloging-in-Publication Data

Hahn, Paul H.
Emerging criminal justice: Three pillars for a proactive justice system / by Paul H. Hahn.
p. cm.
Includes bibliographical references and index.
ISBN 0-7619-1283-5 (pbk.: acid-free paper).
ISBN 0-7619-1282-7 (cloth: acid-free paper)
1. Criminal justice, Administration of—United States. 2. Crime prevention—United States. 3. Community policing—United States. 4. Community-based corrections—United States. 5. Reparation—United States. I. Title.
HV9950.H33 1997
364.973—dc21 97-21187

This book is printed on acid-free paper.

98 99 00 01 02 03 10 9 8 7 6 5 4 3 2 1

Acquiring Editor: C. Terry Hendrix
Editorial Assistant: Dale Mary Grenfell
Production Editor: Sherrise M. Purdum
Typesetter/Designer: Janelle LeMaster
Indexer: Teri Greenberg
Cover Designer: Candice Harman
Print Buyer: Anna Chin

Contents

Foreword

Professor Paul Hahn reveals in this book evidence of a most unusual background. From the point of view of those who work in the criminal justice field, he knows what it is like to be "on the line," facing every day the problems of working with both youthful and adult offenders. Yet as founder and chairman of the Department of Criminal Justice at Xavier University, his knowledge of so many aspects of juvenile and criminal justice has resulted in his being an author, lecturer, and consultant in many states. He has testified before committees of both the U.S. House and Senate.

In contrast to many politicians—and, sad to say, too many desk-bound academicians—Hahn has always resisted "knee-jerk, quick-fix" solutions to criminal justice planning. Well aware of the need for public safety, he focuses "the cool light of reason" on crime in our country.

In fact, this author has always been in the forefront of criminology. He was director of the first work therapy program for juveniles; he established one of the first halfway houses for offenders; he did away with brutal treatment of young adult males in a state mental hospital; he authored one of the very first textbooks on police work with juvenile offenders. He has been an innovative trainer of staff in jails, prisons, and police academies.

Paul Hahn has been recognized for his work by a variety of organizations. To name only a few: The American Correctional Association gave him their highest award for research. The International Association of Correctional Officers gave him their President's Award. Northern Michigan University recognized him as a Distinguished Fellow in Corrections. He was elected

Chairman of the Curriculum Development Committee for the National Institute of Corrections.

Hence, the reader can look forward to a book that proposes a new conceptual framework of "proactivity" in dealing with crime. Community policing, community-based corrections, and restorative justice are looked at in a fresh light. Hahn emphasizes that no criminal justice system can work without citizen cooperation. Though our Constitution emphasizes the "pursuit of happiness," Hahn balances individualism with a community's right to "feel safe."

True safety from crime cannot rest on physical restraint and surveillance alone. The most effective crime control is possible only when individuals and groups realize that law-abiding behavior "works for them" in their life experiences.

Paul Hahn loves and respects all kinds of people. At Xavier, his students came first; he never missed a class. In the corrections field, he always saw the potential in even the worst "losers." This book makes the point that all of us need to play our parts. The "status quo" has clearly not worked in reducing crime in our country.

—*O. J. Keller*
U.S. Parole Commissioner (Ret.)
Former President, American Correctional Association

Preface

Charles Dickens's description of the period of the French Revolution as "the best of times and the worst of times" could easily be applied to today's criminal justice scene. On the dark side, we see a nation embroiled in unsuccessful "wars" on crime and drugs and in many ways on the verge of going to war with its high-risk children by turning juvenile courts into vestibules for the adult court system, building prisons for children not yet born, and tolerating such a high percentage of children living in social, economic, and emotional poverty that population for the future prisons is almost guaranteed. As one police official told us recently, in our criminal justice system, we continue to "swat the mosquitoes and ignore the swamp" with its fetid waters of worsening health, educational, economic, housing, and related conditions. We may need to do some "swatting" for our immediate protection, but if we ignore the source, it will continue to produce more problems faster than any suppression effort can ever control.

Perhaps even more frightening is the frequently heard term *prison industrial complex,* now used to describe the multi-billion-dollar prison-building, furnishing, and maintaining industry. Whereas formerly we waged a "Cold War" during which our greatest growth industry was the building of missiles, now we wage a "war on crime," and our greatest growth industry is the building of prisons.

The overreliance on secure incarceration in our criminal justice planning is only part of an overall approach to crime-control that is purely reactive. This is evident in the neglect of prevention in the early lives and school experience of children, the primary commitment of many police departments only to rapid response and sophisticated crime-solving methods after commission of offenses, probation caseloads so high that offenders need to commit violations to get the attention of workers, and a general level of trust in the effectiveness of deterrence despite high recidivism rates and failure to curb drug usage. Despite the most severe penalties and active enforcement efforts, the subcultures in which crime and delinquency thrive tend to be very resistant, if not impervious, to all the reactive efforts of the criminal justice system.

On the bright side, in the past few years, it has been increasingly recognized that traditional criminal justice agencies alone cannot adequately deal with crime and that the solution ultimately must be found in cooperation with the communities in which the crime is spawned. The movement toward greater use of community-based corrections facilities, application of the "broken windows theory" to halt neighborhood deterioration, community policing, development of concepts of restorative justice, and development of intermediate sanctions and many other program options at both the juvenile and the adult level provide real rays of hope in a scene that would otherwise be bleak.

While politicians win votes by appearing to be "tough on crime" and engaging in inflammatory rhetoric that fuels fear and hatred in the public, many courageous, hard-working, very enlightened professionals, writers, and activists continue to support every movement toward a more proactive system and to encourage a rational debate about what really works in crime control.

In this book, I engage my readers in this debate by presenting suggestions for expanded notions of community policing, community corrections, and restorative justice—the three pillars of a new, proactive criminal justice system. This book certainly does not propose "being soft on crime." But it does propose that we emphasize prevention of crime in its early stages; that we use all sorts of alternative facilities that are as little restrictive as possible, in keeping with community safety; and that we rely on secure incarceration only as a last resort at the end of the criminal justice process.

This book proposes that we consider carefully the existence of the "chain of causality" in the lives of those who become involved in crime. It shows the chain of causality leading to inner-city juvenile violence and suggests that this problem presents opportunities for intervention at any number of points in the lives of the young people who commit these crimes.

Above all, this book urges that we look at the entire criminal justice system as a whole rather than continuing to use "Band-Aids" when "major surgery" is needed. This "major surgery" would be nothing less than the replacement of our traditional criminal justice approach with a whole new paradigm for understanding the system and most of its elements. I argue that community policing requires a whole new mind-set in entire departments and individual officers; that community-based corrections should be understood in an entirely new way as far more than a simple aggregation of halfway houses and other alternative programs; and that restorative justice should be understood as an approach that can promote community safety more than retributive justice, but that demands a high degree of community involvement and has community healing as its most primary goal.

Not only is proactive criminal justice possible, but the necessary conceptual framework and individual program elements are already in place in many locations throughout the country. The need for change is clearly present, the expertise is certainly available, and the base of experience and its evaluation exist in much more than pilot project form. Now all that is necessary is the will to move forward.

As I have said in many places during the several decades of my professional career, we need to focus the cool light of reason on criminal justice planning and be guided by it rather than by the heat of emotion or the darkness of fear, vested interest, and political expediency. To this end this book is dedicated.

Special Acknowledgment

To Mrs. Peg Hubbard, without whose considerable talents and devoted service the thoughts of the author would never have been effectively transposed to the printed page.

Acknowledgments

I wish to thoroughly acknowledge the contributions to the knowledge base in criminal justice of several scholars and professionals whose work is so extensive, accurate, and, in most cases, pioneering that I have relied heavily on it in the sections of this book that deal with their areas of expertise.

The compilation of the most significant research on violence in our society in *Understanding and Preventing Violence* by the National Research Council (1993) provides the structure of Chapter 2 of this book and much of the substantive material in the section entitled "The National Research Council's Matrix of Risk Factors." In the same chapter, the insights of Alfred Blumstein, Elijah Anderson, and numerous others have enhanced my understanding and vivified my expression of many concepts.

In Chapter 3, the historical presentation of the three eras of policing in America is completely attributable to George L. Kelling and Mark H. Moore's report entitled *The Evolving Strategy of Policing* (1988). Likewise, Dennis P. Rosenbaum's *The Challenge of Community Policing* (Sage Publications, 1994) has organized so much of the existing material from so many excellent sources that I have drawn on it extensively for both organization of concepts and substantive material. Finally, throughout the discussion of community policing, the insights of Herman Goldstein and of Robert Trojanowicz and his colleagues at the National Center for Community Policing in Lansing, Michigan, frequently appear because it is impossible to treat this subject adequately without heavy reliance on their voluminous and important work.

In Chapter 4, O'Leary and Duffee's classification of correctional models and their exposition of the reintegration approach, along with the excellent work of Todd Clear on community-based corrections, provide the basis for much of the discussion of these topics. The section "The Use of Authority in Community-Based Corrections" is based on many discussions between myself and John Pettibone, former director of probation services in both Ohio and Maryland during the 1960s and 1970s. The principles, assumptions, and goals outlined in the section "Probation and Parole" should be understood to represent the combined thinking of myself and numerous other practitioners, observers, authors, and lecturers.

In Chapter 5, the pioneering work of Gordon Bazemore, Mark Umbreit, Kay Pranis, Judge Barry Stuart, and others on restorative justice provides the foundation for and, in many cases, much of the substantive content of the chapter and has had enormous influence on my thinking. And in the Epilogue, the contributions of Francis Cullen, Bo Lozoff, and Howard Zehr have also been very helpful.

Finally, it must be acknowledged that the diligence, professionality, and hard work of the copy editor, Elizabeth Magnus, has strengthened this text and contributed to its readability.

PART I

THE NEED FOR A PROACTIVE CRIMINAL JUSTICE SYSTEM

1

Emerging Criminal Justice: Tradition and Reaction Are Not Sufficient

THE "GET TOUGH" POLICY: HOW DID IT HAPPEN, AND WHAT IS THE COST?

The United States is demonstrably the most powerful and wealthiest country in the world. Its riches and might exceed anything that any nation has ever possessed. The same technology that made this world leadership possible has also provided the citizens of this country with a standard of living that makes all of the fabled civilizations of recorded history pale into insignificance. Former rulers of the world, renowned in the annals of history, never experienced even a fraction of the comfort and convenience enjoyed by millions in America today.

Ironically, at the same time that these records are being set, our nation is setting other records of a much less enviable type. Among the most unfortunate of these is that we currently incarcerate a higher percentage of our citizens than any free society and that, in 1995, we executed the largest number of prisoners in 38 years. The setting of these records is the logical result of an overall approach to crime control that is reactive, committed almost entirely to "after-the-fact" solutions and devoid of any proactive approaches in its principal elements.

Commitment to this reactive orientation is visible in the toughening of sentencing in the courts, the hardening of conditions of confinement in the prisons, and the reliance on rapid response rather than problem solving techniques in policing. It is to a great extent based on a trust in deterrence as a principal means of crime control, even though there is little empirical evidence to support this belief.

In the current politically supported "get tough" posture, state legislatures and the U.S. Congress have all rushed to frame legislation providing for more deterrence through mandated longer sentences and fewer opportunities for parole and other means of time reduction. However, this has had little effect on crime rates in general or on violent crime. In 1993, the National Research Council's Panel on Understanding and Control of Violent Behavior (1993) observed that the average prison time for violent crime had tripled between 1975 and 1989, with little apparent effect on the levels of commission of such offenses.

Previously, in 1978, the National Academy of Sciences' Panel on Research on Deterrent and Incapacitative Effects had concluded that they could not find any strong support for the deterrence hypothesis (Blumstein, 1978). The same lack of supportive evidence in the empirical research exists regarding harsh conditions of confinement and police rapid response as effective deterrents to crime. In general, the major ingredients of the "get tough" policy have failed to produce the desired results of crime reduction.

What has resulted from over two decades of "get tough" policies is, among other negative effects, horrendous overcrowding of secure institutions at a level unimaginable just a few short years ago in this country. In just the past 10 years, the prison population has doubled from slightly over one-half million in 1985 to well over 1 million in mid-1994. The average annual growth in the prison population since 1985 has been 8.4%. The Federal Bureau of Prisons operated 26% over capacity in 1995, and state prison systems reported operating between 14% and 25% above capacity. At the same time, secure incarceration of juveniles increased by 17% (Bureau of Justice Statistics, 1996). This "body crunch" has had a serious impact on public policy and planning. The above statistics indicate that officials had to find 1,618 new beds for prisoners in secure institutions every week since 1985 (Bureau of Justice Statistics, 1996).

The Cost of the "Body Crunch" in Corrections

The cost to the individual states for this "lock-'em-up" approach to crime control is staggering. For example, as a result of the 1995 Sentencing Reform Act alone, New York State must create more than 10,000 new prison beds, at a total cost of nearly $2.5 billion, by the year 2005 (Abate, 1996). As the push for more severe sentencing continues, the cost escalation also increases. If Governor Pataki's proposed 1996 sentencing reforms for first-time violent felonies and assaults are enacted, New York State must create more than 13,000 prison beds, at a total cost of over $3.5 billion by the year 2005 (Abate, 1996).

Such steep increases in corrections spending are reported to be the major negative influences on state fiscal conditions that otherwise are reported to be the most positive in many years. General fund collections have increased; the states' "rainy day" and general fund balances are encouraging; and nine states have adopted significant tax cuts, with only three small states increasing taxes. However, in both spending and appropriations, corrections has increased alarmingly. For example, in 1995, whereas the projected budget increase for corrections in 34 states was 7.1%, the actual increase was 11.1%. This actual increase outpaced even the rapid increases in Medicaid, which amounted to 10% (National Conference of State Legislatures, cited in Proband, 1995, p. 4). The percentage change in appropriations for fiscal year 1995 to fiscal year 1996 reflected an increase in the cost of corrections (operations) of 13.3%, whereas the percentage increase for Medicaid (excluding Louisiana) was only 7.2% and for all of higher education was only 5.1% (National Conference of State Legislatures, cited in Proband, 1995, p. 4).

Some states were staggering under the burden of enormous increases in appropriations for corrections. For example, Florida showed a 50.2% rate of increase in appropriations for corrections, and even a state such as Montana that has traditionally had a low incarceration rate ranked second on the list of highest increases in corrections appropriations with a rate of 28.9% (National Conference of State Legislatures, cited in Proband, 1995, p. 4).

The impact that the tremendous increase in spending on prison expansion in Florida has had on spending for higher education was dramatically presented in a recent report by Charles B. Reed (1994), chancellor of the state university system:

> The distribution of Florida's general revenue has shifted dramatically in the last 20 years. Education has fallen from above 60% to below 50%. The State University System has fallen from its historical average of 11% to 13%, to less than 8%. Social service spending (primarily Medicaid) has doubled. Correction spending has quintupled. (p. 4)

It is further reported that in the past 2 years, Florida has increased its prison capacity by 45%. When the current expansion of Florida's prison system is completed, the new beds built in the past few years alone will constitute the fourth largest prison system in the nation—even though the Criminal Justice Estimating Conference recently lowered its forecast of prison admissions and populations through 1999 and even though both the crime rate per 100,000 population and the total arrests in the state of Florida have declined for several years in a row (Reed, 1994).

Florida's experience with the doubling of the inmate population in secure institutions within the past 10 years illustrates not only the enormous strain put on the state budget but also the strain on the corrections system. The lack of available money leads to many internal problems, most important of which is that staffing in Florida's prisons has reached critically low levels. According to Byron Brown of the state's Office of Program Policy Analysis and Government Accountability, "The staffing levels are low enough to create safety concerns. We looked at 2000 shifts, and less than 3% of the time were the prisons fully staffed. About 30% of the time the bare minimum of officers were on duty" (Mendelsohn, 1996, p. 1).

Harry Singletary, Corrections Secretary in Florida, asserted that "time is running out. . . . Draconian measures within the system are putting more pressure on staff and jail space. . . . There is simply not a lot of money available to recruit, train, and retain qualified staff" (quoted in Mendelsohn, 1996, p. 3). This problem is not unique to the state of Florida. In several states, correctional officers unions have protested, either officially or unofficially, because of the dangers inherent in the low staffing levels.

Throughout the country, more prisoners are taken into the prisons each week than the existing facilities can accommodate. Consequently, seriously overcrowded prisons and jails have become the norm, not the exception. At the beginning of 1993, 40 states, the District of Columbia, the U.S. Virgin Islands, and Puerto Rico were under court order for overcrowding or unconstitutional conditions or both. On average, state prisons were operating at 31% over capacity, and the federal system at 46% over capacity (Edna McConnell Clark Foundation, 1993, p. 2).

The results have been described by the Edna McConnell Clark Foundation (1993):

> In many prisons throughout the country, inmates are double bunked in small cells designed for one or forced to sleep on mattresses in unheated prison gyms or on the floors of day rooms, hallways, or basements. Others sleep in make-shift trailers, or tents, or converted ferries. Space that had once been devoted to work, study and recreational programs is now often occupied by dormitories. Violent, predatory inmates can no longer be reliably segregated

> from non-violent offenders or, in some cases, from defendants awaiting trial. Overcrowding has also contributed to the spread of tuberculosis, particularly in its more virulent form, among prisoners and correction personnel. (p. 2)

Many volumes and many reports of grand juries, inspection committees, and professional associations have thoroughly documented the extent and horrible results of the "body crunch" in American corrections today. Any further exposition of the problem here would be superfluous. What is important to address here is how this unfortunate situation has come about.

WHAT HAS CAUSED THE RAPID RISE IN PRISON POPULATIONS IN CONTEMPORARY AMERICA?

No matter how crime rates are reported and estimated, it is impossible to relate the enormous increase in prison populations to any corresponding increase in crime of any type, or even to crimes of violence. Neither can the "baby boom" explain the explosion in prison populations, for the "baby boom" is now over, but the prison populations keep growing at a frightening pace, and even when the portion of the population in the most crime-prone age range *was* contributing to increased crime statistics, the prison-building program tended to outrun any crime increase that occurred.

With these two common misconceptions put to rest, it seems obvious that the prison boom is generated by public policy changes, not by crime rates or demographics. For over two decades, I have been teaching in my graduate corrections classes, and others have been telling much larger public and professional audiences, that public fear of crime and anger about it culminate in pressure on politicians, who in most cases have little knowledge about crime control and little will to advance anything other than simplistic solutions.

The "get tough" policy is just such a simplistic solution. It finds its fullest expression in a "lock-'em-up" correctional policy because the use of secure incarceration is familiar and comfortable as a panacea in crime control, whether it can stand the test of efficiency, effectiveness, and budgetary responsibility or not, and because of a peculiar American phenomenon that I have referred to as the "away syndrome":

> This is the condition of mind in which we simply wish that all of our "problem people" would go away or, better still, be "sent away." . . . This avoidance mechanism type thinking leads us to somehow feel secure if our

> social problems are away, kept securely out of sight, and all of this accomplished with as little expense as possible. (Hahn, 1975, pp. 5-6)

Media coverage of violent crime by the three major networks doubled from 1992 to 1993, and coverage of murders tripled, although the nation's murder rate did not change in the same period. Thus, some have concluded that people's fear of crime in this country does not come as much from the real situation as it does from looking at TV (see, e.g., "Crime Down," 1994).

Because of the media attention, coupled with the inflammatory rhetoric of politicians who feel that they can never be faulted for being "tougher on crime" than their opponents, the American public has been aroused to a state of fear and anger. The resulting outcry of the public to those in authority to "do something" about the perceived threat is loud and persistent. Policy makers then interpret public pressure as a mandate to increase the number of persons sentenced to prison and to make them stay in prison for longer periods and under harsher conditions. Yet although it is generally believed that the overuse of secure incarceration is necessary to ensure that violent offenders are taken off the streets, the majority of people entering state prisons, and the overwhelming majority of people entering federal prisons and local jails, are incarcerated for nonviolent crimes.

A recent report of the American Bar Association (Branham, 1992) addressed the question of whether we are any safer since we have been incarcerating so many people. It showed that during the almost 20 years that the incarceration rate has been consistently climbing, the crime rate, both overall and reported, has sometimes increased, sometimes decreased, and sometimes stayed about the same. The only consistent trend has been the ever-increasing rate of imprisonment. This report criticized the "lock-'em-up" mentality, stating that it makes considerable difference whether we are locking up a murderer or drug offender or pedophile or embezzler or armed robber or shoplifter, but such rational analysis has not generally been used in criminal justice planning in recent years. The emotional appeal and political attractiveness of simplistic solutions continue to fuel the predominance of the "get tough" policy.

Generally Accepted Goals of Incarceration

It is generally agreed that we use prison as a criminal sanction to meet a variety of goals. The goals most often listed are retribution, incapacitation, reform/rehabilitation, and deterrence.

Retribution

Retribution is an ancient goal of corrections dating back to at least the Code of Hammurabi (18th century B.C.). It remains popular in the minds of many even to this day, and it appeals strongly to the common sense of justice. It is based on "the deeply rooted and widely shared moral intuition that criminal punishment is and should be inflicted on criminal offenders because they deserve it" (Gale, 1985, p. 999). It makes no requirement of "utilitarianism," —that is, that some good result must be achieved by the punishment—and it is not concerned with any problematical consequences of punishment. It simply insists that the punishment be administered because it is deserved, independently of any result, good or bad (Gale, 1978, p. 293). Even those who feel that this goal is not suitable for today's criminal justice system recognize that retribution can be achieved by penal incarceration, which does indeed cause one to suffer for the illegal act committed.

Incapacitation

Incapacitation generally is understood as "disablement"—the removal of the offender's capacity to continue committing crime, whether by the death penalty, banishment, mutilation, or imprisonment (though imprisonment does not prevent offenses inside the prison). It can be applied "predictively" before any crime is committed (as in preventive detention) or "after the fact" to prevent continuation of crime (as in execution).

Total incapacitation could be attained if all potential criminals and all actual criminals were rendered physically unable to engage in their activity. Of course, this would violate the civil rights of many, and in many ways it would be morally unacceptable in a free society.

Selective incapacitation is based on the assumption that if enough of the "right people"—those responsible for a high number of offenses—were disabled, the crime rate could be effectively reduced. This seems to be a much more readily justifiable goal in contemporary society, but it has stimulated serious debate because not all researchers agree that selective incapacitation will greatly reduce crime; because selective incapacitation depends on a study of aggregates (the total harm of a crime type or offender type and the amount of suffering required to reduce its incidence); and because such a "cost-benefit" analysis seems to bypass many questions of civil rights and ethics, including the possibility of a high false-positive rate (identifying as high risk those who are not) (Clear & Cole, 1990).

Experiments in the use of incapacitation in our contemporary justice system have been in place since the mid-1970s, when much of the public and quite a few professional planners became convinced that, by building a large number of new prisons, the "crime problem" in the United States could be effectively addressed. Unfortunately, the bankruptcy of this approach is all too apparent in the present result of enormous financial and human costs without the desired effect in positive crime control that was promised.

Reform and Rehabilitation

Reform and rehabilitation have from time to time been seen as goals of the American criminal justice system. Many people continue to see them as at least partial goals of imprisonment or as part of a "wish list." The notion in our society of "reform" as the purpose of imprisonment goes back to the 1790s and the Walnut Street Jail (the forerunner of the "Pennsylvania system," which was fully implemented in the Eastern State Penitentiary a few years later). Developed by the Quakers in an attempt to replace capital and corporal punishment, this system, advocated as "more humane," was designed to bring offenders to penitence, and thus to reform, through silence, solitary work and residence, and Bible study.

The more modern goal of *rehabilitation* is often part of a complex package of similar goals, including resocialization, reeducation, and even reintegration. It is basically a name given to the process of effecting positive change in behavior by treatment (in a generic sense, not limited to clinical programs) in order to restore offenders to a constructive role in society.

Endless discussion can take place regarding rehabilitation and similar concepts. For example, one could ask whether, if social factors prevented someone who had been positively changed from obtaining a constructive role in society, his or her rehabilitation would be invalidated.

There has also been much discussion concerning how to differentiate *rehabilitation,* which has so many traditional connotations, from terms such as *reintegration.* I have always explained reintegration as involving intervention into an offender's life *and community* to reduce penetration into the criminal justice system by presenting positive alternatives to law-violating behavior (within the constraints of community safety needs) (Hahn, 1975). However, goals that involve changing the offender's behavior so that he or she can be readmitted into the community can be grouped for purposes of this discussion in this category of reform/rehabilitation.

Though many correctional programs both within and outside prisons continue to seek to change offender behavior in keeping with this model, it was dealt a blow in the 1970s from which it still has not fully recovered. At that time, the concept of rehabilitation was most popular and was represented primarily by the "medical model," which looked at crime as illness and promised to find a "cure." But the failure of programs based on the medical model to reduce recidivism or to find the causes and cure for crime made the concept of rehabilitation vulnerable to serious attacks that eventually diminished its authority.

It is most unfortunate that because of rehabilitation's close identification with the medical model, all notions of positive intervention in offenders' lives and behaviors have been dismissed as failures and are no longer considered worthy goals of criminal justice planning and administration. Nothing could be further from the truth, as this book will show. Many programs of positive intervention have been shown to work very successfully and to have a much more positive track record than any element of the "get tough" policy, especially the overreliance on secure incarceration.

Deterrence

Deterrence is probably the most popular of all the utilitarian goals of criminal justice in the minds of the American public and of many professionals. It is based on the assumption that if the cost associated with the commission of an offense is sufficiently high, the public will refrain from committing the offense and offenders will refrain from repeating. This cost can be physical pain, loss of time or money, or some other deprivation.

Deterrence can be general or specific. The term *general deterrence* refers to the idea that public knowledge of the penalty for an offense will usually serve to prevent people from committing it. For example, when a criminal law is promulgated that clearly explains the penalty for an offense, it is expected that the public will then refrain from committing that offense in order to avoid the penalty stated.

The term *specific deterrence* refers to the idea that an offender's memory of the punishment he or she received as the result of committing an offense will usually serve to prevent this individual from repeating the offense. Many parents show their belief in this concept when they punish a child for some forbidden act, with the full expectation that the child will then refrain from repeating that behavior.

The research findings, in general, are inconclusive on the effectiveness of deterrence. The literature tends to indicate that when punishment is administered under certain conditions, it can be an effective technique to suppress some behaviors in the short term, but that its effectiveness depends on many variables and that its long-term effectiveness is questionable. Among the conditions generally accepted as requirements for effectiveness are certainty, swiftness, and proportionality. When these are present, the research tends to confirm that a deterrent effect is enhanced (Blumstein, Cohen, & Nagin, 1978; Chiricos & Waldo, 1970-1971; Gibbs, 1975; Newman, 1978; Van den Haag & Conrad, 1983).

Unfortunately, because of the "commonsense" appeal of deterrence, certain absolute requirements for its effectiveness are frequently overlooked. For example, offenders must be rational and free, not only for deterrence to be effective, but for it to be morally justifiable. Consequently, we cannot rely as much on the power of a deterrent effect to restrain the mentally ill or others functioning at various degrees of diminished responsibility. Further, punishment may not be a very effective or legitimate means of controlling the behavior of those who can see no alternative to law-violating behavior. The power of the deterrent effect has also been questioned in relation to (a) crimes of passion, because by definition there is no consideration of the penalty in the "heat of the moment"; (b) adolescents, because it is generally accepted that they are more likely than other age groups to feel that "nothing bad will ever happen to them" and that they are immortal and invulnerable; (c) those with no stake in conformity, because they "have nothing to lose"; and (d) on professional criminals, because they calculate most deterrents as the "cost of doing business" and, if apprehended, are often successful at manipulating the system in such a way as to minimize the consequences.

When we consider the large amount of crime caused by drug and alcohol abuse, the number of inmates serving time who are addicted to these chemicals, and especially the large number of crimes committed at the time of being "high" or "stoned," the use of deterrence as the very backbone of the criminal justice system in America today seems simplistic and unrealistic. Of course, this is not to say that deterrents do not work at all on anyone or that all sanctions should be taken out of the penal code. Rather, it is to say that we need much more than a reactive system based primarily on deterrence if we are to deal with the complex crime problem in our country today.

It seems ridiculous to assume that deterrence will have much of an effect on "subcultures of violence," especially in our large inner cities, where we permit children to be raised more with rats and roaches than with positive human contact, where the absence of every influence that goes into the making of good people causes their life experiences to be stultifying and barren, where their psychological maiming is completed by a process in which the most attractive teachers are pimps and street hustlers, and where the avenue to happiness is seen primarily as either criminality or escape. It seems certainly far beneath our level of understanding as thinking human beings, and it should be beneath our level of decency, to say to such persons: "Now that we have permitted your life experiences to deform your humanity and warp your behavior for the past 15 or 18 years, we are going to threaten you or punish you into becoming a warm human being, a hard-working wage earner, and a good citizen." This is not realistic, and certainly it is not worthy of criminal justice planners in a free and highly developed society. Of course, these considerations do not lessen our need to protect society from the hostile impulses of others, no matter how unfortunate their background. But in criminal justice planning, much more must be involved than a simple reliance on deterrence to control all levels of criminality, especially inner-city violence.

Space considerations preclude in-depth discussion here of the complex subject of the death penalty. But research questioning the deterrent effect of the death penalty is more compelling than that questioning the deterrent effect of other sanctions (Bedau, 1971; Endres, 1985), and when the finality of the punishment and the irrevocability of its consequences are considered, heavy weight must be given to the moral arguments against its usage in the American criminal justice system.

Despite the huge amount of information that calls into question the wisdom of relying on deterrence as the primary method of crime control in our country today, we unfortunately continue to do so. This is probably because fear and anger about crime make us resort instinctively to what is familiar and comfortable to us. The threat of prison, or even the thought of it, is so intimidating to most of the members of the middle class that we feel that it must have the same effect on everyone else, regardless of class differences. Therefore, we try to transpose our middle-class dread of prison, or even of any severe inconvenience, onto the lower class, and this simply does not work. Poor people often have much less fear of loss of family and jobs because their lives are already so disorganized, and they may even gain status in their peer group from their imprisonment.

The Rise of the "Get Tough" Policy

In the 1970s, the medical model of crime became increasingly discredited because of its inability to "cure" the "illness" that was believed to underlie crime and because of the failure of rehabilitation programs based on that model to reduce recidivism or to give us the "safe society" that was being demanded. At the same time, several other factors were causing a public outcry for a more repressive approach to criminal justice.

In the late 1960s and early 1970s, the country was working through the aftermath of terrible racial riots in the inner cities, student rebellion on college campuses, and the bloody prison insurrection at Attica. There was a feeling in some quarters of society that the "forces of evil" were taking over and that perhaps even the basic stability of government was being threatened. Fear and anger gave great impetus to the rising demand that government "do something" to restore order at a level acceptable to the expectations of the larger population. At the same time, crime rates were rising, especially drug offenses and other crimes in suburban America, which previously had known only vandalism, joyriding, and teenage drinking. As a result, disillusionment and fear were pervasive.

Onto this scene, with considerable drama, came several academics who espoused a "hard line" on crime control. Most notable of these was Robert Martinson, who rapidly rose to prominence and became identified professionally with the phrase that "nothing works" in methods attempting to change offender behavior. In a series of articles and television appearances, Martinson (1974) convinced a considerable portion of the American public that a massive survey of a huge number of correctional programs had been completed and had shown that nothing or almost nothing works in criminal rehabilitation.

After an appearance on television's *60 Minutes*, where Martinson repeated his allegations, there was a public uproar. As a result, the New York State government released the report with this alleged evidence in book form (Lipton, Wilks, & Martinson, 1975), and Martinson began touring the country to promote the book. The 735-page book analyzed over 200 reports of research evaluations of correctional treatment programs but did not itself evaluate any programs directly. The conclusions as reported by Martinson were highly debatable but were accepted widely as dogma, especially by the "antitreatment" forces, who welcomed this support for their position. Public support for the notion that "nothing works" rose rapidly.

As the public demand for pure punishment and longer prison terms began to reach legislatures and other funding sources throughout the country, money for program planning and program implementation began to dry up. In many places, Martinson was quoted directly on the floor of the legislatures or in the chambers of county commissioners as having "proved that nothing works" in rehabilitation, and, on this basis, requests for program funding were refused.

Only after about 5 years did the obvious weaknesses in Martinson's position begin to be exposed. Martinson was debated in locations throughout the United States by persons selected by the American Correctional Association, the National Council on Crime and Delinquency, and other organizations, and his conclusions were effectively challenged by exposition of passages in the text itself describing programs that did actually work and challenging the methodology of many of the reports on which his negative conclusion was based.

Perhaps as a result of this, or because his own thinking on the matter changed with time, Martinson eventually stated in an article (Martinson, 1979) and in an interview ("Martinson Attacks," 1978) that he was changing much of his position and recognizing that there were indeed programs that worked. But despite his retraction and the discrediting of his "nothing works" conclusions, the myth that someone has proved that "nothing works" persists even today. Through these years, Martinson's work has supported the position of politicians and other "hard-liners" and contributed to their success in diverting most of the available correctional money into prison building and maintenance.

Another great impetus to the shift from programs attempting to help offenders change their behavior to programs based on a "pure punishment" approach was given by the then-president of the United States, Gerald Ford, in his speech before the Yale Law School in 1975. His address advocated abandoning the treatment model and increasing reliance on imprisonment as the primary means of crime control in this country. Ford's recommendations for criminal justice planning have been summarized by Cullen and Gilbert (1982) as follows:

> Crime flourishes because the criminal justice system, under the influence of treatment ideas, is too lenient on offenders. "Imprisonment too seldom follows conviction for a felony." . . . More punishment, not less, will bolster the deterrent and incapacitative powers of our legal apparatus and cause crime in America to decrease. . . . Strict, legislatively fixed, determinate sentencing is the solution to the nation's crime problem. (p. 102)

Soon it became difficult to find any prominent member of the academic or even the liberal political community who was not in favor of mandatory sentencing for a wide variety of offenses. So-called "liberals" joined with conservatives in an unusual union against rehabilitation, largely because they felt that the system had become unjust in its exercise of the indeterminate sentence options and treatment criteria. A response to this perceived injustice was quick in coming.

In formulating his "justice model" for criminal justice, David Fogel (1975), who had once advocated for humanizing corrections in many ways, now advocated that all sentences be "determinate" or "flat" and that, without exception, every offender be informed before imprisonment exactly how long his or her stay in prison would be, independent of any program or treatment considerations. He also proposed that the principle of "just desserts," and not that of individualized treatment, be used to regulate the sanction that an offender received. This meant that the time that inmates would spend incarcerated would in no way be influenced by their prospects for reform. Sentences were to be legislatively fixed and narrow in range. There was to be no "indeterminate sentence" remaining in the American criminal justice system.

Fogel also argued that prison terms should be reduced substantially and that, except for murder, no sentence should exceed 5 years for any offense. But this aspect of his recommended program was not heeded: Once the indeterminate sentence was removed, sentences did in fact become much longer.

In retrospect, many who were in practice during these years of rapid change toward a more punitive system could hardly visualize how such an enormous regression could take place so rapidly. It is now clear, however, that all the important players in the criminal justice system—politicians on both sides of the aisle, important criminal justice professionals, academics—all for their own and in many cases for differing reasons, united as an invincible adversary to any forces that sought to maintain some emphasis on more positive approaches in criminal justice.

The "get tough" policy took on a life of its own, and, in the early 1980s, prison building and severe sentencing increased dramatically throughout the United States (with the exception of only a few states, such as Minnesota, which "bucked the trend"). The "get tough" policy became the dominant criminal justice policy in the United States, and it remains so today.

Recent Sentencing Policies and Prison Overcrowding

Because the "get tough" policy involves establishing longer sentences and mandatory sentences for an increasing number of offenses, reducing the number of offenses for which one can receive probation, and making parole more difficult (or even eliminating it entirely, along with "good time"), more prisoners are coming in and staying for longer periods of time. The impact on the need for new prisons is obvious. For example, in a 1,000-bed prison, if 1,000 prisoners are sentenced for 1 year, the population can be turned over each year. However, if only 500 prisoners are sentenced for 5 years, after 2 years, there is no longer any room to take in any new prisoners for another 3 years.

SENTENCING POLICIES AND PRISON OVERCROWDING

Drug Penalties

The Comprehensive Crime Control Act of 1984 and the Anti-Drug Abuse Act of 1986 and its amendments (all at the federal level) turned almost every conceivable drug violation into a federal crime and made all penalties harsher. They drastically changed the federal court system and in many ways negatively affected the federal and state prison systems. Also, the U.S. Congress passed the Sentencing Reform Act in 1984 and its amendments in 1985; these drastically changed the federal corrections system by abolishing parole and reducing "good time" for drug and firearm offenders. The act was amended and made even tougher in 1986, in 1988, and again in 1990. These mandatory minimum sentencing laws were signed with much fanfare and public applause. However, by requiring offenders to serve a predetermined long number of years solely on the basis of the weight of a drug or the presence of a firearm, and by eliminating parole and reducing good-time opportunities for such offenders, these laws soon began to cause a serious backlog in the prison system.

Following the lead of the federal government, 46 states almost immediately adopted sentencing laws just as strict, and in many cases stricter. The message that we were jailing serious drug dealers for longer periods of time, in some cases with no hope for parole, was powerful politically because it showed that the laws' supporters "would not tolerate this cultural cancer in our midst" and so forth—but what really happened? There is evidence that some law enforcement officials chose easy arrests and prosecutions as a way of compiling impressive statistics for the numbers of offenders that they were "bringing to justice." Thus, an enormous number of low-level drug users and sellers were arrested, convicted, and sentenced. Meanwhile, the "big fish" often managed to elude apprehension or to mitigate prosecution and sentencing by "copping a plea" and informing on other dealers. In many cases, the people receiving the harshest sentences were first-time, often young, and mostly low-level offenders. These individuals got sent away for long periods of time because they had no important contact person on whom to turn state's evidence and thus could not bargain effectively. Also, the enormous differences in the penalties imposed for "crack" cocaine versus "white powder" cocaine raised questions in the courts about possible racial discrimination, in that crack is primarily an inner-city, African American drug, whereas white powder cocaine is primarily a white, middle-class drug.

According to the U.S. Bureau of Prisons, drug offenders made up 59.6% of all inmates serving federal terms in 1993 (Edna McConnell Clark Foundation, 1993, p. 14). Convictions for federal drug offenses increased 213% from 1982 through 1991. Drug arrests doubled, but drug incarceration has been estimated to have increased about 5 times in the same 10-year period (Edna McConnell Clark Foundation, 1993).

The average sentence for a drug offense was about 6.5 years in 1992, whereas for manslaughter it was only 3.6 years and for all sex offenses 5.8 years. In a 1993 report, it was estimated that, at the federal level, the average prison sentence for drug offenses had risen from less than 4 years in 1980 to almost 8 years in 1991. Because of mandatory laws, most drug offenders serve out their full sentence, whereas the average sentence served for murder in the states is just 6.5 years of a typical 17-year sentence (Edna McConnell Clark Foundation, 1993).

On June 27, 1991, the U.S. Supreme Court held that a sentence of life in prison without the possibility of parole for a first-time nonviolent drug offender does not constitute cruel and unusual punishment. In this case, *Harmelin v. Michigan,* the court, in a 5-to-4 ruling, said that Ronald Harmelin, a 46-year-old former Air Force Honor Guard from Michigan, could be kept in prison for the rest of his life for carrying 1.5 pounds of cocaine in his car. The drug cargo was found when he was stopped by the police for a traffic violation.

Under a 1978 Michigan statute that was supposed to incapacitate major drug traffickers, conviction of possessing more than 650 grams of cocaine requires a sentence of life imprisonment without parole. Harmelin had 672 grams in his car when he drove through a stoplight in Oak Park, Michigan, on May 12, 1986. It is important to note that this is just 22 grams over the requirement for the life-without-parole sentence. If Harmelin had possessed the same amount of cocaine on the other side of the state border in Ohio, he would have faced a maximum sentence of only 1 to 10 years. Even though the federal government had recently tightened its sentencing guidelines, he would have been sentenced to only 5 to 6 years behind bars in the federal court for the same offense. In fact, the only other state with the mandatory sentence of life in prison without parole for any kind of drug possession at that time was Alabama, and then only for carrying more than 10 kilograms (15 times as much as Harmelin possessed). This terrible disparity in the sentences given by the separate states and the federal system results from sporadic efforts by politicians in state legislatures to "look tough" and therefore pass strict antidrug legislation.

In a dissenting opinion on the Harmelin case, Supreme Court Justice Byron White wrote:

> Not only is it undeniable that our cases have construed the Eighth Amendment to embody a proportionality component, but it is also evident that none of the court cases suggest that such a construction is impermissible. In this light, any prison sentence, however severe, for any crime, however petty, will be beyond review under the Eighth Amendment. The death penalty is appropriate in some cases and not in others. The same should be true of punishment by imprisonment. This majority opinion provides no mechanism for addressing a situation in which a state legislature would make overtime parking a felony punishable by life in prison. (p. 34)

Unfortunately, the statistics indicate that of the more than 120 drug offenders given life sentences under the Michigan statute, more than half are first-time offenders like Harmelin. Such mandatory sentences for drug offenders have reduced the meaning of a total lifetime record of good conduct apart from the present offense. One's record as a good citizen seems to count for little; only the present offense means anything in the sentencing process. This seems to ignore or reverse all of the traditions of American jurisprudence.

In the 1980s, all of the elements of the criminal justice system sought to enforce new drug laws more zealously. More money was put into policing; consequently, the number of arrests for drug manufacture, possession, and distribution soared. Prosecutors brought more drug offenders to trial until 78% of all drug suspects were prosecuted (more than any other type of criminal defendant). These developments have swamped the courts during the past decade.

Investigations of drug offenses were intensified as prosecutors increased their efforts. As a result, the conviction rate for drug crimes rose from 74% in 1980 to 85% in 1987. All of this resulted in a huge increase in the proportion of convicted felons who were drug offenders. In 1991, drug offenders accounted for 35% of all federal convictions, as opposed to 17% in 1980 (Edna McConnell Clark Foundation, 1993). In 1990, 28% of all criminals convicted in state courts in 1990 were drug offenders, and by 1994, this percentage had increased to 31.5% (12.5% for possession and 19% for trafficking) (Langen & Brown, 1994).

In recent years, arrests for drug possession, manufacture, and sales have gone down, although they are still high by pre-1986 standards. Yet there has been no relief for the overcrowded prisons. Even if arrests continue to go down, the prisons will still be forced to house huge numbers of drug offenders sentenced to long prison terms under the mandatory sentencing laws that still remain in effect. The terrible drain on state budgets continues as a result of these draconian sentencing policies.

The drug sentencing experiment in this country provides a unique and thought-provoking opportunity to see firsthand the folly of a purely reactive and punitive attempt to control actions that have been declared criminal (in my opinion, properly so) but that have deep roots in numerous social problems. One reason that the "get tough" sentencing policy for drug offenders has failed is that when one drug dealer is sentenced, he or she is quickly replaced. This indication of the essential role of drugs in the "street economy" and the widespread demand for the product should certainly lead us to take a more serious look at other means of control than simply the punishment of dealers and users. Punishment and accountability for personal behavior are still an appropriate part of drug control policy, but the error is relying on this approach to the exclusion of other approaches and applying it in a severe form across the board to even minor offenders.

As I discussed in a previous work (Hahn, 1978), several problems indigenous of American adolescents make them potential customers for the drug market:

- Alienation from or disillusionment with family and traditional groups
- Insecurity heightened by a sense of imminent nationwide or worldwide collapse of traditional structures and socializing institutions
- The gnawing feeling of being unwanted, useless, or out of place
- Diminution of parental authority reasonably exercised by involved and caring parents
- Overt challenges to traditional morality exerted by peer groups influenced by TV, rap music, and so forth

- Frustration and disenchantment resulting from exposure of corruption in politics, heroes with "feet of clay," and seemingly insurmountable national problems
- The desire to escape the responsibility and/or boredom of the day-to-day business of living

In addition, many troubled youths become involved in drug usage to escape from extremely painful living situations or personal problems or use drugs "medicinally" to deal with adolescent anxiety heightened by the pressures of adapting to an increasingly complex work world for which they are not prepared and an increasingly violent urban subculture. All sorts of alternative programs are available to address the economic and social factors underlying the "drug problem" and to prevent and stop drug use, ranging from drug courts through the entire spectrum of traditional and innovative individual and group treatment. Thus, it seems unconscionable for our advanced society to continue to devote itself to a reactive, negative, punitive "war on drugs" that there is little chance of winning, at a huge cost to the community at large and to the viability of the criminal justice system.

"Three Strikes" Laws

The "war on drugs" is just one striking example of a simplistic, flawed approach to the complex problem of crime in our society. Another is the "three strikes" laws that 22 states and the federal government have recently passed in an attempt to control recidivism by serious felony offenders. Such laws require that people with third convictions (for crimes that in some states are narrowly specified but in others can include most or even all felonies) be given life sentences without hope of parole (with moderation in some states, but still involving the imposition of sentences of enormous length).

California's law is both the most punitive and the most frequently used of all those passed since 1993. Therefore, it has been the most frequently observed and evaluated. So far, the results are mixed, in part because of the widespread variations with which the law is being applied, despite its simplistic intent and its unambiguous language. In Torrance, for example, a 27-year-old man was sentenced to 25 years to life in prison for his third felony conviction, which was for stealing a slice of pizza. In contrast, juries in San Francisco have refused to convict people when they learned that it would make the defendants third-time felons.

According to a 1995 article in *Corrections Digest,*

> California's three strikes law requires people with a serious or violent felony conviction on their record to receive twice the usual sentence when they are convicted of a second felony and 25 years to life for a third felony conviction. . . . When it comes to a third strike, the law makes no distinction among the 500 crimes that are felonies in California, ranging from placing a bet on an office pool to homicide. . . . The most comprehensive study of the law's effect, conducted by the Legislative Analyst Office, the nonpartisan research arm of the state legislature, found that 70% of all second and third strike cases filed in 1994 were for non-violent offenses. The largest categories were for drug possession and burglary. . . . In Los Angeles County, only 4% of second and third felony convictions were cases of murder, rape, kidnapping or carjacking, according to a study released last month by the county-wide criminal justice coordinating committee, which is made up of judges, prosecutors, city officials and community leaders. ("No Plea Bargains," 1995, p. 6)

An objective report on the effectiveness of "three strikes" laws in general has been compiled and distributed by the Campaign for an Effective Crime Policy in Washington, D.C. This group, which includes hundreds of top-level correctional administrators, sheriffs, police chiefs, academics, and including at least one former attorney general of the United States, has strongly advocated a "rational debate" about crime policy in the United States, founded on an objective analysis of evidence from all crime programs and policies currently in place.

In their report, the Campaign for an Effective Crime Policy (1996b) examined the evidence to date in California, as well as the available information from other states, and drew the following conclusions.

To begin with, the laws have been used very infrequently in most of the states. For example, Wisconsin has applied its law only once; and the law has not yet been used in Tennessee, New Mexico, or Colorado (at the time of the release of this report). Most jurisdictions have drafted laws much more narrowly than California, and for this reason, or because they have not seen the need, prosecutors nationwide have not extensively applied "three strikes" legislation. And although the federal "three strikes" law received great attention during the crime bill debate of 1994, only 9 offenders have been sentenced under it (and 24 additional cases are pending).

In California, 1,300 offenders have been imprisoned on "third strike" felonies, and over 14,000 have been imprisoned on "second strike" felonies. Analysis of the results is still disputed. Though political leaders have claimed that the law is responsible for a substantial reduction in crime, others have pointed out that the crime rate had already declined substantially before the law was passed. Two possible reasons for this decline were a reduction by over 100,000 men in the crime-prone age category and a 2% decline in the unemployment rate.

The vast number of offenses targeted under California law means that the law is applied to many nondangerous offenders. Of all the offenders sentenced under this law, 85% were sentenced for nonviolent offenses.

The California law has resulted in the early release of some offenders, thus obscuring its effect on crime. The crowding caused by people accused under the "three strikes" law has been most evident in the jails, where offenders with sentences of 1 year or less are being released early in some jurisdictions. In Los Angeles, offenders with 1-year sentences are serving only 71 days, down from 200 days before the enactment of "three strikes" legislation.

Because of the severity of the penalty in "three strikes" cases, many defendants insist on going to trial. The effects have been an increased workload for judges, prosecutors, and defense attorneys and delays in other criminal and civil cases.

It appears that the law is being used as a tool in plea bargaining and that there is a great variation throughout California. For example, in San Diego, "three strikes" charges have been reduced in 20% to 25% of the cases, whereas in Sacramento, they have been reduced in 67% of the cases. Similarly, the law is not used for drug cases in San Francisco, whereas it is in Los Angeles.

Racial disparity in the application of the law is a matter of concern. One California study indicated that African Americans are sent to prison under the law 13 times as often as whites.

Although the report acknowledges that the risks posed by dangerous repeat offenders present an important problem, it states that we must consider other, more viable ways of dealing with this problem that would not have the deleterious consequences of "three strikes" legislation and would be more effective and fair.

Unintended and Hidden Costs of Prison Crowding and Building

Some of the unintended effects of our present system of crime policies have an enormous impact on the quality of life of the average citizen in the affected states. For example, the cost of the overuse of secure incarceration, which we discussed previously, is certainly not intended, but it is an absolute consequence of the need to accommodate more and more prisoners in secure settings. The billions of dollars required for construction and operation add up to a staggering figure and, as previously mentioned, represent funds cut from education, welfare, and other important programs in state budgets.

However, these are only the most obvious costs. There are also enormous hidden costs. One such cost is interest rates on state payments for prisons. For example, in New York State, 27 new prisons were opened between 1983 and 1990. To pay for their construction, the state issued $1.6 billion in bonds. When interest rates are factored in, the total cost to taxpayers over the next 30 years will be $5.4 billion (Correctional Association of New York, cited in Edna McConnell Clark Foundation, 1993, p. 4). Just as any private citizen contemplating purchase or building of a new home expects to pay out 2 to 3 times the purchase price because of interest over the long term of the debt, so citizens must realize the cost of financing these new prisons. Some other hidden costs of building and operating prisons are as follows:

- Costs of contractual services for medical, educational, or other needs of inmates (sometimes charged to the "central office" or to other state departments)
- Costs of the physical plant, such as maintenance or utilities (sometimes drawn from "the general services budget" or some other department)
- Contributions of grant monies and special foundation studies for special programs and services
- Costs of pensions, some vacation and sick leave, and even other fringe benefits, often accounting for 20% of operating expenses (in some places, charged off to other state budgets, such as the department of personnel)
- Architectural fees and cost of construction supervision, which may range from 8% to 10% of the actual cost (sometimes charged to certain other sources rather than to the prison)
- Expense of "loss of use" or "opportunity cost" resulting from taxes or rent forgone from alternative use of land or buildings
- External administrative overhead, which can include a prorated share of the expenses of centralized executive offices and administrative offices (such as personnel, purchasing, and data processing)
- External oversight costs, including inspection, program monitoring, administrative or judicial reviews, appeals of decisions, auditing, and other comptroller expenses

- Legal services, including defense of the government and its employees and public funds for inmates as plaintiffs or defendants
- Liability costs, successful legal claims, punitive damages, fines and court costs, insurance or cost of administering self-insurance plans, and so forth
- Staff training, when provided or subsidized by another agency or service
- Transportation services, sometimes provided by the department of transportation or local enforcement officials
- Food costs when other government agencies provide surplus food or subsidies
- Treatment or program costs when other government agencies provide hospitalization, medical and mental health care, education, job training, recreation, counseling, or other such programs and services (Logan & McGriff, 1989)

When all of these hidden costs are taken into consideration, the impact on monies available in the budget for other essential services can be clearly seen.

Another important unintended result of a simplistic crime control policy that is merely reactive and punitive is the current conditions of confinement caused by the "body crunch" in the prisons and jails. Great costs accrue in the harmful effects on the inmate population, the further lessening of any opportunity to promote positive inmate behavioral change, and the maintenance of a safe and orderly institution.

This problem was summarized in a U.S. district court decision (*Adams v. Mathis*) in 1978: "Forcing inmates to live in too close proximity to other inmates is psychologically debilitating and leads to an increase in tensions and problems. This overcrowding also poses a protection problem" (p. 4). When there is an increase in tensions and a protection problem, it is obvious that the welfare of the inmates, including their physical and mental health, and the ability of the administration to provide positive programming are the first casualties. Though it has long been recognized that prisoners subjected to a high degree of sustained overcrowding have a higher death and suicide rate, more disciplinary problems, and a larger number of illness complaints than those in better conditions, such deplorable overcrowding has often been rationalized and excused by authorities.

In his dissenting opinion on the celebrated case *Rhodes v. Chapman* in the U.S. Supreme Court in 1981, Justice Thurgood Marshall argued that putting two prisoners in one cell is not based on the concept of just punishment but is simply an expedient to cope with more prisoners than the facility was designed to hold. He pointed out that "in a doubled cell, each inmate has only some 30 to 35 square feet of space. Most of the windows in the supreme court building are larger than that" (p. 20). In expressing his outrage over some of the crowded conditions in penitentiaries throughout the country, he stated further:

> Too often state governments truly are insensitive to the requirements of the 8th Amendment. . . . With the rising crime rates in recent years, there has been an alarming tendency toward a simplistic penological philosophy that if we lock the prison doors and throw away the keys our streets will somehow be safe. In the current climate, it is unrealistic to expect legislators to care whether the prisons are overcrowded or harmful to inmate health. It is at that point, when conditions are deplorable and the political process offers no redress, that the federal courts are required by the Constitution to play a role. (p. 23)

Much as studies in experimental psychology have demonstrated repeatedly that increasing population density of mice causes an increase in their assaultive behavior, current prison conditions show this relationship for human beings. The reported increase in assaults in the federal system, the horrible riot at Lucasville in Ohio, and lesser disturbances in other places recently all have taken place under conditions of severe overcrowding. Because the criminal justice system is designed to increase the safety of society and thus to enhance the quality of living for all of our citizens, the corrections component should not be forced to administer under conditions that increase frustration and raise the hostility of the prisoners.

Besides the cost and the problems created inside the prison community, high rates of incarceration in some communities may have social and economic effects on the "outside" that counteract whatever crime control impact the prisons have. Marc Mauer (1996), Assistant Director of the Sentencing Project in Washington, D.C., summarized much research on this subject by pointing out that

> in African-American communities, in particular, where 7% of all adult males are locked up on any given day, high imprisonment rates have a host of negative consequences: diminishing numbers of employable and marriageable males, ex-prisoners increasingly serving as negative role-models, and a destabilizing of more traditional neighborhood and family controls on individual behavior. (p. 24)

In addition, the high rate of incarceration of young African-American males adds fuel to the fire of the rampant feeling in many inner-city communities that the entire criminal justice system is racist and that it is a "them-against-us" operation. When an already isolated, deprived, and frustrated portion of any community struggles with interpretations of police as an "occupying army" and the courts as "administering white man's justice," the additional obvious condition of overuse of the most severe sanction on the young members of that community is indeed unfortunate.

Prison Populations Are Controlled by Public Policy

The rapid increase in incarceration rates in the United States is not due to an unprecedented "crime wave." Rather, as Robert B. Hawkins, chair of the Advisory Commission on Intergovernmental Relations (ACIR), has stated, "The overloading of our prisons, courts and other criminal justice agencies has been driven more by public policies, especially sentencing policies, enacted by our state and federal officials, than by increased crime or arrests" (quoted in "A.C.I.R.," 1993, p. 1).

Changes in crime rates seem to have little impact on the amount of prison building. The more prisons are built, the more prisoners are sentenced to occupy them. This was confirmed by two important studies done in the 1970s, which found that the single most important contributor to the prison population was not crime, or even unemployment, race, inflation, or family background, but simply the availability of cell space (Carlson & Mullen, 1980; Nagel, 1980). Nagel's (1980) study indicated that the 15 states that did the most prison building and the 15 states that did the least prison building over a 20-year period had startlingly different increases in prison population. The 15 states that had done the most prison building (increasing cell space by 56%) saw a 57% increase in prison population during the same period. The 15 states doing the least prison building saw an actual decrease in prison population of 9% during the same period. Nagel argued that one of the principal solutions for prison overcrowding was to give judges sentencing options: "Judges without alternatives definitely send people to prison; judges with options more often do not."

An obvious conclusion from all of the above is that prison populations can be controlled. The use of prison space is not at the mercy of fluctuating crime rates. An outstanding example of controlling prison population growth was provided by the state of Minnesota, which controlled its inmate population so successfully for many years that it was able to lease prison bed space to states that were seriously overcrowded. But since 1989, and the enactment of more than 40 significant sentencing enhancement bills, sentence lengths for many offenders in Minnesota increased sharply, in some cases quadrupling. As a result, although the Minnesota state prison system continues to be among the smaller systems (approximately 4,700 inmates), institutional crowding has become a chronic and serious problem in recent years (Wood, 1996).

Despite the present problems, Minnesota continues to have some key system elements in place that will enable it to continue to deal more effectively with prison population and cost control than many other jurisdictions: most notably, the implementation of restorative justice, a long-standing commitment to community corrections, and legislation favorable to community corrections (Wood, 1996).

The overwhelming message from Minnesota and from the studies cited above is that crowded prisons are created by public policy decisions. Changing corrections policy, especially mandatory sentencing legislation, can lessen the use of incarceration without affecting crime rates substantially.

Challenges to the "Get Tough" Policy

Criticism of the public policy and legislation that have precipitated the crisis of prison overcrowding has been escalating from many professional sources, including sources within corrections itself. In 1994, Ms. Bobbie Huskey, president of the American Correctional Association, stated, "We need to look at a broad range of sanctions. . . . The absence of a notable reduction in adult crime-rates, as incarceration rates have climbed, raises serious questions about the efficacy of America's sentencing policies" ("ACA Calls," 1994, p. 3).

A study published in 1994 that surveyed 157 prison wardens in eight states showed widespread dissatisfaction with the policies that have created prison overcrowding. More than half the wardens surveyed stated that they did not support mandatory minimum penalties for drug offenders, and 85% said that elected officials had failed to offer effective solutions to crime. In addition, many wardens stated that the nation was wasting scarce prison space on nonviolent offenders and urged greater use of alternatives, such as home detention and halfway houses. They also called for additional prevention programs, smarter use of prison space and resources, and expanded alternatives to incarceration ("Wardens Reject Mandatory Terms," 1994).

Results of a study conducted by the National Council on Crime and Delinquency (NCCD) on behalf of the Illinois Department of Corrections

(Austin, 1994) revealed that reducing prison time served is effective in reducing prison crowding and prison costs and has a negligible effect on public safety. The study observed that since 1980, the Illinois Department of Corrections has been authorized by the State Legislature, in a program called "meritorious good time" (MGT), to shorten sentences as much as 90 days for inmates who qualify. In 1990, in House Bill 3838, the legislature permitted the department to shorten eligible inmate sentences by an additional 90 days via supplemental meritorious good time (SMGT). The NCCD study found a savings of over $7,000 per inmate released an average of 4 months earlier and showed a recidivism rate the same as, or in many cases lower than, that of those serving their full term. It was also noted that the vast majority of the rearrests of persons having gone through this early-release program were for nonviolent misdemeanor crimes. These findings indicate that a well-administered policy of moderately reducing sentences can work without jeopardizing public safety and at considerable savings to taxpayers.

In May 1992, police and civil rights groups joined with the correctional commissioners of three states to hold a special press conference in Virginia to challenge the recommendations of the "Corrections Summit" held in April 1992 by then Attorney General William P. Barr and his associates at the Justice Department. At that summit, Barr and his associates had recommended even more prison building to lock up an increased number of offenders. At the press conference, the speakers challenged the basic premise of the summit that locking up more people for longer periods would result in less crime. They stated that in fact "the over-reliance on incarceration has not made our streets safer" (p. 1). Citing figures from the National Prison Project, they stated that California is a perfect example of a state that has spent billions of dollars within the past 10 years, only to wind up with terribly overcrowded prisons, no impact on its crime rate, and slashed budgets for drug treatment, education, and other vital programs ("Police, Civil Rights," 1992).

In an excellent policy statement on sentencing, the American Correctional Association (1994) has sought to encourage a rational approach to sentencing that, if properly implemented, would effectively address many of these problems. Among the 10 points of the policy statement, the following three are especially important:

1. Encourage the evaluation of sentencing policy on an ongoing basis. Monitoring of the use of various sanctions should be done to determine their relative effectiveness based on the purpose(s) they are intended to have. Likewise, monitoring should take place to ensure that the

sanctions are not applied based on race, ethnicity, gender, or economic status.

2. Community-based programs should be utilized for those offenders who, consistent with public safety, can be retained there.
3. Sentencing should be linked to the resources needed to implement the policy. The consequential costs of various sanctions should be assessed. Sentencing policy should not be enacted without the benefit of a fiscal impact analysis. Resource allocations should be linked to sentencing policy so as to ensure adequate funding of all sanctions, including total confinement and the broad range of intermediate sanctions and community-based programs needed to implement those policies. (pp. 30-31)

If these policy recommendations of the American Correctional Association were followed in actual practice, the ineffectiveness, the social inequity, and the exorbitant financial cost of our present sentencing policies would be reduced dramatically.

In "An Open Letter to the Next Drug Czar" (Hahn, 1991), I told Robert Martinez, director-nominee for the Office of Drug Control Policy at the federal level:

> Let's be honest enough with ourselves to recognize the futility of present sentencing policies that overload already crowded prisons with drug offenders. Too often, this forces the release of truly dangerous offenders who present a much greater threat to society. We must also recognize the myopic vision of programs that do not see the failure of any effort that spends billions on prison building and hardware. . . . If ever there was a time for focusing the cool light of intellect on a problem, instead of the blinding heat of emotion, it is at this juncture. Unfortunately, the tendency has been to do what is popular rather than what is needed; to choose the politically safe over the professionally challenging; to cling to what we always have done rather than to launch into the unfamiliar. Certainly the violent and dangerous, who present a real threat to their communities, must be controlled; but this common-sense axiom cannot justify a professional policy of incarcerating all those whose behavior is offensive. (p. 19)

The present "get tough" policy advocates the process of locking up more and more people for longer times under harsher conditions. It continues to be carried out, with little thought given to all the hard evidence and accumulated professional opinion as to the absolute failure of such an approach. To attempt to control crime by a totally reactive system is unrealistic. Given the small percentage of crimes being reported, the small portion of that percentage actually resulting in an arrest, and all the delays and complexities within the court system, simply heaping more punishment at the end of the system on the few unfortunates who are unable to manipulate their way into lesser sentences will not control the aggregate amount of crime or its rate in this country.

The Present System Does Not Emphasize Prevention

The greatest tragedy probably is that such a reactive system almost totally neglects the kind of preventive efforts that could really influence the behavior of the demographic group that gives us most of the crime problem. A brief realistic look at two contemporary phenomena of frightening proportions to all concerned citizens, gang formation and the immersion of so many youthful offenders in the "drug world," indicates the importance of preventive efforts addressing the erosion of traditional socializing institutions and the consequent warping of young lives.

Thousands of children who are not bonded to a loving parent, who are pushed out or have dropped out of the educational system, and who are unattached in a way that sets them simply adrift in society quickly find that they lack the human capital of socialization, education, and employment readiness that is so necessary to succeed in the job market. Lacking the developed skills, the perseverance that comes with the ability to delay gratification, and the motivation that comes with hope, such children soon realize that they are "surplus" to the mode of production and earning, but in our materialistic, hedonistic, and commercially hyped culture, they are nevertheless very involved in the mode of consumption. This causes great frustration, resentment, and often rage. In addition, the steady diet of extreme violence and constant gore on television, the sexual overstimulation in some contemporary "art forms" in music and in video presentations, and the debasement of much of what has always been upheld by the Judeo-Christian ethic as wholesome effectively dilute, and in many cases destroy completely, the efforts of those trying to maintain most standards of behavior. Thousands of young people thus "prepared" are buying into a lifestyle of instant gratification and activities without thought of consequence. As a result, very early they steal or hustle for consumer goods, practice random sex, idolize those who have "made it" as pimps or pushers, and dull their brains with ever-increasing chemical indulgence. And for many, the gang is always available, with its promise of a way to belong and have status.

When we take all of this into consideration and especially when we apply it to groups who have been subjected to poverty and prejudice for generations, gangs, drug trafficking, and crime probably should be seen not as aberrations but as something to be expected. Consequently, to say to children who are poor, have been abused, have never had any limits constructively set for them, have been influenced primarily by sordid TV, rap music, and easy money, or are crazed with drugs and "bombed" with booze, when their behavior is completely out of control, "Now we are going to threaten or punish you into being good," is certainly highly questionable, both in its effectiveness and in its ethics.

The "get tough" policy has promised the effectiveness of deterrence and incapacitation but really has delivered only the bankrupting of governments through prison building and maintenance and untold human misery resulting from incarceration of the highest percentage of our citizens of any free society in the history of the world. To continue to maintain, as a national crime control policy, the building of prisons that, with a projected life of 30 to 50 years, will be available for our grandchildren not yet born, not only is poor planning but is morally unacceptable in a free society.

If a disease were looming on the horizon that seriously threatened the lives and well-being of our grandchildren, we would probably be marshalling all our forces and working together in a massive effort to prevent it; we would not just be preparing secure facilities in which to quarantine those infected. Such an epidemiological model seems much more rational than that of a "war on crime," which divides our society and gives us permission to hate those whose offenses disturb our peace and safety. Certainly, we should hate the offense—to hate crime is both normal and, in my opinion, constructive—but the Great Teacher and many others after Him have taught for centuries that we must "hate the sin but find it in ourselves to love the sinner."

A prominent warden recently commented that "you want to vote against paying an extra thousand dollars per kid to improve education, and then you turn around and give me $18,000 per inmate to watch them the rest of their lives" (Godinez, quoted in Lindenman, 1995, p. 19). He went on to say that our present philosophy of crime control has the basic principle in reverse:

> Tough on criminals, yes; but tough on crime, no way. . . . Don't get me wrong. I'm no liberal. If someone does a crime and is convicted, they deserve to do their time. I'm just saying, if you treat the symptoms and do nothing about the causes, this is what you get. You build 40 more prisons, thinking that's going to solve your problems, and I guarantee you you'll fill the prisons. (quoted in Lindenman, 1995, p. 19)

WHERE DO WE GO FROM HERE?

To move toward a more effective criminal justice system, one that will address many of the difficulties previously discussed, we need to acknowledge, as Mauer (1996) stated, that

> while the criminal justice system is the appropriate venue for controlling mass murderers and serial rapists, it is not the best arena in which to solve most other crime problems. This is not to suggest that criminal activity should not have any consequences; but these punishments are no substitute for more pro-active intervention. (p. 24)

If we know that our traditional reactive approach to criminal justice has not been successful, common sense would indicate that we need to change to a proactive approach. For example, there is little hard evidence to confirm that traditional policing, depending primarily on rapid response and high technology, has any real impact on crime control, even in relation to the more "public" crimes, and when performance is evaluated relative to more "private" crimes (e.g., corporate offenses, domestic violence, sexual abuse), it is even less effective. When we add to this assessment the lack of success of traditional policing in dealing with the drug problem and the proliferation of gangs, and the negative race relations that often result from such efforts, the need for proactive policing becomes even more evident.

This need can be well met by properly developed and implemented community policing programs. However, such programs cannot be a token effort or a minor commitment. The presence of a police officer mounted on a horse in a shopping center of an affluent area of a community where well-scrubbed middle-class children pet the horse and stand in awe of the officer may be good for police community relations and can be part of a larger program, but by itself it is not the kind of community policing that is required. Officers knowledgeable about and interested in inner-city areas, working on tough streets, interacting with high-risk youth, and committed to improving the quality of life in the area for all citizens because they feel the pain, frustration, isolation, and hopelessness that are rampant and criminogenic, are both the sign and the most important component of the community policing that can have an impact on the proliferation of drugs, gang life, and inner-city violence.

Courts can also be proactive and thus more effective in crime control if they have multiple alternatives to incarceration at their disposal and if they are sensitive to the needs and input of indigenous community members. Prosecutors and defense counsel can be located in the communities served.

Corrections can work with the other elements of a proactive system to deal much more effectively with the problems presented to them on a daily basis if they have relief from overcrowding in the prisons and adequate funding for the many alternative programs that have proven track records of success. Further, programs must be staffed by properly paid and educated officers who have cultural sensitivity and communication skills and are dedicated to the "human salvage business" rather than the "junk business."

All of this requires willingness to depart from traditional thinking regarding the role of criminal justice in our society. The beginnings of these changes are already under way and can best be seen in the recognition of the need to include communities in larger roles at every level of criminal justice.

The progress being made in various community policing efforts in America is just the beginning of efforts to involve communities more actively in the provision of public safety. This partnership was recently stressed by Michael E. Smith (1996a), Professor of Law at University of Wisconsin-Madison: "Establishing and maintaining these conditions for public safety is properly the work of parents, neighbors, schools, churches, athletic teams, voluntary community service groups, the labor market, and, on what needs to be relatively rare occasions, the local cop" (p. 7). The recognition of the important role of communities in criminal justice that began with community policing now is informing national criminal justice planning efforts throughout all the other elements of the system as the need for a more proactive crime control policy is becoming more widely discussed.

As discussed earlier, one of the brightest spots in advocacy for more enlightened criminal justice in America today is the Campaign for an Effective Crime Policy in Washington, D.C. It has urged the public and its policymakers to understand that the safest communities are not those with the most police and prisons but those with the strongest community structures, including socializing institutions, families, and economic opportunities (see Campaign for an Effective Crime Policy, 1996a).

The National Center for Disease Control in Atlanta has repeatedly called for the use of an epidemiological model to deal with the serious problem of juvenile violence in our society (Friday, 1994). I and others have urged that this model be used in dealing with other types of crime as well. The protocol that flows naturally from the adoption of this model constitutes a much more proactive approach to crime control because it includes

1. *Definition of the problem:* developing health surveillance systems that will allow us to measure, document, and monitor the problem over time
2. *Identification of causes:* identifying the causes, or risk factors, so that we can design and implement preventive interventions
3. *Development and testing of interventions* that are based on information learned in the earlier stages—a controlled process of evaluation research that will show us what kinds of interventions work in what settings
4. *Implementation of interventions and measurement of prevention effectiveness:* applying the field-tested interventions, including education interventions, such as public awareness campaigns, in a broad range of real-world settings to evaluate how well they work; assessing their benefits, costs, and consequences (Friday, 1994)

The use of this model provides an emphasis on prevention and early positive intervention in children's lives at the point when the first delinquency would begin. At this point, children can be helped to develop a sense of wholesome accountability for their acts, can receive relief for many of the problems that are crimogenic in their life, and, above all, can become aware that they are not "invisible" and certainly not worthless. If ever there was a situation in which "an ounce of prevention is worth a pound of cure," it is criminal justice, in which the terrible results of a nonpreventive policy are visited on entire communities daily.

The epidemiological model also takes into account that crime is not one-dimensional and consequently that it demands a multidisciplinary approach if it is to be dealt with effectively. The inner cities present what is practically a "laboratory" for testing the epidemiological approach to the problem of youth violence, especially homicide by firearms. The chain of causality in the lives of the violent youth who kill in the most deprived sections of our communities can be clearly seen by all those who dare to get close enough to the problem. It presents enormous opportunities for positive intervention. The chain of causality begins, for some children, in infancy or even before birth, with poor medical care of mother and infant. It proceeds through the preschool years with inadequate supervision and nutrition, through the school years in an educational system that in many places is facing bankruptcy in funding and in effectiveness, and on to the streets, where the same children are frequently victimized or introduced to drugs and gang activity. The potential for enlightened community police to arrange positive intervention very early in this chain and for sensitive, concerned, and community- oriented courts, legal services, and corrections to stop early delinquent activity before it becomes intractable is evident.

In the present system, a nonviolent young drug offender may well find himself among the approximately 60% of inmates currently in state prison for nonviolent offenses and may therefore be forced to learn to survive in a predatory environment, in the society of the 20% to 30% of the prison population who are dangerous offenders. His situation should lead any truly honest, objective observer to recognize the need for a more proactive system of crime control. Certainly, the nonviolent drug user, or even the child committing his or her first act of delinquency at an early age, needs to be held accountable for his or her behavior, but programs of accountability should not be more restrictive than community safety requires.

Even community safety needs can be best evaluated from community input collected by agents of the criminal justice system who are actively involved in the community. When police are seen as an "occupying army" by neighborhood residents, courts are seen as inscrutable, uninterested, and even hostile to neighborhood interests, and jails and prisons are "revolving doors" or warehouses with no real correctional impact on most prisoners when they return to the neighborhood, the criminal justice system receives little input from community members concerning community safety needs and little of the information necessary for solving crimes or assisting the community in any other practical way. Conversely, a system emphasizing real partnership with the community and maintaining constant daily contact at a grassroots level with neighborhood residents enjoys information flow and a level of comfort and confidence that eliminates "them-against-us" perceptions and effectively defuses many of the tensions that exist today between community residents and the various elements of the criminal justice system.

To accomplish this, not only must the various elements of the criminal justice system adapt and, in many cases, replace traditional policies and procedures, but a whole new philosophy must be developed to replace the traditional dominance of retributive justice. This new philosophy must be committed to and capable of preserving an emphasis on community safety at every level. At the same time, it must be based on the recognition that the criminal justice system by itself cannot control crime. It must acknowledge that strong families and communities can more effectively prevent crime, and control the crime that cannot be prevented, than the traditional system can.

Chapter 2 will explore the chain of causality in inner-city juvenile violence to show the viability of a proactive criminal justice system.

2

Understanding and Controlling Juvenile Violence: The Need for a Proactive Approach

To understand the concept of violence, it is necessary to understand its complexity. The word *violence* evokes in the mind of the hearer a wide variety of behaviors. Both an ax murder and a school playground fistfight are acts of violence, yet the levels of violence involved are very different. Likewise, a sadistic rape by a stranger in a woman's own home, the lynching of a civil rights worker on secluded farmland, and the use of multiple automatic weapons on an open gang battlefield in an urban area are all acts of great violence, but the causes, effects, and necessary means of prevention and control are almost generically different. And our means of calculating and reporting violent offenses in this country vary so widely that there really is no national profile of all violent events summarized in one report.

We generally depend on three nationwide measurement systems that count and report violent behavior. The first is the Uniform Crime Report (UCR) of the Federal Bureau of Investigation (FBI), which reports violent crimes known to the police, including homicides. The second is the National Crime Survey (NCS), which counts and reports all nonfatal violent victimizations of persons age 12 and up. The third is the National Mortality Statistics (NMS) of the National Center for Health Statistics (NCHS), which tabulates and reports only homicides, including those of persons under the age of 12. (For a more thorough discussion of these statistics, see National Research Council, 1993, pp. 42-45.)

Clearly, there are enormous differences in the way violent offenses are counted for the purpose of determining number of violent crimes and number of offenders and their victims. For example, if a violent event takes place in which a robbery results in a homicide, the UCR will count only one violent act, the homicide. This is because the UCR is concerned only with the most serious crime in the event. However, the NCS will count no violent act at all because the death of the victim disqualifies this event from being included in the "nonfatal" category. Similarly, there are wide discrepancies in the manner of reporting number of victims and events where there is group victimization. Some statistical sources report group offenses as one offense, whereas others report one offense for each perpetrator. For example, if a gang rape is perpetrated by four boys, one agency will tabulate only one offense of rape, whereas another will count four offenses, one for each of the boys involved.

Even within specific crime categories, where one might expect to find a greater degree of conceptual simplicity, there is wide variety. For example, homicides may be classified according to the victim's relationship to the offender (stranger vs. nonstranger homicide) or according to the age of the offender (adult vs. juvenile murderer). However, the greatest variety can be seen in the motives or causes of these offenses, which may include "thrill killings" by excitement-seeking youth under the influence of alcohol, calculated murders for financial gain, killings for hire, sadistic murders in connection with sex crimes, murders committed by youth who habitually "stuff" their feelings but suddenly explode in rage, unintentional or accidental homicides, and drug- and gang-related killings. These homicides differ so widely in their meaning and purpose that it is difficult to consider them all as one category.

If the category of homicide alone is so complex and so variable, the larger category of all violent acts is even more so. All classification schemes seem inadequate for it, and no clear picture seems to emerge. Thus, as Phillip Heymann (1995), a former deputy attorney general of the United States, said recently in a speech on violent crime, "The discussion is full of unknowns and disputed statistics. No one is certain how much of it there is, what kind it is or exactly how much it is increasing or decreasing."

From 1992 to 1993, the national news media coverage of violent crime, especially by the three major networks, doubled, and coverage of murders tripled. Yet the nation's murder rate was actually constant over those years and had even dropped 9% between 1980 and 1992. The media have convinced the

American public that a tremendous wave of crime, especially violent crime, has been occurring. This simply is not the case.

Further, although we are currently seeing some incidents of vicious, inhuman crimes committed by young people, there is no general crime wave in this age group. In fact, according to the most recent U.S. government statistics, violent crime by juveniles declined 25% between 1994 and 1995, and a large portion of the decline was due to declining gun homicide by black juveniles (Sickmund, Snyder, & Poe-Yamagata, 1997, p. 13). This is indeed encouraging, although it is not clear whether this will be a lasting trend.

Of course, the great concern of the American public and law enforcement officials rightly continues to be juvenile homicide, especially in the inner cities. Despite the recent reported decline, it remains true that the number of juvenile homicide offenders aged 15 to 17 increased 195% from 1984 to 1994 and that the homicide rate for 18-year-olds more than doubled. The smaller number of juvenile homicide offenders aged 12 to 14 also increased dramatically, by 174% (Office of Juvenile Justice and Delinquency Prevention [OJJDP], 1996, pp. 5-7). This decade of dramatic increase is the backdrop for the surprising and encouraging statistics of decline in 1994-1995 and a reminder of the depth and extent of the continuing problem.

Although it is important to understand and control violence of all types by all age groups throughout our society, the problem of juvenile homicide by firearms in the inner city can serve as a kind of "laboratory experiment" in understanding a particular kind of violence: a specific offense committed with a specific type of weapon by an identifiable population subgroup. Consequently, we are presented with the opportunity to plan rationally for its control.

The focus on juvenile violence is also important because of the continuity between juvenile and adult violence. Violent behavior that begins before the 18th birthday tends to continue after it (Hamparian, Davis, Jacobson, & McGraw, 1985). Further, according to a study by Chaiken and Chaiken (1982, pp. 15-17), the most violent adults (those classified by the authors as "violent predators" or "robber assaulter dealers") tended to have

1. Committed violent crimes before age 16
2. Committed violent crimes frequently as juveniles
3. Used hard drugs frequently as juveniles
4. Been convicted of a crime before age 16
5. Have had multiple commitments to juvenile institutions

GUNS IN INNER-CITY JUVENILE VIOLENCE

An important contributing factor to the juvenile homicide rate has been the easy availability of guns. From 1981 to 1994, the entire growth of homicide by juveniles was firearm related, and in 1995, 83% of murdered juveniles over age 12 were killed with firearms (Sickmund et al., 1997, p. 11). From 1980 through 1994, 70% of all juvenile homicide offenders killed with a firearm (20% used a knife or blunt object, and 5% used their hands or feet). Older teens were more likely than younger juveniles to kill with a gun. Guns were used by 71% of homicide offenders aged 15 through 17, 66% of offenders aged 12 through 14, and 54% of offenders younger than 12 (although anecdotal reports at that time seemed to indicate a rise in the number of weapons offenses by younger juveniles) (OJJDP, 1996).

The arrest rate for juveniles carrying weapons is at a historic high. In 63,400 juvenile arrests in 1994, a weapons law violation was the most serious charge. Unfortunately, this is only the tip of the iceberg because the FBI's reporting procedures classify offenses only by the most serious charge involved. For example, if a person rapes, robs, or kills in an offense with a gun, only the most serious charge is reported. In such a case, this charge would be the homicide, robbery, or rape and not the weapons violation. Therefore, the use of guns by juveniles is far greater than the number of weapons violations reported officially.

A study by the National Institute of Justice (Decker & Pennell, 1995) based on interviews with 4,000 arrestees in 11 cities (Atlanta, Denver, Detroit, Indianapolis, New Orleans, Los Angeles, Miami, Phoenix, San Diego, St. Louis, and Washington, D.C.) found that 40% of the juvenile males arrested reported possessing a firearm at some time; over a third admitted owning a firearm in the previous month; 22% reported carrying a gun all or most of the time; 55% reported that they had been threatened with a gun; 50% had a gun fired at them; 11% had been injured by a gunshot; and 38% believed that it was okay to shoot someone who hurts you. In another survey, almost half of high school students reported weapons in their schools in 1993, and about 40% reported the existence of gangs (National Center for Education Statistics, 1994). Most significantly of all, non-firearm-related homicides with a juvenile victim remained relatively constant from 1984 to 1994, whereas juvenile homicide victimizations with guns nearly tripled in the same time period. In addition, gun murders by acquaintances increased 156%, and gun murders by strangers increased 120%. A report for 1995 (Sickmund et al., 1997) still indicates the predominance of guns as murder weapons.

The problem is clearly (despite the encouragement offered by recent statistics) a high incidence of gun violence resulting in death, perpetrated by young offenders and taking place mostly in the inner-city areas of this country. Two elements of this problem are new and very properly of great concern: More people are dying, primarily because guns are being used more often, and both killers and victims are younger (for 1984 to 1994, though the 1994-to-1995 decline adds some hope here with its report of a large decrease in homicide in the "under-15" group; see Sickmund et al., 1997, p. 11).

Although there is certainly evidence of violence among suburban and rural youth, and even gun carrying in some instances, much of this is "copycat" or gang activity seeking to emulate the inner city. There is simply no comparison with the inner city as to the numbers or rates of homicides by gun-carrying juveniles. In 1995, five U.S. counties reported 25% of all known juvenile homicide offenders, and 84% of the 3,139 counties in the United States reported no juvenile homicide offenders. The problem is concentrated in the counties containing the cities of Los Angeles, Chicago, Houston, Detroit, and New York (Sickmund et al., 1997, p. 19).

THE QUESTION OF RACE

Violent juvenile offenders are disproportionately likely to belong to a racial minority group and to live in inner-city areas populated mostly by racial minorities. African Americans are disproportionately represented in all arrests, more for violent crimes than for property crimes, and they are overrepresented in the most serious violent crimes, including gun homicide. But none of this can be attributed to factors of race, and those who attempt to draw racially prejudiced conclusions from these figures commit a great error. Factors of social class and limited opportunity structure explain this overrepresentation much more adequately than race. All underclass groups have always been overrepresented in the "crime problem" in this country. There has been an ethnic succession in our early history of Irish and Italian immigrant crime, and, in more recent times, Appalachian migrants into the big cities, Hispanics in the Southwest, and so on. If race were the explanation, how could we explain the low crime statistics for successful middle-class blacks who have extricated themselves from the inner city and live law-abiding lives in suburbia? How could we explain the law-abiding populations of native Africans in their homelands—even in those countries where a few national leaders may be criminal and exploitative? How could we explain the fact that some of the most prominent mass murderers in all of history have been Caucasian (e.g., Hitler and Stalin)?

Furthermore, racial categories of "black" and "white" are arbitrary and not at all distinct. Many American "blacks" have mixed European blood (just as many "whites" have mixed African blood). How much "black blood" would someone need to be predisposed to criminality—20%? 30%? 51%? How much "white blood" would keep a person from committing crimes—20%? 30%? 51%?

The race hypothesis simply does not stand the rigors of objective examination. The remainder of this chapter explores the influences that create a violent juvenile offender.

THE ROLE OF DRUGS

The surge in violent inner-city juvenile crime coincided with an increase in drug arrests, particularly among nonwhites in urban areas. According to a National Institute of Justice report (Blumstein, 1995),

> After a ten year decline, juvenile drug arrests began to increase sharply for non-whites in 1985. This reflected in part the degree to which drug enforcement has focused on street drug markets, which more often involves African-American drug dealers. The number of arrests rose from approximately 200 per 100,000 in 1985 to twice that amount four years later; for white use, drug arrests declined, in part because of a policy shift, begun in 1975, that reversed the rapidly growing drug arrest rate, primarily for marijuana. The increase in arrests for non-whites (particularly African Americans) reflects the appearance of large crack markets on urban streets and the recruitment of unemployed inner-city youths as drug marketers. (pp. 1-2)

What many scholars and observers have described as a "crack epidemic" had enormous significance for the increase in violence from 1984 to 1994. After peaking in 1980, the homicide rate in general in this country was down considerably until the "crack epidemic" in 1985. Then it quickly jumped to the 1980 level and increased among juveniles very rapidly from then up until 1994, when a decline occurred.

Juveniles are recruited for serious work in the drug trade, which often requires the use of a gun. They tend to work for lower pay than adults and to have less fear of the risks involved. Children respond to these opportunities because the money is attractive and easily made and because carrying and using a gun brings high status. This may seem foreign to middle-class experience, but not for inner-city minority youth it is very real. Trapped in circumstances that afford them little or no hope of achieving status legitimately, they need to show "nerve" and "street smarts." This often includes the willingness to kill or be killed—a very effective status-gaining mechanism among disadvantaged youth.

Further, as Blumstein (1994) pointed out, inner-city youth are often pushed into the drug market to earn money because of the lack of employment opportunities (in some areas, the unemployment rate for teenage African American males is as high as 70%). Consequently, they enter a very violent subculture.

THE VIOLENT SUBCULTURE OF THE INNER CITIES

Anthropologists and historians tell us that in all human societies, male status has been determined to a great degree through fighting. However, in contemporary Western society, cultured persons settle differences verbally or through written exchange of ideas. If country club members do not frequently assault each other over differences, it is because status in that setting is not measured by the ability to fight.

In most modern mass societies, the state has prohibited individual combat and enforces laws against it—if necessary, even by the use of official state violence against those who break this law and engage in individual violence. Nevertheless, in settings where the state's rules and social structures break down, as in today's underclass society, where the state can no longer totally guarantee the safety of the individual, it becomes necessary for people to threaten individual violence and demonstrate a willingness to carry it out. In such situations, violence is deemed legitimate, and male inclinations to violence serve to enforce male demands for respect (Daly & Wilson, 1988).

One historical precedent in America for this condition is cited in at least one source as visible in the "wild West" of the 19th century. In that setting, where there was little structure and little law, there was an enormous amount of violence and regular gun carrying by individuals. Today the same conditions exist to a great extent among the underprivileged in the inner city (Goodwin, 1995, p. 73).

Within this setting, physical aggression is regarded as completely normal. These juveniles live in a "jungle" where they must expect to be attacked and whipped if they cannot defend themselves. Thus, it is common for them to reply to questions in surveys about their environment with statements such as "There's a lot of snakes around here, and they will hurt you bad if you let them," "Most everybody carries a gun, and I have to also unless I want to get hurt bad," and "What do you mean be nice, there ain't nobody around here that's nice."

According to Blumstein (1994), carrying a gun not only provides protection for inner-city children but enables them to participate in their peer group, all of whom seem to be armed. The widespread carrying of guns by inner-city youth (and now even suburban youth) is partly attributable to the fact that youth form a tight network. They talk to each other, they notice the habits of others from TV and other mass media, and they are quick to pick up what is the "in thing." Thus, they blend toward one style or mode of conduct that is generally accepted (see also Blumstein, 1995).

The values in this violent inner-city world of drugs and guns differ greatly from accepted "middle-class values" in our country. "Street values" center on toughness, "nerve," "street smarts," excitement (including thrills, risk, danger, change, constant activity), "trouble" (including law violation), autonomy (freedom from external control), and, of great importance, the sense of belonging that one can gain from the peer group (identification as a "homeboy," or as someone who "hangs with us"), and the status in the peer group that comes from being considered "cool" and "bad" (reflecting acceptance of the group's values and willingness to engage in risk-taking behaviors).

Even in the inner-city world, however, some children will gravitate toward the violent subculture and some will not. It is generally accepted that one of the most important determining factors is early childhood experience and family environment.

THE IMPORTANCE OF EARLY CHILDHOOD AND THE FAMILY

The amount of violence experienced in the home seems to be crucial in predisposing people toward violent behavior. Although not all children who grow up in violent homes become violent, there is great support for the notion that "violence begets violence," especially when it is experienced in childhood—probably because abuse in childhood encourages the victims to use aggression as a means of solving problems and prevents them from feeling empathy for others as readily as people who have not been victimized as children. Straus, Gelles, and Steinmetz (1980) found, for example, that over

20% of adults who had been abused as children later abused their own children (pp. 107-108). Others have reported strong relationships between (a) child abuse and later parricide (Ewing, 1990, p. 11) and (b) harsh discipline and later serious delinquency (Farrington, 1989). My own 40 years of work in juvenile corrections has convinced me that there is a high incidence of abuse of all kinds in the histories of incarcerated delinquents and that this abuse often continues in the state institutions. There are some professionals who strongly agree. For example, in the 1970s, Dr. Robert ten Bensel (1980), a pediatrician, pediatric historian, and expert on child abuse, expressed his opinion that if studies were conducted, probably 100% of death row inmates in some prisons would prove to have histories of childhood abuse.

Although Widom (1989b), in a review of the literature, cited methodological limitations relating to many of the studies and concluded that some of the studies that are methodologically sound result in conclusions that are at best mixed, the importance of childhood experiences in general is clearly indicated. For example, one well-designed study (Widom, 1989a), carefully controlled for age, sex, and race, found that persons who had been abused or neglected as children had a significantly greater likelihood of arrest for a violent offense than did persons in a control group (15.8% vs. 7.9%).

The evidence continues to mount that supportive family relations are essential to the socialization of children. This is especially true in the first 3 years of life, when appropriate, loving stimulation in the child's environment and the provision of good health care and nutrition combine with genetic inheritance to determine how intelligent and capable the child will be.

Early supportive family relations are especially crucial for healthy personality and the development of the capacity to bond emotionally with others. Particularly important is the child's attachment to his or her first caregiver, usually the mother. Attachment is perhaps best understood as an intense bond of affection that is lasting and can survive many difficulties. It empowers us to become more fully human by enhancing our motivation, self-reliance, empathy, and conscience.

When the process of attachment works properly, newborn infants learn that a caregiver responds quickly to comfort them and minister to their needs, especially when they cry. The touch and the sense of the presence of the mother's body and the looks, smiles, and obvious approval continually flowing from the mother provide the necessary nutrients and stimulants for positive personality development. Conversely, the lack of opportunity for such bonding, or an early, sudden break in the process, is devastating and often irreversible. Thus, every child absolutely requires a primary caretaker or "significant other" to whom attachment can be established (Fahlberg, 1979; Kennell & Klaus, 1976).

As early as 1915, in his book *Juvenile Offenders,* Morrison observed that "among social circumstances which have a hand in determining the future of the individual, it is enough for our present purpose to recognize that the family is chief" (p. 121). This observation has since been borne out by an enormous body of research suggesting that family functioning variables are indeed inextricably linked to delinquent behavior (see, e.g., Geismar & Wood, 1986). Loeber and Stouthamer-Loeber (1986) concluded from their analysis of 300 studies that the most powerful predictors of juvenile delinquency were lack of parental supervision, parental rejection, and low parent-child involvement. They also found correlation to a lesser degree with parents' marital relations and parents' criminality. And Wilson (1994) summed up the research by stating that "the closer the mother's supervision of the child, the more intimate the child's communication with the father, and the greater the affection between the child and the parents, the less the delinquency" (p. 55). He noted as well "the powerful effect on aggressiveness and delinquency of being raised in a family that is discordant . . . or given to inappropriate disciplinary practices" (p. 59).

Clearly, when parents feel overwhelmed or defeated, or when they abdicate their child-rearing responsibilities, children do not receive the stimulation, supervision, care, or role modeling that they require. The children then obtain it from other sources, usually TV or the streets.

Further, as Snyder and Patterson (1987) concluded from their analysis of approximately 100 studies, poor family socialization can lead to delinquency through its tendency to cause antisocial behavior and lack of social skills in children. Socially inept and antagonistic children, on being rejected by teachers or peers, are more likely to enter into association with children like themselves, who then encourage each other's delinquency.

However, research findings are not clear in relation to the impact of broken homes per se as causal factors in either delinquency or violence. Self-report studies have found little or no overall relationship simply between family intactness and reported delinquency (Austin, 1978; Canter, 1982; Dentler & Monroe, 1961; Gold, 1970; Hennessey, Richards, & Berk, 1978; Hirschi, 1969; Nye, 1958; Wadsworth, 1979; all cited in Wright & Wright, 1994). Numerous studies indicate that adolescents who are processed through the juvenile justice system are disproportionately likely to come from broken homes (California Youth Authority, 1971; Chilton & Markle, 1972; Glueck & Glueck, 1950; Smith & Walters, 1978; all cited in Wright & Wright, 1994).

But the connection may be spurious because of confounding socioeconomic factors. In general, the poor are more likely to be processed through the juvenile justice system and are also more likely to have families that are not intact. Higher arrest, adjudication, and incarceration rates among the children of the poor (who incidentally are more likely to come from broken homes) may also *increase* the likelihood of their becoming violent because of "contamination" by older and more violent offenders during periods of incarceration, especially when they occur early in the child's life. It may well be that the quality or strength of the parent-child relationship, rather than the intactness of the family itself, matters most in determining the actual behavior of the children (McCord, 1982, cited in Wright & Wright, 1994).

The chain of family causality factors for juvenile violence can probably best be outlined as follows. Predisposing or preventative factors often are present at the very beginning of life, sometimes in the prenatal stage and certainly during the first 3 years, when brain development is in its crucial stages. The most critical factor seems to be the development of an emotional bond with a parent or parent surrogate. When this does not take place, the child adopts a stance of having no real feelings for or trust in anyone. In extreme forms, this leads to "affectionless psychopathy," but even in the best of circumstances, it makes the development of normal guilt, empathy, loyalty, and other important personality characteristics very difficult (McKelvey & McKelvey, 1987). Tragically, these same children most often find themselves immersed not only in dysfunctional families but also in a dehumanizing larger environment.

The child's "multiple-problem family" is likely to have problems with family relationships; family unity and stability; behavior and adjustment of individual members; child-rearing practices; household practices and personal hygiene; use of money and other resources; lack of positive social, recreational, and cultural activities; and a whole host of other individual and collective lacks. There are often few shared experiences, for such "survival-oriented families" tend to be atomistic rather than nuclear. Individual planning and goals replace family and structured activities, and there is little communication of family members' need for each other or even any positive communication at all.

Such families are composed of persons under serious stress, often overwhelmed and unable to cope, and frequently frustrated and confused. As a result, family members withdraw and deny, retreat, become sick, or attack and strike out. Their best attempts often meet with failure because of lack of preparation or necessary background or resources, and they then react to failure by often behaving more irresponsibly and creating more problems for themselves and others. This cycle causes feelings of rage. The anxiety often becomes unbearable. Attempts to extricate themselves from problems become more poorly planned, more crude, and more poorly executed in many cases. Despair is an ever-present possibility.

Such families often resist or reject the services of social agencies by not using services when offered, missing appointments, breaking probation, dropping out of school, or failing to participate in job training. They often meet with rejection or punitive responses as a result.

Conversely, in a very large recent study of the causes of violence crime and delinquency, researchers reported lower rates of violence in neighborhoods with a strong sense of community and values. They cite a willingness on the part of residents to intervene in the lives of neighborhood children in order to stop truancy, street-corner "hanging out" and graffiti as strong prevention factors. They refer to "collective efficacy," interpreted as common values, a sense of trust and neighborhood cohesion, as the factor of most importance in predicting violent crime rate in a geographical area. While not denying the role of poverty, unemployment, racial discrimination, and single-parent families, the study's authors cite "collective efficacy" as a strong prevention force, even in neighborhoods where all of the negative factors are also prevalent.

This large study has been under way since 1990; and it is expected to continue until 2003. Until now, 8,872 residents in 343 Chicago neighborhoods were interviewed in depth (Sampson, Raudenbush, & Earls, 1997).

IMPACT OF THE MEDIA

To this volatile mix of factors predisposing to violence, the media often add another destructive ingredient with the presentation to an enthralled child audience of the glitz and glamour of a totally unattainable lifestyle. And all too often, they present degrading sex and violence that are not wholesome even for fortunate children from a stable home background with loving parents and other caring adults who can guide TV viewing or interpret negative events when these are presented. Disadvantaged children are again disadvantaged in this regard, having no one to limit their viewing or to give a proper interpretation of the stimuli parading before their eyes.

The electronic media contribute to a general climate that tolerates violence, instant gratification, and self-indulgence without concern for consequences. The extent of their destructive influence on the most vulnerable members of their audience is very great. The impulsive, impressionable, undisciplined, undirected child sees violence used as a solution to problems not only by the "bad guys" but also by many of the "good guys." Explosions, raging fires, live firefights with automatic weapons, close-up shootings, knife assaults, and dismemberment are often the fare presented, and always in an atmosphere of stimulation and excitement.

The impact of such TV viewing was described recently by the prominent criminologist Dr. James Fox, who stated that, for children, "Murder is not just the taboo that it once was. A lot of that is television. . . . We used to blame television and the movies for not showing consequences of violence. Now, they do. And kids have become desensitized" (quoted in Urschel, 1995, p. 2A). The importance of TV as a cause of violence in children was also highlighted in the report *Understanding and Preventing Violence* by the National Research Council (1993). It concluded from a review of the literature that "overall, the vast majority of studies, whatever their methodology, showed that exposure to television violence resulted in increased aggressive behavior, both contemporaneously and over time" (p. 371).

Disadvantaged, unsupervised children often become immersed in video games that are so violent that a reward is given for tearing off the head or tearing out the heart of an opponent. One youth worker well acquainted with "street kids" was recently dismayed by the report of a video game in which the player captured girls and drained their blood by drilling into their necks. These vivid acts of violence, in which the game player vicariously participates, might be dismissed by some as fantasy or simple entertainment, but for the very vulnerable they can be overstimulation and seduction.

Glamorized presentations of violence—especially the possession and use of weapons and the "cool front" needed to use them without conscience—are extremely seductive to a youngster who has no legitimate access to status or who is already involved with a violence-prone peer group. Such a child was recently overheard to say, "I like the rough, really tough stuff, like when a guy puts a gun to somebody's face and then says something real cool, and pulls the trigger."

THE DEADLY COMBINATION OF CAUSAL FACTORS

I have frequently told my classes in juvenile justice at the university that there are three obvious causes of violence among underprivileged inner-city children:

1. *Alienation,* caused by lack of bonding and the frustration of nurturance needs
2. *Dehumanization,* caused by subhuman living conditions
3. *Brutalization,* caused by violence in the home, in the streets, and on TV

For the development of the truly violent child, this is the "deadly combination." It produces strong feelings of deprivation, insecurity, and powerlessness, resulting in fatalistic resignation or rage.

The sense of powerlessness engendered by subhuman living conditions and violence was graphically described some years ago by Attorney General Ramsay Clark (1970):

> You are powerless if you live where there is no hospital, and psychoses, drug addiction and alcoholism go untreated; where poor health and retardation are common place, and where infant mortality is many times more frequent than elsewhere in the same city; where most of the people die much younger than the rest of the population; where you pay more than people in suburbia for poor quality meat and bread; where your house is a fire trap; the only stairwell unlighted and unsafe and the wiring is more than forty years old; where the wiring is chewed off by rats; where you share a two room flat with the remnants of three families and the derelicts sleep on the landing, all despite the prevailing building, safety and health codes; where you cannot afford to sue even when great wrong has been done to you; where the risk of assault on your person is very real and robbery is common, and murder is frequent; where all around you the drug dealers peddle, the whores hustle and loan sharks cash in and are ignored sometimes by the authorities. If this is where you live, then you are powerless. (pp. 247-248)

Such powerlessness is perceived to an exceptional degree, especially by the young, in economic terms. The sense of being unable to consume in our consumer economy is one of the principal sources of embarrassment, insecurity, and hostility among many of these children. In a consumer-oriented society that tells us through the media on a regular basis that our worth is measured by what we wear, what we drive, and so on, it is to be expected that many impoverished young people will commit crimes of violence to obtain coveted consumer goods.

Children raised in the conditions described above arrive at school much better prepared to flee or to fight than to learn. Thus, they quickly find themselves uncomfortable and in many cases unwanted. Hertha Reise (1962) movingly addressed this situation over 30 years ago, and her observations are still apt today:

> As the ghetto youngster disengages himself from the school, at the first allowable moment, he feels relieved, for it has given him no pleasure and has consequently caused him to feel failure. . . . For such youngsters, the schools, community centers and often even the Job Corps centers are foreign lands with values and expectations beyond him. He doesn't understand their demands, scheduled activities, forms, nor does he have the skills to achieve in their activities. He therefore closes off the school from his meaningful life, which then begins to exist only outside of the school. (p. 30)

In the world outside school, children have few or no experiences with successful adult role models, and the criminal model is ever present. They are constantly aware of the need for peer approval and their lack of sufficient money to buy the right clothes and keep up with the current fashions. The resulting threat of further isolation, embarrassment, and failure heightens their feelings of hostility, humiliation, inferiority, self-doubt, and in many cases even self-hatred. In these circumstances, according to Reise (1962),

> The community has become a rejecting parent to which the child extends his hopeless longing, but to which his approach now is by hostility and negation. These children are aware of the inequality of fate that has placed them in an underprivileged position. Deprivation as well as "badness" are taken as an unavoidable destiny against which they must either revolt or obey the verdict. In effect, they resort desperately to badness, which is not only the main source of alleviation of their misery but becomes a compensation for their deprivation. It also becomes the language spoken by the resourceless child. Their own needs are too concrete, their attitude toward life and human society too negative in every conceivable way, their sense of isolation and incompetence too overpowering for finding a common ground for communication. (p. 30)

Children in such circumstances, lacking the capacity for attachment developed very early, and then immersed in subhuman living conditions, are pushed further toward delinquency and violence by the brutalization that they witness or suffer in their homes and neighborhoods. Such children at the earliest ages frequently suffer physical abuse and neglect, witness terrible fights and even murder, and are subject to gang pressure and aware of gang violence. In many cases, they are given graphic evidence that "crime does pay," for they witness the success of drug dealers and enforcers, and they learn very early that "tough guys" are left alone while others are exploited.

These children grow up fast because they are exposed to life crises from which children in other circumstances are protected to a higher degree. They have more than their share of fear and worry because their families are more often struck by disease, the end of marriage and love relationships, arrests, mental hospitalization, and other calamities. They are confronted very early with the ill, the injured, and the dying. Already at preschool age, they have listened to family discussions about unemployment, desertion, murder, adultery and institutional placements. Consequently, their fear of disaster and pain is much less than that of the middle-class child because they live with these features in their everyday lives.

Inner-city children are constantly exposed to two competing orientations. The first is the example of those who continue to display a commitment to mainstream values even under very difficult circumstances by going to church, working hard, promoting the education of their children, and generally living law-abiding lives. The second is the example of those living lives of almost total disorganization, failing to perform in most areas of responsibility, and adhering to a code that sees violence as an acceptable response.

When high-risk youth are drawn to this latter orientation, they place an extremely high value on an exaggerated posture of "manhood." Their need for "respect" becomes all important, and because they cannot earn it through ordinarily accepted legitimate accomplishments in the intellectual or economic arenas, they must earn it by establishing a reputation of being "someone not to mess with." In its most extreme form, such youth would rather risk death than to be "dissed" (disrespected). Consequently, they do not hesitate to engage in illegal behavior to obtain the objects of "style" that support this image, such as gold jewelry or expensive sneakers, and they are willing to fight to the death if need be to defend these objects from anyone wishing to take them.

Observers of these dynamics of street life such as Anderson (1994) point out that other children in deprived areas often eventually assume this orientation because they must wear the trappings of "style" if they are not to be ridiculed but then must also be prepared to defend them with violence, if necessary, from predatory youth who would take them. In this context of intimidation, children with a more law-abiding orientation find themselves needing to take on the language and posture of someone who has the potential for violence in order to appear less vulnerable and receive "respect." The felt need of even so-called "good kids" in the inner city to possess firearms becomes much more understandable when these dynamics are recognized. Of course, nonviolent, law-abiding children and adults are still present even in the most violent neighborhoods, but they need to struggle mightily to maintain that orientation. (For a more complete discussion of this topic, see Anderson, 1994.)

I have always felt that when children steal or kill for material things (gym shoes, gold chains, etc.), it is generally because of an "emptiness" inside of them. In the opinion of many observers, this emptiness is caused by a lack of meaningful relationships, a lack of commitment to anything bigger than oneself, and the materialistic culture in which so many children are immersed today (especially lower-class children, but also the middle-class children of suburban America to a greater extent than in years past), which teaches us to satisfy only our material needs in our quest for happiness.

When children are constantly struggling to achieve material things but are unable to get them, then they are constantly frustrated. Even if they succeed in getting some things, without also having important human relationships and commitment to higher values, they quickly become emotionally and spiritually bankrupt. Some have said that such children have a "hole in their heart." When they find that the hole cannot be satisfactorily filled with material things, their level of frustration is increased dramatically.

This concept can explain most addictions. The addictive behavior (whether to drugs, alcohol, sex, or gambling) is an attempt to fill the "hole" in the self. As the person attempts to fill it more and more with the addictive substance, the level of frustration increases. The sense of shame that often exists along with the addiction also increases, thus making the situation continually worse.

In today's culture, TV and the example of professional athletes, entertainers, and other media figures continually teach deprived inner-city children that they must fill that "hole" with material things. The message is, "If you just have the right gym shoes/jacket/car, you will be happy." This is a seductive message for all American citizens, but for unattached, left-out inner-city children, the seduction is overwhelming.

Similarly, many children soon gravitate toward a "street-corner society" of peers because the family has not provided essential functions of bonding, affection, security, education, sharing of new experiences, and satisfaction of spiritual and emotional needs. Thus, the only solid, lasting group with any stability in the area is one's "buddies." They, at least, seem to be always there, in comparison to the family, which may be quite unstable, with frequent starting and stopping of sexual and friendship relationships, marriages, jobs, and school programs and frequent relocations to find affordable housing.

The group exerts a strong pressure on the individual not to break up the group by leaving or "listening to others" because the group performs very necessary functions. It fulfills essential needs for intimacy in many cases. It confers a "group rep," which, though it often depends on illegal or immoral acts, becomes the individual's one true status as self-recognized and recognized by others. Finally, it confers "adult" status, which in this subculture means, not the assumption of adult responsibilities such as getting a driver's license legitimately, graduating from school, or holding a job, but the outward trappings of freedom to smoke, drink, stay out late, drive legally or not, and in general be "on their own."

As a result, from an early age, such children are immersed in a culture and a set of motivations that differ almost entirely from those of middle-class children. However, when they enter school, the juvenile court, a social agency, or any other professional setting, it is generally the middle class that deals with them, and it is middle-class expectations that they are expected to fulfill.

PROFILE OF A VIOLENT JUVENILE OFFENDER

The following description of a hypothetical violent juvenile offender presents more graphically the influences described above. This offender is perhaps 14 or 15 years old and may be African American, Hispanic, or poor white. He deals in petty vice and drugs, and his life evolves around "getting high" and being a "big man" in the eyes of his peer group. He may live in the "projects," the child of a single mother who is beset with personal, financial, and social problems herself. She is unable to adequately supervise her children or to satisfy most of their legitimate needs. He carries all the outward trappings of "style," represented especially by expensive sneakers and the latest in jeans. He is either a "dropout" or a "pushout" from the school system, is practically illiterate, and has few salable job skills. He is not actively seeking work because he believes that entry-type jobs are for "chumps." He takes great pride in his ability to "hustle" on the streets and has met most of his needs in this way since he was about 9 years old. He spends his days and much of his nights "shooting hoops" or playing video games and sleeps either at home or at the home of one of his girlfriends until late afternoon hours. His life revolves around "getting high" and seeking excitement. He does not hesitate to use violence to protect his portion of the drug trade, and he regularly carries a firearm. He has witnessed many fights with severe injuries and several deaths as a result of gunshot wounds. Although this is perhaps an extreme illustration, there are literally thousands of children in the big cities of America who closely resemble this boy.

In speaking of serious violent habitual juvenile offenders, it is important to exclude occasional offenders—those who habitually commit nonviolent offenses or those who hurt someone in an isolated high-stress incident or under extraordinary provocation. We are talking about young people who have violence so inexorably woven into their lives that a homicide is in fact predictable at some point in their career (Vachss & Bakal, 1979). According to Vachss and Bakal (1979), the characteristics of such juvenile offenders are

1. A complete lack of apparent empathy for other human beings
2. A lack of perception of the future
3. Inability to relate their behavior to the consequences
4. Assumption that everyone commits crimes of some kind
5. "Translator mechanisms" such that, for example, the need to earn money becomes the need to take it

This profile points up the need for positive intervention early in the developmental process and the difficulty of trying to correct violent behavior that has become integral to the individual's personality and way of life.

Although they can be responsible for great harm, the great majority of violent delinquents are not psychotic or seriously disturbed emotionally. They can probably best be characterized by extremely poor impulse control and inability to delay gratification. Some research identifies a group of juvenile murderers who fit the clinical description of "psychopath" or who show psychotic symptoms or neurological impairment before committing the violent act ("Compromise Is Needed," 1986). This group, however, is relatively small.

Far more crucial than psychobiological factors in developing the traits listed by Vachss and Bakal (1979) above and in facilitating their expression through violence are the kinds of environmental factors that have been discussed in this chapter: the amount of violence seen in the home, the neighborhood, and the news and entertainment media; the economic and social rewards for committing violence; and the cultural practices that tend to instill or disable empathy for victims (National Research Council, 1993, p. 302).

The National Research Council (1993) stated that "no one influence in isolation is likely to account for the development of potential for violence" (p. 363). They then listed the following influences that in combination tend to produce a violent individual:

1. Born with a particular temperamental profile
2. Living in a particular family constellation
3. Living in a disadvantaged neighborhood
4. Exposed to models of aggression and patterns of reinforcement of aggressive behavior
5. Having a particular school experience
6. Having a particular set of peer relations
7. Experiencing certain chance events that permit the actualization of violent behavior

And research prepared for the Winter Meeting of the U.S. Governors' Association in 1994 ("Youth Offer Advice," 1994) identified significant risk factors for violent behavior more explicitly as

1. Chronic parental unemployment
2. Substance abuse
3. Early onset of aggression and antisocial behavior
4. Family characteristics such as poor parenting skills, inconsistent discipline, child abuse, and out-of-home placements
5. Inappropriate peer relationships
6. Victimizations (e.g., being a victim of violent offenses or witnessing chronic violence in the family or the community)
7. Poor performance in school and attendance at schools characterized by limited resources
8. Co-occurrence of problem behaviors such as illegal ownership of guns, drug use, and involvement in gangs
9. Living in socially isolated neighborhoods that fail to meet the basic needs of the residents, including access to health care

In sum, it is not at all surprising that the highest incidence of violence is among the rejected and disenfranchised members of society. Though it is not limited to them, such persons, deprived of most positive experiences and immersed in a culture of violence, often see crime as the only way out or up. Given children who are faultily bonded to parents; unattached to any other positive adults; underachieving or outside the school system; struggling to survive in a street culture of violent peers; immersed in a TV world of unattainable glitz, glamour, sex, and violence; masking their pain with soft or hard drug use; unemployed and probably unemployable; desperately seeking status and respect in the only way they know in a situation where the very symbol that will earn them instant respect, the gun, is readily available, is there any reason for surprise that there is an epidemic of gun violence among them?

THE NATIONAL RESEARCH COUNCIL'S MATRIX OF RISK FACTORS

The National Research Council (1993, p. 20) classifies risk factors for violent behavior by temporal proximity to the violent event and specifies the four levels at which the risk factors exist. Under the category of temporal proximity,

1. *Predisposing risk factors* increase the probability of violent events months or even years before they take place.
2. *Situational risk factors* are circumstances that surround an encounter between people and that increase either the chance that violence will occur or the harm that will take place if it does occur.
3. *Activating events* are those that immediately lead to a violent act (also often referred to as "trigger mechanisms").

Of the four levels at which the risk factors exist, two are social and two are individual:

1. *Macrosocial* (characteristics of large social units; e.g., countries, communities)
2. *Microsocial* (characteristics of encounters among people; e.g., exchange of insults, reaction of bystanders to escalating confrontation)
3. *Individual psychosocial* (characteristics of individuals or "temporary states" that influence interaction with others; e.g., ways of expressing anger or acting when drunk)
4. *Individual biological* (chemical, electrical, and hormonal interactions, primarily in the brain)

(For the complete exposition of these risk factors and their explanation, see National Research Council, 1993, pp. 296-306.)

Within the conceptual framework of this matrix, a violent event requires a person with some predisposition; a situation with elements that create some risks; and, normally, a triggering event. The *predisposition* to a particular act could be internal (e.g., genetic factors, brain damage, or chronic use of psychoactive substances) or external (e.g., limited opportunity structures or neighborhood gang activity). Whatever "sets the stage" for the violent act internally or externally is a predisposition. The *situational risk elements* could range from weapons access to current drug use or even a crowd of bystanders who support fighting. The *triggering event* may range from miscommunication between intoxicated participants to something as remote from the individual as the announcement of an unfavorable court verdict in a police brutality case. When a predisposed person is in a situation favorable to violent behavior, a violent act can be triggered by an almost infinite variety of individual or social factors.

An important conclusion of this study is that there is no single type of person who is violent and that no single influence in isolation is likely to account for the development of an act of violence. Rather, a complex network of risk factors creates a high risk for a violent event.

In this conceptualization, every violent event is a "chance occurrence" in the sense that no human characteristic, set of circumstances, or chain of events makes violence inevitable. If this is correct, it seems reasonable to assume that some intervention might have prevented each violent event. Unfortunately, however, the most effective intervention cannot always be known in advance for every individual case. There are well-documented risk factors that increase the odds that violence will occur, and timely intervention to mitigate these risk factors is the best opportunity for prevention.

Some risk factors definitely can be modified to reduce the odds. There is always a chance that violence will occur in a low-risk setting or fail to occur in a very high-risk setting, but the odds of this occurring are much less than when there is a substantial presence of the high-risk factor. Therefore, any positive intervention that reduces a risk factor is helpful in reducing the probability of violent behavior.

It is important, especially for prevention purposes, to view violent events as the outcome of a long chain of preceding events, which might have been broken at any of several links, rather than as a product of a set of factors that can be ranked in order of importance. For example, the accumulated humiliations of an explosive rage killer should not be designated as "more important" than his drinking at the time of the event. Both are important in the chain of causality.

As we look carefully at this chain of risk factors from a standpoint of both temporal proximity and individual and social levels at which the risk factor may operate, it becomes apparent that community concern and activity far beyond the purview of the traditional criminal justice system are required for interventions. Prenatal services, nutrition, parent training, preschool, in-school programs, social agency services, and more are all required.

A NEW MODEL OF TOTAL INTERVENTION

Communities can do a great deal to provide front-line prevention of juvenile violence and delinquency. For example, in Mountlake Terrace, a Seattle suburb of about 20,000 people, a grassroots coalition of community residents has been assembled to deal with homeless teens, gang members, "copycats," and others. The program, funded through community support and matching federal Americorps dollars, provides training in interpersonal skills, anger management, and the work ethic. There are also educational programs on drug and alcohol abuse, HIV awareness, and domestic violence; recreational activities such as basketball, volleyball, and air hockey; and a TV room. Between 175 and 250 youth aged 12 to 21 participate each evening that the center is open. It is staffed by volunteers, who logged more than 10,000 hours in the first year of operation. In answer to charges that the program was just another "soft prevention program," statistics showed that serious crime among youth in the community had dropped about 20% in the first year of the program's operation and that minor crimes had dropped about 60%. Further, during a 6-week period in the summer of 1994, when the center was closed for remodeling, local police received 72% more calls for service during the hours that the program would have been open (Gregoire, 1996, pp. 4-5).

Although proactive, preventive crime control activities must involve much more than just the criminal justice system, the traditional criminal justice system has a significant role to play. Research and experience indicate that the justice system must intervene early to interrupt developing patterns of antisocial behavior and that chronic offenders must be made aware that there are predictable consequences for their behavior.

These "early interventions" and "consequences" should not be interpreted as early and expanded use of secure incarceration. Though simple "leniency," which often implies doing nothing, must be carefully avoided, early interventions should be as positive as possible in the circumstances, and secure incarceration should be reserved as the "last resort," used only when necessary for public safety (Hamparian et al., 1985).

An excellent example of such a positive proactive program, which certainly rebuts the criticism that advocates of nontraditional approaches are "soft" or "too lenient," is Boston's very successful program to reduce juvenile homicides with guns. The Boston Police Department, the U.S. Bureau of Alcohol, Tobacco and Firearms, the U.S. Attorney General's Office, state probation, parole, and youth services departments, and other agencies have worked together for several years, and they fully implemented the program just last year. It tracks guns found in the hands of youth and prosecutes suppliers when possible, responds quickly and firmly to gang violence, forewarns gang members of "zero tolerance" for violence, and urges gangs to explore nonviolent means of conflict resolution. The program's success is illustrated by a 71% reduction in the number of murder victims for youth aged 24 and under in 1996 and a two-thirds reduction in the homicide rate for the same age group, according to a recent report compiled by David Kennedy (1997) of Harvard University's Kennedy School of Government.

Programs that effectively combine interdiction of guns, personal accountability for antisocial behavior, and incapacitation when necessary for community safety with positive interventions such as teaching nonviolent problem-solving skills, providing job preparedness training and placement, and addressing other competencies required for healthy community living can and do address the problem of juvenile violence very successfully. But an extremely high level of community involvement is necessary for such programs to be effective. This is best coordinated by a community "Criminal Justice Coordinating Council" that ensures the commitment and cooperation of all players at every point of intervention. Success in these programs also presupposes an entirely new model for crime control planning, encompassing all of the points of intervention and especially emphasizing a proactive stance, as opposed to the traditional reactive stance, for all elements of the criminal justice system. Early efforts to do this can be seen in many places already, especially in community policing.

All of this requires a new concept of crime as an injury to all members of the community and not just as an affront to the state. It also requires that the goal of all crime control activity become "community healing" and the restoration of the torn fabric of the community caused by the criminal act. (This concept is explained in detail later in Chapter 5 of this book.) In this model, community-oriented police and community-based corrections workers are in close contact with neighborhood groups and family councils, who are intimately aware of the development or existence of early risk factors at all four levels of the matrix: macrosocial, microsocial, individual psychosocial, and individual biological.

These conditions, when brought to the attention of the community, trigger response from appropriate agencies and necessary support from the community itself. Such concern and activity provide a "front line" of prevention.

The understanding of behavior of individuals in a given residential area readily leads to the ability to predict and prevent offenses. It also facilitates a more efficient response to offenses at the enforcement level and provides more accurate information to the courts when offenses are committed and court action is necessary.

Certain information about risk factors can be known only within the intimacy of the community. The economic pressures on families, the activity of gangs, the availability of drugs and guns, illegitimate rackets, how someone behaves between epileptic seizures, how individuals act when intoxicated, important events of political concern, and a whole host of other related pressures and events cannot be known and understood from a distance. They require personal observation and information from families and neighbors.

The emphasis on prevention, followed by the use of the "least restrictive alternative" and the least intrusive measures when violent acts have not been prevented, becomes a natural progression in the "chain of intervention" that closely parallels the chain of causality. In the present model of the "war on crime," such close cooperation and communication are impossible. In the new model, based on the three pillars of community policing, community-based corrections, and restorative justice, such cooperation and communication are the stuff of which the system is made. The remaining chapters of this book will deal in detail with these three essential elements of a proactive criminal justice system.

PART II

THREE ESSENTIAL ELEMENTS OF A PROACTIVE CRIMINAL JUSTICE SYSTEM

3

Community Policing

Historians through the ages have admonished their listeners that we cannot understand where we are going or even where we are without a good understanding of where we have been. This axiom is eminently true for present and future policing in the United States.

HISTORY OF POLICING IN THE UNITED STATES

The history of policing in this country is complex and does not lend itself to coherent narrative. It is composed of the experience of thousands of departments, some small and some large, located in highly diverse geographic areas and serving populations of vastly differing ethnic and racial composition. The picture is further complicated by the fact that within some larger departments, all sorts of experiments in policing have been tried in various bureaus and divisions, often in competition with other developments.

But despite all this variation, some major trends are clearly identifiable. Kelling and Moore (1988) divided the entire history of policing in this country into three eras. Although their schema has met with some criticism for perhaps failing to emphasize sufficiently the aspects of class struggle that have influenced policing (see Williams & Murphy, 1990), it is helpful for understanding where we have been, where we are, and what the dynamics and essential elements are of each era based on a concept of "corporate strategy" as originally presented in the work of Kelling and Moore (1988).

The authors' three eras are

1. The *Political Era,* so named because of the close ties between police and politics during this period. It dates from the introduction of police into municipalities during the 1840s up through the early 20th century.
2. The *Reform Era,* which developed in reaction to abuses that took place during the Political Era. Its origins are placed in the 1930s, and it is considered to have reached its zenith in the 1950s and 1960s. By the late 1970s, it was exhibiting signs of decline, although it still endures today with great strength in some places.
3. The *Era of Community Policing,* also referred to as *community empowerment policing* or *problem-solving policing.* This period began in the early 1980s and reached full flower by about 1988, certainly by the early 1990s.

These three eras do not have clear boundaries: There is overlap and coexistence, especially today, when the two latter styles can be seen existing side by side in geographically contiguous departments and, more important, even within individual departments. Also, this schema does not imply that, during a given era, every department policed in the same way. There were many exceptions during each era. With these admonitions in mind, it is helpful to look at each era as Kelling and Moore (1988) originally presented them.

The Political Era

In the Political Era, from about 1840 to well into the 1930s, the police were authorized by local municipalities. Unlike the British police, police in the United States had no central national police authority to give them their mandate. Being locally based, they were dependent on local political leaders for their resources. The local leaders were often ward politicians, so the police were brought into close proximity with the local political machines. Often, these relationships were so close that the police were seen as simply adjuncts to the local political machine. The political machines recruited and maintained the police, and the police reciprocated by encouraging citizens to vote for certain candidates. At times, they were even involved in the rigging of elections.

Their organization was decentralized. Although they appeared to have a central office and a unified chain of command, the precinct was actually the most important unit. It frequently was run in cooperation with the local political leaders. Because of their distance from central command, and because communication and transportation were quite primitive, police officers were given substantial discretion in handling affairs within their immediate area of influence.

Generally, officers lived in the same areas that they patrolled. Often, they had been recruited from the same ethnic stock as the dominant political group in the area. These factors, combined with the close relationship with the local political leaders, made them truly "local officers," with few relationships beyond the precinct boundaries.

They provided a vast array of services to the citizens, whose needs they knew well. They helped in finding jobs, providing coal in the winter, giving Christmas presents to children, providing food for the needy, and a whole host of activities that would fall under the general title of "social services" today. These altruistic, humanitarian efforts could extend to the running of soup kitchens, the provision of lodging for newly arrived immigrants, and other expressions of practical concern about the general welfare. However, the police also carried out their essential responsibilities of crime control and order maintenance.

The demand for their services came primarily from the local politicians and from citizens directly to the beat officers. The service demands were received, interpreted, and responded to at the precinct or street level. The officers were primarily involved in foot patrol. They walked beats and related to problems of crime and disorder as they confronted them or as citizens requested. They had few or none of today's technologies. When call boxes became available, they were used for supervisory and managerial purposes, and when automobiles became available, they were used to take officers from one beat to another, but although these new developments certainly increased officers' range, they did not change the local focus of police activity.

There were primitive detective divisions, but these did not have the preeminence that they do today. Caseloads were composed of "persons" rather than "offenses." Police relied heavily on these "persons" to inform on other criminals. In interviewing of criminals, the "third degree" was a common technique for obtaining information.

Just as they are today, the police were expected to control crime and riot and maintain the general order, but they were also judged by their ability to relieve many social problems, such as hunger and homelessness. Their success was measured by the satisfaction of the citizens of the area and the local politicians.

The Reform Era (the Era of "Professional Policing")

The Reform Era got under way in the 1930s, after August Vollmer first rallied police executives around the idea in the late 1920s in Berkeley, California. It reached its zenith in the 1950s and 1960s and began declining in some places in the latter part of the 1970s. This era was the era of "police professionalism." It owes much of its structure and character to two early proponents: O. W. Wilson, a police chief in Chicago and later a professor of criminology in California, who is often called the principal administrative architect of the organizational strategy; and J. Edgar Hoover, who reformed the FBI and molded it into a professional police organization. The FBI was and in many places continues to be seen as the model of police professionalism.

The movement toward professional policing was impelled to a great degree by some of the corruption, brutality, unfairness, and incompetence of local police during the first era. As a reaction to these abuses, Reform Era officers were to receive their legitimacy and authorization not from local politicians but from the law itself and from the very concept of professionalism. The political influence had to be rejected and, in fact, began to be seen as one of the problems in American policing.

Very early in this period, the position of police chief became a civil service position to be obtained through examination (in Los Angeles and Cincinnati). In some cities, such as Milwaukee, chiefs were given lifetime tenure by a police commission. In other places, such as Boston, their terms were staggered so as not to coincide with the mayor's term in office. The rejection of the local control concept became so clear that in some places, such as Philadelphia, it became illegal for the patrol officers to live on the beat in which they patrolled.

In the new era, police officers generally saw their role as one of "enforcing the law." When they chose not to do so in situations where they considered the use of discretion necessary—such as riots, where they might isolate and disperse certain groups instead of arresting—they would justify their action by claiming professional knowledge, skills, and values that uniquely qualified them to make these decisions. As a result of this claim of professionality, along with the removal from the influence of local politicians, police departments quickly became one of the most autonomous public organizations in urban government.

The focus of police became narrowed to crime control and criminal apprehension. Police departments became "law enforcement" agencies. Their goal was basically to control crime. Any other activities that caused police to engage in community problem solving or the delivery of other services were seen as "social work" to be avoided if at all possible. These "nonpolice" functions were looked on with disdain and even ridicule in many cases. They were seen as inhibiting the police officer from doing "real police work." In this atmosphere, the provision of emergency medical services was transferred to firefighting organizations or other agencies. All of these developments were supported in the documents of the 1967 President's Commission on Law Enforcement and the Administration of Justice.

An entire generation of police officers was developed with the idea that they were to enforce the law and do little else. Attempts were made to limit discretion in patrol work. If special problems arose, the typical response was to create a special unit (e.g., vice, juvenile, drugs).

These special units were put under central command rather than local control. All of this contributed to the control of the workers through a bureaucracy, with a constant flow of instructions downward and information upward, along with complicated record keeping and layers of middle managers. Tasks were broken down into components so that workers could highly develop their skills in particular areas. Elaborate mechanisms were put into place to evaluate performance. Economic reward was linked to productivity.

The professional officer, in this model, was an impartial law enforcer who was neutral and distant in his contacts with citizens. The best personification of this style was Sergeant Joe Friday in the TV program *Dragnet,* whose response was always "Just the facts, Ma'am." His only concern was crime solving; it was not his job to respond to any emotional need or crisis.

The citizen, in this model, was simply a passive recipient of the officer's professional services who was supposed to "stay out of the way." Any involvement of citizens in defending their own community or defining the police function was seen as inappropriate interference. Just as doctors would take care of the community's health problems, the police would take care of the crime problems.

The concept of the "thin blue line," portraying the police as the only defense against dangerous external threats to the community, emphasized police heroism, but it also implied, in many cases, a suspiciousness or even antagonism toward the citizens being policed. Just as J. Edgar Hoover had sold the FBI to the American public, the local police began to engage in a media selling campaign that constantly pushed the image of police as "crime fighters." Even though many citizens were still demanding foot patrols, the police developed the rapid-response technique to calls for service, and citizens were discouraged from going to their neighborhood police officer or district. All calls were being channeled through central communication facilities.

After the 911 systems were installed, extensive efforts were made to discourage citizens from seeking services at the district or local level in any way. Rapid response to calls for service became one of the principal ingredients of the professional police program, along with preventive patrols by automobile, detective units using highly technical forensic services, and other specialized units. Most of these units were controlled by central headquarters. Police performance was measured primarily by crime control and criminal apprehension outcomes. Individual officers' effectiveness was judged by the number of arrests they made, and "social service" functions were virtually dismissed.

By the 1960s and 1970s, police departments had increased in size very rapidly and had huge expenditures for new technology. Nevertheless, crime was rising, and the public was expressing dissatisfaction in several ways. Citizens ceased using public transportation and began abandoning city parks and even moving from their neighborhoods because of fear of crime. Only much later (the early 1980s) was the connection between disorder and fear seen to be more important than fear of crime. This is important because order maintenance was one of the functions that had been downplayed by the police all through the Reform Era. No data had been collected on it, and officers had not been trained in these activities.

Increasingly, minority groups voiced the perception that their treatment was not equitable or adequate. They rioted, and the police response was often seen by the public as brutal. Civil rights groups challenged police methods, and there was greater insistence that minorities and women be adequately represented on the police force.

Studies pointed out that "pure law enforcement" took up a very small portion of the time of police officers and that huge amounts of discretion and all sorts of other activities characterized actual policing at all levels.

The social changes of the 1960s and 1970s created unstable conditions in which the situation of the police changed radically. Some of the major changes were the civil rights movement, the migration of minorities into the cities, the changing age of the population, increases in crime and fear, increased oversight of police actions by the courts, and the decriminalization and deinstitutionalization movements. The Reform Era model simply could not accommodate to all of these changing social circumstances. It was obvious that communities needed, and were expecting, a more proactive stance on the part of police and more community involvement, if not control. The challenge for police all over the country was to create, build, and maintain organizations in which change was seen as the norm rather than the exception and as an opportunity rather than a threat. Things were rapidly changing, and the clock could not be turned back. Many enlightened police administrators saw this clearly; they felt that the legalistic and paramilitary structure of traditional police departments inhibited creative responses to change and that it would be necessary to make bold moves toward a whole new model with new lines of authority, approaches to community, use of resources, and techniques of evaluation, as well as a whole new image of what it meant to do policing in the contemporary United States. The public began insisting that they wanted more from the police. (For complete original discussion see Kelling and Moore, 1988.)

The need for a new model was given special urgency by the rapid rise and continued expansion of the drug problem, especially in the inner cities of America. People felt more and more frustrated as their neighborhoods were taken over by drug dealers and "nothing was done about it." But because police did not tap this potentially positive energy, it often turned into socially destructive vigilantism, which only undermined respect for the law even further (Trojanowicz & Bucqueroux, 1992c). There was growing concern about the police corruption connected with drug enforcement. Several celebrated cases received wide publicity, so there was additional demand that the community be given a more important role in combating this problem. The need to move away from central control to local involvement, and from elite tactical units to more cooperation with the public, was well stated by Trojanowicz and Bucqueroux (1992c):

> Studies show that far from fostering corruption, the involvement of line officers and street level anti-drug initiative prevents corruption. The dynamic most likely to promote widespread corruption and police abuse appears to be when an elite unit is put on the task, especially if the unit is cloaked in secrecy (see "Prince of the City," the most notable drug case out of New York City involving an elite police unit). (p. 5)

The Era of Community Policing

According to Kelling and Moore's (1988) schema, this era probably began about 1982 in Houston, Texas, but came into its own around 1988 and has been increasing in its acceptance in police departments throughout the United States ever since. However, there are some who see the origin of the community police concept as far back as the 18th century, when Sir Robert Peel introduced his "Coppers" to the streets of London. Still others place its beginnings in changes that commenced after the riots and disturbances of the 1960s, or in the inauguration of the Kansas City Experiment in the early 1970s (Ward, 1991).

Whatever the specific date of origin, community policing can be seen as the result of a real transformation in police thinking. Clearly, this transformation is not complete because the Reform Era model of professional policing remains the dominant style in most places. However, there are strong pressures to change (Hartmann, 1988).

The emphasis on the need for a new model, far from attacking the notion of police professionalism, demands that we view professionalism itself in a new light. This is in keeping with some of the finest "traditional" police thinking. Patrick V. Murphy, President of the Police Foundation and Former Police Commissioner of New York, said so eloquently years before community policing began:

> Professionalism in policing, at a minimum, involves not being mired in the untested traditions, the folkways, the inherited ruts that govern police departments. Professionalism means questioning, through research, old and new policies and tactics, and contributing to a growing body of knowledge about what works and doesn't work in controlling crime and maintaining order.
>
> Professionalism means obtaining education in many areas so that we can understand our work and do it effectively. Professionalism means contributing to a developing Code of Ethics which helps to guide police behavior in its daily passage through the narrows of ambiguity about right and wrong.
>
> Professionalism means debating our differences publicly, speaking out on issues that involve our work and our goals. (quoted in "Forum," 1984, p. 10)

In the truly highest spirit of professionalism, top-level police administrators throughout the country began challenging what had been a way of life for police departments for decades. They no longer viewed the accepted wisdom as adequate, and they listened carefully to the noted futurist Alvin Toffler when, in an address to the FBI National Academy in 1982, he warned that law enforcement had two options: "to cling to the status quo" or "to facilitate social change" (quoted in Tafoya, 1990, p. 13).

They recognized that the "tried and true" methods had become so ingrained as to be considered practically sacred doctrine. And in the actual state of affairs, they saw a real failure of traditional policing methods to resolve some of the most important problems confronting policing: dealings with minority communities, drug trafficking, gang activity, and even violent crime itself. According to Rosenbaum (1994), the persistence of these problems

> only hastened the push to find a more effective and just paradigm for policing in the 1990s. In a nutshell, hundreds of cities . . . decided that "business as usual," asking the police to drive around randomly in squad cars and respond to radio calls, does little to address or alleviate persistent community problems. (p. xi)

It was quickly concluded that the Reform Era model had to give way to something new. This conclusion was well stated in a report of the Boston Police Department Management Review Committee: "The traditional tactics of patrol, rapid response to 911 calls, and detective investigation must be replaced by a system in which officers are given authority to work with community residents to identify and solve the problems that contribute to crime, and are held accountable for achieving those goals" (quoted in "Boston Mayor's Panel," 1992, p. 6).

While traditional policing, relying almost totally on the application of the criminal law, was being considered less and less effective in confronting contemporary problems, a new approach that depended on a variety of methods to control crime, far beyond the simple application of the criminal law, was quickly evolving. Addressing the root causes of crime, educating the community to take an active role in its own defense, and understanding community needs and values all began to be considered, along with other "strange" new directions for the police enterprise. New deployment of resources, chains of command, and overall police strategies began to emerge in support of this effort to achieve a new effectiveness in crime control.

This new approach had two characteristics that immediately set it apart from the old model. First, it involved a whole new set of relationships with the community and a recognition that, as Kennedy (1993) commented, "the police alone cannot solve many crime and order problems, but in partnership with others, who have time, money, expertise, ideas, energy, equipment and more, perhaps they can" (p. 6). Second, it emphasized the search for specific solutions to problems rising from particular circumstances, thus departing from the old pattern of applying one solution generally to all problems that occurred. The first new emphasis, on community involvement, gave rise to the term *community-oriented policing,* and the second led to the development of the term *problem-oriented policing.*

The community and problem-solving approaches together seem to be a "commonsense" response to the more major problems of crime control in contemporary society. It seems unrealistic to expect any solution without the involvement of the community or to expect any one solution imposed from above to deal effectively with the problems presented by a highly complex crime picture, civil disorder of numerous types, the ever-changing drug scene, and citizens' fear of crime of differing types in various communities with highly differing needs.

The literature suggests that social order is best maintained by the informal social processes within neighborhoods and not just by police activity. This makes clear the importance of having citizens participate in the crime control efforts in their area and the need to marshall all community resources to prevent crime (Goldstein, 1993).

Recognizing all of these things, enlightened police leaders worked toward the development of new processes within their departments that could fill gaps in existing strategies and entirely replace strategies when indicated. In effect, they were attempting to develop a new set of goals for policing and all of the necessary strategies to support those goals.

DEFINITIONS OF COMMUNITY POLICING

What has evolved in community policing is not one simple, clear concept but a broad range of approaches with several readily identifiable commonalities. It seems that, even after years of evolution, there is no accepted fixed definition of community policing either in the literature or in actual police practice. As Goldstein (1994) commented,

> The concept community policing is often used without concern for its substance. Political leaders and unfortunately many police leaders hook onto the label for the positive images it projects, but do not engage or invest in the concept. . . . In many quarters today, community policing is used to encompass practically all innovations in policing, from the most ambitious to the most mundane, from the most carefully thought through to the most casual. (p. viii)

Similarly, Bayley (1988) stated that although community policing is

> widely, almost universally said to be important, it means different things to different people—public relations campaigns, shop fronts and mini-stations,

> rescaled patrol beats, liaison with ethnic groups, permission for rank and file to speak to the press, neighborhood watch, foot patrol, patrol detective team, and door-to-door visits by police officers. Community policing on the ground often seems less a program than a set of aspirations wrapped up in a slogan. (p. 225)

There are so many differing opinions on what constitutes community policing, and so many different terms and phrases used in treating the topic, that summarizing the essential elements of the concept is a challenging task. However, the differences reflected in nomenclature are minor when set against the obvious similarities. The common elements were well summarized recently on the cover page of a report of the International City Management Association (1989):

> Whether they are called "community-oriented policing" or "neighborhood policing" or "problem-oriented policing," the idea is to take the police officer out of isolation as a lone crime-fighter and make him or her part of a team that includes not only the staff resources of the police department, but also the resources of the local government and the resources of private citizens. Traditional lines of command are replaced with new group arrangements that emphasize problem solving and personal interaction.

Community policing, in the broadest sense is an overall philosophy of policing that encompasses concepts and strategies generally included in the notions of community-oriented policing and problem-solving policing. Although programs may vary widely, they always include a proactive (rather than reactive) stance and a new and much higher level of involvement with the community. They most often also include decentralization of control, affiliation with and responsibility for a particular geographical area, reallocation of resources, greater use of foot patrols (return to the beat), development and use of many new and different skills by officers, and new and different methods of evaluating individual officers and departmental performance.

A mere reallocation of resources or use of a tactic that is generally part of community policing, such as foot patrols, does not constitute community policing. Only if resources are reallocated as a result of a participative decision-making process with community members, or if foot patrol is assigned along with specific geographic responsibilities (beats) and is accompanied by a sense of "ownership" of an area and close communication with its residents, can such efforts be considered signs of a department's commitment to a program of community policing. Partnership with the community and a proactive stance are the necessary elements; verbal commitments to the concept or individual tactical demonstrations alone are not sufficient.

NEW PHILOSOPHY AND ROLES

One of the most obvious unifying elements in the multiple approaches to community policing is the general agreement on its intended outcome. Whereas formerly the performance evaluations of police were based on quantifiable factors such as number of activities and response time, now the quality of life in neighborhoods and citizens' satisfaction with their community become of paramount importance. The relationship between the police and the community changes dramatically from a distant and sometimes almost adversarial relationship to one of consultation and collaboration.

Police consultation with members of the public can mean merely that the police listen to the community to improve the quality of service without affecting their operational policy. But it also can mean that the police listen to the community to determine police priorities and policy and have some system of public accountability. The latter is referred to by Skolnick and Bayley (1986) as police *collaboration* with the community. This is a relationship in which the police and the public work together to achieve common goals. In this model, the police and the public are coproducers of the public safety. According to the National Institute of Justice (1995c), this approach "re-orients police philosophy and strategy away from primary reliance on reactive tactics toward the view that crime, disorder, fear and other community problems can be better redressed and prevented pro-actively—through multifaceted consultative and collaborative relationships among police, diverse community groups and public and private sector institutions" (p. 1).

The need for such collaboration is especially marked in relation to the drug and gang problems, where the totally reactive programs simply do not work. The effort to find out what causes persons to enter gangs or get into the drug market in the first place requires close communication with the community, and efforts to deal with it require a partnership approach.

For some years now, without this partnership, communities have been inflicting great pain on themselves by making drastic changes in their own lifestyle and landscape rather than working toward a new paradigm for crime control. People have begun to avoid activities that were once sources of comfort and joy, like family visits, church attendance, and visits to the theater, and have altered their homes and business places to the point that these resemble fortresses in some cases. This trend has been changing recently with the introduction of community policing. The interaction of the community with the police breaks down the isolation syndrome and encourages a sharing of concerns and proposals in a process of effective two-way communication.

Essential to community collaboration and the building of a partnership in crime control is the presence of the officer on foot in the neighborhood. People have the opportunity to know their officer by name and as a person with strengths and weaknesses. They can assist and encourage the officer in performing his or her functions, and they can hold the officer directly accountable if he or she exceeds his or her authority or engages in any destructive behavior.

The officer in these daily contacts also learns the strengths, weaknesses, problems, hopes, and fears of the people of the neighborhood. He or she learns whom to trust and whom to keep an eye on and develops very valuable sources of information as the trust level increases. Citizens soon become aware that the officer is an intimate and viable neighborhood presence who does much more than simply arrest people or disperse crowds. When successful, he or she helps to solve problems, to organize positive programs, and to provide a sense of empowerment to the neighborhood citizens (Trojanowicz & Bucqueroux, 1992a).

Community police are officers who walk a beat, but they are much more than that. Their foot patrols are really the means of developing a working relationship, understanding problems, and pinpointing where service delivery is necessary. Their presence and the exercise of these positive functions provide great support to neighborhoods in dealing with disorder and help to allay the fear of crime that more and more is found to be linked with neighborhood disorder problems. Officers are no longer anonymous but well known. They are seen no longer as threatening but as helping. Their presence is no longer to be feared but to be welcomed.

This "new breed" of police officer is especially valuable in establishing much-needed relationships with "hard-to-reach" young people who are at risk for drug problems and involvement in crime. Because these youth often have no satisfactory relationships at home and have been rejected by or rejecting of school, the opportunity to relate positively to an authority figure is an opportunity to prevent entrance into gangs, experimentation with drugs, and eventual serious crime. In some places, resourceful police officers have even provided mentoring services, brought together groups and agencies to address youth problems on a much wider scale in the area, and succeeded in raising the awareness of the entire community as to the needs of youth.

Critics of community policing refer to such service involvement as "social work" and not "real police work." Often they call officers involved in these important programs "super nice guys" or "lollicops" and describe their work as being "soft on crime." But crime—and the fighting of crime—cannot be separated from the social context in which it occurs. As the chief of police of one large metropolitan area expressed it, the police cannot "do anything about true crime in the sense that there are so many underlying social policies that create environments where crime flourishes. We're sort of the firefighters at the back end" (Potter, quoted in Clark, 1993, p. 7). Community policing, by addressing the social dimension, at least on a neighborhood level, expands the possibilities for dealing with crime. Thus, "Community policing isn't a gimmick; it's not smoke and mirrors. It works—and not just in the soft, touchy feely areas that are important, but in terms of law enforcement as well" (Potter, quoted in Clark, 1993, p. 7).

When officers engage in social service activities, they are actively preventing crime, but such officers also engage in traditional activities such as solving crimes and making arrests. To criticize them for being "soft on crime" or engaging in nonpolice work seems unfair. There is little evidence that police officers involved in various aspects of community policing are unable to engage in other police activities as necessary. In fact, it seems that in combining the best of both approaches, the "new policing" becomes more effective. As Walters (1993) has argued,

> Although both of these approaches have merit, the reality is that with the complex crime problems facing society today, law enforcement administrators need to synthesize the two strategies into a comprehensive response to crime. Both approaches, swift police response to incident and disorder, and problem-oriented policing, are critical to serving communities in a balanced manner. The combination of these two law enforcement strategies provides an even more dynamic form of law enforcement—community-oriented policing (COP). (p. 20)

APPEAL OF COMMUNITY POLICING PROGRAMS

Flexibility

One reason that the community policing approach is becoming more accepted is its flexibility in dealing with the specific problems of particular communities. As Walters (1993) argued,

> Today's police managers must resolve new problems within their communities through cost-effective, innovative ways. Community-oriented policing offers an interesting possibility to departments nationwide.
>
> A combination of problem-oriented policing and response to incidents, community-oriented policing offers a comprehensive and balanced approach to maintaining high levels of safety and security throughout neighborhoods. However, in order to ensure effectiveness, managers need to adapt the strategy to the changing demands of their jurisdiction. (p. 23)

The awareness that flexibility and the decentralization of control that makes it possible are difficult to attain under the traditional policing model is fast becoming a part of the contemporary wisdom in policing:

> Existing police structures tend to be mechanistic and highly centralized. Headquarters is the brain that does the thinking for the whole organization. Headquarters, having thought, disseminates rules and regulations in order to control practice throughout the organization.
>
> . . . New ideas are never conceived, evaluated and implemented in the same place, so they are seldom owned or pursued enthusiastically by those in contact with the community.
>
> Why is this state of affairs a hindrance to the ideas of community policing? Because it allows for no sensitivity either on a district level (to the special needs of the community) or on an individual level (to the particular considerations of one case). It operates on the assumption that wealthy suburban districts need to be policed in much the same way as public housing apartments. While patrol officers may be asked to behave sensitively to the needs of the community and to the individuals with whom they deal, there is little organizational support for such behavior. (Sparrow, 1988, p. 4)

In contrast, under the new model, community officers are constantly encouraged to engage in problem solving based on their observations and communication in the community. They feel a responsibility for their geographic area, and they are not saddled with demands and directives from central headquarters that seem to have little relevance to their beat as they perceive it.

Cultural Sensitivity

The need for establishing better trust with, and delivering services more effectively to, racially and ethnically diverse groups of citizens is one of the major forces impelling the shift to community policing. This endeavor shows great promise for success.

An enormous amount of historical baggage is carried by law enforcement officers in minority communities. Although improvement has been made in many places, few observers would say that the problem is relatively solved or that great tension between the police and racial groups does not still exist.

The two opposing viewpoints of minority group members and police officers were recorded recently by Sadd and Grinc (1993). A large number of community residents indicated that a major reason for lack of involvement in community policing programs or even outright hostility was the historically negative relationship between the police and the residents of economically disadvantaged communities. Such relationships, most common in areas of the city usually chosen as the target sites for community policing demonstration projects, will not be easily changed. Police officers in many of the sites interpreted the refusal of the residents to become involved as apathy or lack of interest in bettering their own lives. The lack of involvement may, however, be due less to apathy than to this long-standing antagonism. There is a tremendous amount of work to be done in police-community relations in many communities throughout the country, and a racial subtext underlies many of the issues that face police officers in contemporary America.

Many professionals and scholars agree that community policing presents the best hope to deal effectively with the distrust and often the hostility toward police in many neighborhoods, especially in African American communities. As Williams and Murphy (1990) pointed out, some of the most eloquent advocates of community policing are African American police executives.

The opportunity that community policing presents to break down barriers with minority groups, especially with the young, is also being professionally recognized. According to McGlothian-Taylor (1992),

> Many minorities view police as the oppressor. Community-policing offers minority children the chance to experience positive interaction with police at an early age. . . . Children at early ages are given the opportunity to call officers by their first name and see them do very positive things instead of just making arrests, giving tickets or beating and shooting people. (p. 4)

Reactions in the minority community immediately after a well-publicized arrest of a minority member, especially when injury or death is involved, and certainly the vivid memory of the frighteningly brutal beating of Rodney King, continually remind us of the need for programs that will provide us with measurable improvement in police-minority group relations. In a publication of the National Center for Community Policing at Michigan State University (Trojanowicz, 1991), this fact was forcefully stated:

> The ugly crime of police brutality, with its subtext of racism, is dangerous not only because of the threat it poses to potential victims, but because it jeopardizes the overall credibility of the police.
>
> . . . Most of the discussions about solutions so far have focused on training and minority recruiting, and on the need for police chiefs to send an unambiguous message that abuse and harassment will not be tolerated. . . . All are essential pieces of the puzzle, yet equally if not more important is the need for fundamental reform in the relationship between people and police—a shift from confrontation to cooperation that only community policing can supply. (p. 1)

It has been argued that community policing, by establishing relations of trust and an intimate knowledge of the neighborhood and its residents, actually contributes to better crime control and in some cases can even prevent tragedy. For example, Trojanowicz and Bucqueroux (1991) pointed to the recent highly publicized police reaction to an incident at the end of the horrible serial killing career of Jeffrey Dahmer:

> Dahmer apparently persuaded the officer that the young Laotian boy was his adult homosexual lover with whom he had quarreled. As tapes of telephone conversations with concerned neighbors later confirmed, the officers put more credence in Dahmer's explanation, the explanation of the white middle-class male, than in the concerns expressed by the lower-class minority females who called wanting to know if the Asian boy was all right.
>
> A community officer in Dahmer's neighborhood would at least have given the police department a better chance at uncovering his crime sooner. (p. 18)

Under the traditional, reactive policing model, minority communities are especially likely to feel that police are unresponsive to their concerns. An outstanding example of police indifference to and neglect of the public is found in the recent report of the Independent Commission on the Los Angeles Police Department (1991):

> Of the 2,152 citizen allegations of excessive force from 1986 through 1990, only 42 were sustained. The Commission has found that the complaint system is skewed against complainants. People who wish to file complaints face significant hurdles. Some intake officers actively discourage filing by being uncooperative or requiring long waits before completing a complaint form. In many heavily Latino divisions, there is often no Spanish-speaking officer available to take complaints. (p. 13)

Such unresponsiveness results in high levels of citizen dissatisfaction and seriously inhibits good police performance. In the community policing model, in contrast, the familiar police officer "on the beat," listening to his or her neighbors and engaging in group problem solving on a regular basis, develops a sense of trust in advance of the need for any call for help and provides a constant line of communication to the police department from the neighborhood.

SUPPORT FOR COMMUNITY POLICING AMONG POLICE

Community policing has found widespread support in law enforcement agencies throughout the country. A 1993 survey of more than 2,000 law enforcement agencies sponsored by the National Institute of Justice (1995b) found strong support nationwide for the community policing approach and for the need to develop and train practitioners. Although 48% of the police chiefs and sheriffs polled felt that implementation of community policing would require major changes in organizational policies and goals, and although 56% anticipated that rank-and-file employees would resist such changes, these officials overwhelmingly endorsed the concept of community policing. They especially cited the following benefits:

1. Fewer problems on issues of concern to citizens
2. Improved physical environment in neighborhoods
3. More positive public attitude toward law enforcement agencies
4. Decreased potential for conflict between citizens and police
5. Increased officer satisfaction
6. Reduced crime rates

Of the officials polled, 99% reported improved cooperation between citizens and police, 80% reported reduced fear of crime among citizens, and 62% reported fewer crimes against persons. It is true that 81% of these police executives thought that crime might just be displaced to a non-community-policing area, and 43% believed that response to calls for service would decline. But despite these reservations, overall support for the concept was strong, and it remains so, as evidenced by the fact that, in the past 4 years, over a dozen national conferences have been held on the subject, each drawing a large attendance of professional police officers.

Although hundreds of departments have at least partially implemented the concept, full implementation of community policing in many places is severely inhibited by resistance from within the police culture (Sparrow, Moore, & Kennedy, 1990). Some officers steeped in the traditions of Reform Era policing continue to feel hostility toward community policing. Such hostility was described in 1991 by Doug Elder, president of the Houston Police Officers Association: "I think most officers feel it's a hoax, renaming things and using a lot of buzz words and the like. . . . I think a lot of officers probably feel they are expected to be more like social workers than police officers" (quoted in "Study Criticizes Community Policing," 1991, p. 132). The emphasis on "traditional police work" as an ingrained value within the police subculture, as opposed to the delivery of other necessary services, was discussed as early as 1978 by Charles Silberman:

> Unfortunately, the police have become prisoners of their own mystique. They have been avid readers of detective stories since modern policing began, and many are fervent fans of Kojak, Columbo, Baretta and other heroes of the television screen. The police definition of their role, indeed their whole sense of self, has been shaped by these fictional accounts of their exploits. "We are all recruited like little boys to play cops and robbers" was stated by Joseph McNamara, Chief of the Police Department in San Jose, California.
>
> The playing cops and robbers is only a small part, in some ways the least important part of what the police do. (p. 202)

Silberman reported that "because their self-image is bound up so closely with their crime-control mission, policemen tend to look down on every other activity as not real police work" (p. 202).

Of course, as many observers have pointed out, the image of police work presented in TV, movies, and detective stories is not really true to life. It is generally accepted that police spend only a small portion of their time arresting criminals and engaging in other crime control activities; they spend the majority of their time doing traffic control, paperwork, and service activities. Further, media crime dramas are misleading in that they perpetuate a "value-free" image of police work (e.g., Kojak is free to kick down doors, assault suspects, and in other ways do as he pleases in fighting crime). Nevertheless, the "crime fighter" image is cherished by many police who have been trained and have operated under the traditional system.

The impact of the new policing model on police subculture is very great and is threatening to those who wish to maintain the status quo. But, according to Goldstein (1993), many aspects of police subculture need to be changed in the ways that community policing would encourage:

> Currently, for example, one of the greatest impediments to improvement in policing is the strength of the police subculture. That subculture draws much of its strength from a secret shared among police: that they are compelled to bend the law and take shortcuts in order to get the job done. Providing the police with legitimate clear-cut means to carry out their functions enables them to operate more honestly and openly and therefore has potential for reducing the strength, and as a consequence, the negative influence, of the police subculture. (pp. 4-5)

SUCCESS OF COMMUNITY POLICING PROGRAMS

To varying degrees, hundreds of departments are currently actively involved in the evolution of community policing in America today. In the past 2 years, as a result of the Community Oriented Policing Services (COPS) Program authorized by the 1994 Crime Act, hundreds of communities have either begun to develop or expanded community policing programs. In 1995, the Justice Department's COPS office awarded more than $1.5 billion, which enabled communities across America to hire more than 31,000 community officers, and in 1996 the program was budgeted at $1.6 billion.

Evaluating the success of community policing programs is complex because of the varying definitions of "success" and because of the wide variety of program elements included under similar names in various jurisdictions. Further, it is difficult to compare evaluative results across varying stages of program implementation. Partial implementation and the interference of random problems such as budget deficiencies, personality incompatibilities, and spontaneous outbursts of criminal behavior have obscured the evaluation picture many times.

However, in some enlightened departments that are totally committed to the community policing concept and in which the entire department's mission is formulated in terms of enabling work in partnership with local communities, the record of success has been striking. One such department is the Chicago Police Department, which in 1992 began its Chicago Alternative Policing Strategy (CAPS) in five districts chosen as prototypical. There was much preparatory work before the program was actually launched, most notably the training of 1,700 officers in problem-solving techniques. In addition, the department hired a management consultant to analyze the department and recommend a strategy. It also studied the efforts of several other cities so that their mistakes might be avoided.

Despite many difficulties of internal and external resistance and suspicion, the program went forward. In 1994, the city contracted with the Chicago Alliance for Neighborhood Safety (CANS), the organization that had taken the lead in advocating community policing in Chicago in the beginning, to train the community in problem-solving techniques and techniques of working with each other and in cooperation with the police. The Chicago effort has been so successful that it is being expanded into all 25 police districts (National Institute of Justice, 1995a).

The Chicago experience clearly indicates that police departments with long histories of traditional approaches to policing can change and move toward shared decision making and a proactive stance. Similar results were reported by the evaluators of a community policing program in Madison, Wisconsin: "The most dramatic finding is that it is possible to 'bend granite'—it is possible to change a traditional control-oriented police organization into one in which the employees become members of work teams and participants in decision-making processes" (Wycoff & Skogan, 1993, p. 84). The Madison research also suggested that the community benefited from the departmental change because there was some indication of a reduction in crime and in levels of citizen concern about crime. And there were indications that treating employees in the police organization as internal customers made them better able to understand what it meant to treat citizens as external customers. According to Wycoff and Skogan (1993), the data showed that "officers' attitudes can shift from more traditional views of policing to ones that are more in line with police community involvement and problem identification and resolution, even among officers with many years of service" (pp. 84-85).

REQUIREMENTS FOR SUCCESSFUL IMPLEMENTATION OF PROGRAMS

Community Partnership and Participative Management

The need for both rank-and-file police officers and the community to be actively and meaningfully involved in the planning of community policing programs is shown by a recent study of Innovative Neighborhood Oriented Policing (INOP) programs in eight cities (Sadd & Grinc, 1996). INOP uses the principles of community policing and problem-oriented policing and relates them to drug demand reduction. Its central thesis is that partnership between police and the community can be effective in reducing both crime and fear in neighborhoods.

Within the INOP program, intensive local street-level enforcement was combined with prevention and treatment efforts. The intensive enforcement attempted to make it considerably more difficult for buyers and sellers to establish links and thus to discourage new users from becoming more heavily involved. This relative short-term strategy was combined with more long-term efforts to involve the community in programs of prevention, education, and treatment. The comprehensive program held great promise of success in effectively reducing the demand for drugs in the targeted areas. Unfortunately, however, one of the major difficulties encountered in this project was gaining police acceptance. It is significant that in all eight cities, the police administrators were the initiators and formulators of the program. Rank-and-file police officers had little if any input into program design and development. Police officers in the areas generally had little training in the goals of the program or even in community policing in general. As a result, officers showed considerable resistance when asked to change from their traditional roles.

Perhaps just as important, representatives of city agencies and neighborhood residents were for the most part excluded from the planning process. The role of the community was never properly interpreted, so many citizens felt that their involvement meant simply giving information to the police about crime. There seemed to be a two-way communication problem, with the neighborhood not knowing its expected role and the police not being able to discover what the community really wanted from the program.

The INOP experience is not unique. Here, as elsewhere, internal resistance points to the need for total department understanding and acceptance of the concept, strong leadership from top administration, and widespread participation in the planning process before the program is initiated. Further, the INOP findings suggest that without adequate training for community residents as to their expected roles, and without participation by all other agencies in the development stages, community policing programs can never realize their full potential (Sadd & Grinc, 1993).

The need for long-term strategy and a high level of community involvement is also shown by the outcome of the Hartford COMPASS program. This program, a "Weed and Seed" (reclamation and stabilization) program, was designed to "weed out" the drug problem in the target area and then to "seed" the target area with business and activities to replace the "weeded-out" drug businesses and activities. In such a design, intensive policing activity is only the beginning stage of the overall project (Tien & Rich, 1994).

With the community's input and help, the police were able to reclaim a targeted area. They did this by performing a drug market analysis and by employing a variety of community policing and antidrug tactics. This step is essential in keeping with the basic premise that street-level drug sales are a key contributor to the declining quality of life in urban neighborhoods.

At the end of the "weeding" operation, evaluations showed extensive positive publicity for the city and particularly the police department. Because of the positive results of the first step, success for the next step of the program was anticipated. But despite a positive community attitude, the "seeding" program never became fully developed because of turmoil in city government and a negative budget climate that made funding difficult. In the final analysis, COMPASS actually became only a "weeding" program, with the police as the dominant player.

The story of COMPASS suggests that although an intensive, coordinated police effort can have positive effects in even some of the poorest areas of the community, long-term improvements in the area are likely to be elusive at best without a "seeding" program to offer alternatives to persons previously involved in the drug trade. The evaluation of the COMPASS program stated that the city and entire community, including businesses, must cooperate to plan and implement a program that is citywide. Police efforts alone cannot have the desired effects, especially if the results are to be long term (Tien & Rich, 1994).

One recent evaluation of a community policing project (Rosenbaum & Wilkinson, 1993) concluded that full involvement of line officers in the decision-making process greatly reduces resistance and enhances the likelihood of successful implementation. A rigid paramilitary model, the authors argued, does not easily support development of community policing. A community policing program can be conducted under such circumstances, but it requires informal support or independence as a unit for some time during the development period if it is to have a chance of survival, and it may never develop to its full potential.

Total Quality Management

Community policing readily incorporates many of the ideas of total quality management (TQM), particularly an emphasis on consumer satisfaction as the primary goal, the importance of evaluating quality over quantity, the need for participative management and continual input from all those involved in a project, and the importance of teamwork.

Of particular relevance to policing is the move away from numerical goals for production or service and numerical standards for evaluation of employees. As Scholtes (1991) pointed out, such evaluation pays little if any attention to processes and systems or to the real capabilities of the organization as a whole. A problem resulting from strict adherence to numerical goals and standards is that eventually workers, supervisors, and even managers get caught up in playing games involving these numbers.

First, meeting the immediate goal becomes much more important than quality. When quotas are imposed, people will meet them at any cost, and quality suffers (Deming, 1986). Thus, for example, a large steel corporation that constantly emphasized quantity of output found that although its employees consistently met the quotas, the quality of the product became so degraded that the corporation eventually went out of business.

Further, personnel in organizations tend to focus on the things for which they are immediately rewarded, and these are usually the measurable short-term objectives. These get the attention because the immediate results get the priority of emphasis, even though the long-term goals of the agency, such as consumer satisfaction, may not be well served.

Yet another problem is the concern with "looking good" that numerical goals create. This frequently causes conflict within an organization in that one unit or person's short-term gain is opposed to the gain of another unit or person. Thus, when salespeople are pushed to sell in order to meet quotas, they often end up making promises that production or warehousing cannot fulfill. Such conflicts between departments or persons lead to "finger pointing" and an endless series of excuses shifting the blame to others (Scholtes, 1991). In relation to criminal justice, courts are constantly blamed by police and corrections officers, corrections officers are blamed by the other elements, police are blamed by probation and parole officials, and so the game goes on. Within police departments, detectives are often criticized by patrol, patrol by other specialized units, and vice versa, all to the diminishment of the overall effectiveness.

Still other abuses can readily result, such as manipulation of figures when desired outcomes are not readily available; creation of an atmosphere of fear among employees who are threatened by loss of raises or promotions; and, ultimately, a tendency to become more and more blind to the "outside world" in which the persons who receive the organization's services live. Finally, when accomplishment is seen as resulting from meeting numerical goals, it is difficult for employees simply to take delight in providing a service that works and satisfies the consumer (Scholtes, 1991).

Obviously, it is necessary to develop a whole new set of mechanisms for evaluating officer and department performance in the move toward community policing. David Couper, chief of police in Madison, Wisconsin, argues that community policing must be "quality policing." He strongly believes that "in policing, the process of improvement is a never-ending search for ways to improve quality police service" and states that

> the goal is citizen-customer satisfaction. . . . Conceptually, community policing provides a wealth of opportunities for managers to innovate and challenge many of the long held myths that have characterized the field for more than a century. Everything from the quasi-military model to reactive patrol has come under scrutiny; and the future promises continuing change, if community policing advocates continue to hold the spotlight. (quoted in Ward, 1991, p. 19)

Changes in the way effectiveness is evaluated are fundamental if community policing is to be implemented in a department. Response time and number of arrests may still be helpful in measuring how well police handle emergency incidents, but they provide no adequate measurement of the overall effectiveness of a community policing approach. More important are measures of the community's satisfaction with the service being provided and the community's input into the decision-making process.

It is obvious that the paramilitary model of policing facilitates the close supervision of officers in the traditional role, but this model is inappropriate for supervising officers in the broader, more discretionary role mandated by community policing. Thus, new issues are raised about employee performance evaluation, including the means by which supervisors and managers hold officers accountable for the use of their greater discretion, the inclusion of the community in the evaluation process, and the evaluation of the team or unit or organization as distinct from the evaluation of the individual officer (Wycoff & Oettmeier, 1994).

The challenge of evaluating community police officers has been said to be one of "finding ways to express quality as quantity—in other words, to make quality an accountable commodity." This means "identify[ing] quantifiable outcomes that truly relate to the job, and . . . ensur[ing] that this does not corrupt community-policing (or any other orientation to policing) into policing by the numbers (Trojanowicz & Bucqueroux, 1992b, p. 16).

The emphases of a TQM approach to policing are reflected in the list compiled by one professional (Stephen R. Harris, President of the International Association of Chiefs of Police and Chief of Police in Redmond, Washington) of attributes of police agencies that have adopted a more progressive approach in their departments:

1. A sense of agency mission that reflects community or constituent needs and expectations
2. Community/constituent organizational-based objectives with measurable results
3. Teamwork, both internally and with other services in other communities
4. A commitment to problem solving, using data to make thoughtful decisions
5. Imagination to devise and attempt creative approaches to different problems
6. A commitment to sensitive, humane, and professional behavior
7. Honest evaluation of accomplishment against objective

According to Harris, "Perhaps most important of all is a willingness to take risks and try new approaches to continuously improve. Quality is a moving target and one can never be sure that there isn't a better way—just over the horizon—to accomplish an objective" (quoted in "Seavey Award," 1993, p. 13).

Personal Qualifications and Education of Community Policing Officers

Far from lowering the level of police professionalism, community policing demands that it be raised. Community policing is an awesome responsibility. It demands that officers be suited by personal characteristics and education to earn the trust of the community and their own confidence in their ability to perform in this new way.

Under community policing, individual officers are valued for, and evaluated on, communication skills; sensitivity to cultural diversity; abilities to engage in interagency networking, problem solving, mediation, negotiation, and community organization; and a host of other skills that have not appeared in police evaluations previously. Their job requirements extend far beyond making arrests and maintaining the general order. Whereas formerly their discretion was rigidly contained as far as possible and their responses were to be as predictable as possible, now their ability to use discretion and develop new solutions is crucial to their performance. Input from the community becomes a primary source of guidance and direction, as far as possible, and programs mandated from headquarters become much less frequent and perhaps eventually almost nonexistent.

What kind of officer is required for successful community policing? Lee Brown, former Commissioner of Police in Houston and New York City, emphasized the need to recruit and train officers with a spirit of service, not just a quest for adventure or macho experiences. He stated in a recent interview that the successful community police officer must "be knowledgeable about people and problems" (quoted in Rosen, 1992, p. 10). Moore and Trojanowicz (1988) similarly described the need for "generalist patrol officers who are as comfortable outside their cars as in, and as capable of organizing meetings and mediating disputes as of making arrests" (p. 11).

While developing an intimate knowledge of the community and of individual persons within that area, officers must also be keenly aware of their own strengths, limitations, and needs. Self-knowledge is probably an even more important requirement than knowledge of the community. When people exercising great authority and discretion fail to understand others, they are capable of doing great damage, but when they fail to understand themselves, they will almost certainly be a negative force.

In medicine, law, and nursing, higher education has always been the key to professional recognition and authorization to exercise a wide latitude of discretion in the performance of one's duties. Higher education of community police officers is important for the same reasons. Unfortunately, there are some who believe that "too much education" for community police officers would inhibit their ability to relate in the culturally diverse atmosphere in which they must function. This is not a valid criticism because raised self-esteem is one of the first fruits of higher education, and those who "feel good about themselves" are always better able to relate to those with different opinions and diverse lifestyles. Further, as Patrick Murphy (1989), former chief of the New York City Police Department and currently with the Police Foundation, has stated, "A college-educated police force has the potential to proactively, rather than just reactively, address the crime and drug problems that plague society today" (p. 1). This is so because problem-solving, analytical, and especially writing and verbal communication skills are greatly enhanced by higher education. An especially crucial need in the years ahead will be knowledge of languages other than English. According to McCord and Wicker (1990), "By the year 2000, a major thrust [in police training] will likely be toward communication with non-English speaking communities, perhaps with incentives for bilingualism" (p. 31).

One national study indicated that only 14% of the reporting law enforcement agencies required education beyond high school in 1989 but that a substantial proportion (22.6%) of the officers in the study had already obtained college degrees. Raising the educational requirements may present a problem in minority recruitment, which is essential to the success of the community program, but this can possibly be dealt with in other positive ways (Carter, Sapp, & Stephens, 1989).

Networking in the Community

It is generally recognized that the future of community policing depends on the police and the community to identify needs together and pool their resources. Trojanowicz (1994), for example, stated that

> there needs to be the commitment from all the "Big Five," the police, the community, social agencies, political leaders and the media. Citizens need to do more for themselves and volunteer to help rejuvenate their neighborhoods; social agencies need to do their share; political leaders need to provide long-term commitment and support; the media needs to educate the public and the police cannot conduct business as usual. (pp. 258-259)

The ability of the police to network becomes a key to evaluating the effectiveness of the entire department. Marshalling the resources of all the social agencies and community groups enables police to do things that are far beyond the limited resources of the police department itself. The essential nature of the community role in the partnership cannot be overemphasized. As Friedman (1994) argued,

> To the degree community policing reaches beyond the problem solving methodology toward partnership, it is a coordinated strategy, and the role, knowledge and effectiveness of the partner is critical to its success. In community policing the quality of the community's participation is decisive. If community policing is to contribute to the reduction of crime and disorder and the improvement of a neighborhood's quality of life, more than dialogue

> between professionals and even more than real police organization is necessary.
>
> The community must have a voice in the forums that define community-policing itself; must be a ready and knowledgeable ally to the forces of reform; and, in the neighborhood, where the benefits are supposed to be delivered, must have a serious part in implementing solutions as well as nominating problems. (pp. 263-264)

The neighborhood network center of Lansing, Michigan, applies this concept well. According to one report, "Officer Don Christie serves as protector and unofficial leader for the other agency people who followed his lead 'out on the beat.' He has direct contact with and assistance from school psychologists, social workers, student nurses, drug treatment counselors and other specialists and a host of community volunteers" (Weaver, 1992, p. 3).

Another example of successful networking is the community-oriented policing office that was opened in Newport, Rhode Island in 1990 because of serious crime, violence, illegal drug trafficking, and quality-of-life problems. As Weaver (1992) has reported,

> A multi-faceted program was put into place under the guidance of the community police officer in conjunction with other social agencies and neighborhood persons, including the housing authority, schools, city agencies, etc. This center now publishes a community policing newsletter, sponsors neighborhood watch groups, and utilizes Turn-in-the-Pushers (TIPS) Program and drug awareness programs for parents and youth. Additionally it provides basic and advanced women's self-defense courses and aerobic classes, mens night programs providing basketball, fitness, weightlifting, etc. . . . , field trips for youth, parenting skills seminars, substance abuse outreach programs, youth and peer counseling and teen and youth dances.
>
> An evaluation, done after two years of operation, showed "encouraging" results. Street corner dealing seems to be virtually eliminated, with trafficking constrained to residential units and alleys in the early morning hours. The local gang has been interrupted, and out of town drug trafficking has been reduced substantially. Other crimes seem to have fallen off considerably, most likely as a result of increased enforcement and improved neighborhood attitude. Malicious mischief incidents dropped 34%, attributed to the neighborhood's overall improvement and new found respect. (p. 3)

The networking function of community policing is especially clear in the efforts being made to assist in providing mental health services. Traditionally, the police were summoned only when a situation got "out of hand" and some person's behavior became totally unmanageable. In these situations, the police were always seen as the last recourse, yet because of a lack of available services, they were frequently called on. According to Murphy (1986),

> One of the main reasons the police become involved with the mentally ill is that in most communities they usually have the only 24-hour, 7-day-a-week, mobile emergency community-response capacity. Add to this the authority the police agencies have and the fact that they are a non-charging service, and it becomes easy to understand the extent of their involvement in various community services. Without the existence of 24-hour emergency mental health services, the public has but one option—call the police. (p. 12)

In the community-based police model, the officers are in the neighborhood and working actively with mental health agencies in a proactive stance. Several police agencies around the country have developed very exciting programs working intimately on a continuing basis with mental health agencies. Marans (1995) reported how

> police in New Haven embarked on a new community-based approach that relied on the development of relationships between officers and the neighborhood residents for whom they work. In both fields, it became clear that we had to find other approaches to being useful, to augment traditional policing and clinical responses with more sustained and systemic intervention in the lives of children and families at-risk.
>
> . . . We recognized our shared concern about the same groups of children and families . . . who came to the attention of clinicians as traumatized, anxious, and angry youngsters who defied attempts at treatment.
>
> . . . The new officer has a preventive role and an early intervention responsibility; the officer does not consider himself or herself successful through making more arrests, but through helping to reduce crime, diverting children from adverse outcomes and helping the victims, not simply capturing the villains. (p. ix)

In the New Haven program, seminars concerning mental illness and adolescent development are arranged, and officers are given materials as to available resources for appropriate referrals. Consultation and on-call services are arranged to assist police in handling situations. The mental health professions have had to adapt by getting out of their consulting rooms and making home visits and being exposed in the field to the violence that really exists (Marans, 1995). The police and the mental health professionals meet on common ground in partnership for the good of the community. This is a practical illustration of community policing in action successfully.

SUMMARY AND CHALLENGE

The new philosophy of policing is a major change from the traditional understanding of the police function, organizational design, relationships to consumers, measurement of outcomes, tactics and technologies, and a whole host of other elements of policing. Most notably, the organizational design shifts from highly centralized to decentralized, and the police function begins to be legitimized by community support as well as by the traditional sources of law, the political structure, and professionalism.

While continuing to defend the values of law and professionalism, community policing emphasizes the need to listen to community concerns. Foot patrols, intimate knowledge of the neighborhood, and problem solving become important means of working toward the intended outcome of quality of life in the neighborhood and citizen satisfaction with the community in general. Some metropolitan departments commit themselves to increasing the growth and livability of their city in mission statements or other official documents.

Implementation of this new approach requires enormous flexibility within police organizations that have traditionally been paramilitary, authoritarian, and highly structured. As they become more open and more committed to a participatory management style at every level, training, both in the academy and in the field, along with evaluation techniques and reward systems, will have to change markedly.

Top-level administrators may feel that their job security is threatened, mid-level managers may sense a considerable loss of control, and many officers in the field may feel inadequate or even "asked to do the impossible." As a result, in numerous departments, lip service will be given to adopting the new style, but at best a limited effort will be made. Token programs may be started but given little support.

However, many totally committed top-level executives are successfully marshalling the support of all levels of their department, the political structure, the media, and the community at large. As a result, this nation is currently the scene of exciting developments throughout its policing establishment, ranging from major metropolitan areas through suburban departments and into rural areas. Goldstein (1993) described the challenge that they face with great insight:

> The policing of a free, diverse, and vibrant society is an awesome and complex task. The police are called upon to deal with a wide array of quite different behavioral problems, each perplexing in its own way. The police have tremendous power . . . to deny freedom, to use force and even to take a life. Individual officers exercise enormous discretion in using their authority in making decisions that effect our lives. The very quality of life in this country and the equilibrium of our cities depends on the way in which the police function is carried out. (pp. 1-2)

Community policing, when understood properly, is part of a general trend in our society toward greater sensitivity, tolerance of diversity, decentralization of control, and participative decision making. Thus, it can be the cutting edge of a criminal justice system much more responsive to this country's needs today. Along with progressive programs of community-based corrections (Chapter 4) and restorative justice (Chapter 5), community policing can be one of the most exciting and successful elements of a new criminal justice system.

4

Community-Based Corrections

A NEW DEFINITION OF COMMUNITY-BASED CORRECTIONS

Traditionally, the term *community-based corrections* has referred to correctional programs and services that are administered in the community rather than in secure institutions. Sometimes it has been a general term to refer to various types of therapeutic, support, and supervision programs forming a continuum of options for dealing with offenders within the community.

Such definitions are descriptive of community-based corrections as it has been implemented so far, but they are not sufficiently encompassing to provide a conceptual framework for the system's overhaul. Community-based corrections needs to be progressively defined, not merely as a collection of noninstitutional alternatives, but as a sequence of positive interventions at every point of the chain of causality, extending from prevention of crime through control of offenders. Only then can it become one of the three pillars of the emerging criminal justice system.

Several years ago, I drew up the following broad definition:

> Community-based corrections is a concept which views the criminal justice system as a whole process, emphasizing due process and the development of service delivery systems at every level, to divert the maximum number of offenders, and which employs a reintegration approach to develop alternatives to incarceration consistent with public safety and local community

needs, so that secure facilities can be reduced in size, located close to the offender's community, and utilized only when necessary. (Hahn, 1975, p. 25)

Although this definition is an obvious departure from the traditional definitions, I believe that it is necessary because of its inclusion of the following elements that do not seem to be present in other definitions:

1. *Sufficient consideration of the need for community safety.* This definition insists on "develop[ing] alternatives to incarceration consistent with public safety and local community needs." It calls for the use of secure facilities, thus making it evident that all incarceration is not eliminated from the program.
2. *Compliance with the U.S. Constitution and the safeguarding of the rights of the individual.* This definition calls for "emphasizing due process" at every level.
3. *An emphasis on diversion before entry into the system.* This definition calls for a maximum effort to divert every possible person from entering the system at the juvenile or adult level so that the system can begin to function without being overwhelmed by numbers.
4. *Recognition of the need for both residential and nonresidential programs and the fact that success will not be guaranteed at any level.* This definition seeks to avoid the utopian notion that all offenders will automatically or swiftly be successfully reintegrated into society. It simply suggests that the probability of such be increased.

Two essential components of community-based corrections are diversion and reintegration. Although both of these concepts reached some degree of prominence as early as the 1970s, they have often been misunderstood or narrowly interpreted. Both were neglected and rejected to a great degree when the "get tough" policy became popular, with its heavy emphasis on institutionalization and punitive approaches to crime control. Here, these concepts will be defined more broadly, in keeping with this book's larger vision for community-based corrections.

Diversion

The popular definition of *divert* is "turn aside or deflect" (*Webster's New World Dictionary,* 1957, p. 427). The term *diversion* as it was first used in the criminal justice system denoted an intervention in which the offender was referred to a community agency outside traditional criminal justice institutions. But now the concept has come to include almost any conscious effort to prevent initial or further penetration into the criminal justice system.

This interpretation very easily embraces the concept of using the "least restrictive alternative": that is, in all interventions, making every effort to minimize the amount of intrusion and restriction of liberty in keeping with the demands of public safety. This means making every effort to use agencies outside the justice system if at all possible; to use probation in preference to institutionalization; and, in my view, to use lesser degrees of security and more open programs when at all possible within the institutional framework.

The notion of diversion has several important implications that present difficulty to some persons both in and outside the justice system. First, in the goal of preventing entry into the criminal justice system, there seems to be a conscious admission of failure of the criminal justice system and its programs. If the best thing that one can suggest is to divert people out of the system, then we are admitting that there are drawbacks to placing people in the system. These include long court delays, problems with plea bargaining, overcrowding in institutions, the existence of criminal subcultures in institutions, and certainly the enormous financial costs. Further, it is thought by some that the notion of pretrial diversion challenges some of the basic concepts of our criminal justice system, such as the presumption of innocence, the adversary procedure, and due process (see, e.g., Ehrlich, 1993; Gibbs, 1975; Newman, 1978). Finally, diversion demands systemic change and a higher degree of tolerance on the part of some members of the community in their attitude toward offenders. The very prevalent public desire to "get tough" by incarcerating a larger number of offenders, extending the use of mandatory sentencing, giving longer sentences, and hardening conditions for offenders who are incarcerated is directly challenged by the concept of diversion.

However, these difficulties are not universally perceived, nor are they insurmountable. One enlightened congressman, Lee H. Hamilton (1971), was especially eloquent in addressing "get tough" objections to diversion. "Be prepared for accusations that you are letting hoods and murderers loose on the innocent people of your community; but that is just what is done every day anyway," he told proponents of criminal rehabilitation programs.

> Moreover, when your son or nephew, or the boy next door, gets busted, skillful lawyers and psychiatrists usually get him out of jail and into probation for a carefully designed program of treatment or supervision. Generally, the middle-class and the rich are horrified at the prospect of putting their children into the infectious garbage heap of the present correctional system. The same horror should prevent such treatment for the children of the poor. (p. 235)

Hamilton urged that people "do everything possible to get offenders out of the traditional court jail process. As a general proposition, courts and jails cannot handle and really don't know what to do with offenders. And offenders for their part seem to be generally worse off for the association" (p. 235).

Diversion that embraces the notion of prevention can precede even the commission of any offense by providing conditions in which law-abiding behavior is much more readily chosen than criminal behavior in the community at large. At the earliest stages, such conditions include adequate nutrition and medical care during childhood and even during the pregnancy of the mother. Later, "Head Start," tutoring, and special attention in school, before the commission of any offense, continue to provide prevention. When these are not completely successful and behavioral problems begin, children can be appropriately referred to agencies for status offenders and early minor delinquency offenders. After commission of offenses, opportunities for community service and restitution, mediation programs, and other programs offered to juvenile and adult offenders can prevent further criminal entanglement. All these programs can be important elements of a series of positive interventions producing diversion at every point of the chain of causality.

These are not unrealistic "pie in the sky" proposals. They are being used with much success in numerous jurisdictions. Their track record is well documented by research findings. Most recently, a RAND Corporation study (Greenwood, Model, Rydell, & Chiesa, 1996) analyzing four types of diversionary programs concluded that the alleged reduction in crime that California received for $5.5 billion (the cost of a "three strikes and you're out" policy of incarceration) could be doubled "for less than an additional billion dollars, spent on diversion programs" (p. 25). This study particularly endorsed the cost-effective crime control benefits of three programs: parent training, monitoring of high school students with delinquency experiences, and cash incentives to induce disadvantaged students to graduate.

Reintegration

Reintegration is intervention into the offender's life and community in order to present positive alternatives to law-violating behavior that, when properly used, reduce penetration into the criminal justice system. This definition of *reintegration* is broader than most traditional definitions, which construe the concept as the rehabilitation of the offender by supervision in the community. Although many of the traditional definitions are excellent for the purposes for which they are used, they are too restrictive in the context of a whole new system of criminal justice planning. Although they often include the notion of the least restrictive alternative, the need for involving the community in the correctional process, and the provision of opportunities to achieve legitimately in the community, they differ fundamentally from my definition in that they do not describe the use of reintegration techniques anywhere *except* in the community, whereas my definition extends the use of such techniques even to the secure institutional setting.

Reintegration traditionally is based on the premise that crime and delinquency are primarily symptoms of community disorganization and not generally evidence of the psychological, moral, and behavioral problems of individual offenders. My proposed model allows for recognizing individual pathology, poor judgment, and any other causes internal to the offender where these exist. However, it also insists on the need to focus to a great extent on restoring the offender to the community, using the community in positive programming, and remedying community lacks. This community-oriented approach in positive intervention is emphasized whether the offender is in the community or in an institutional setting.

Simply stated, reintegration, when understood in this way, tends to maintain the offender's existing positive ties to the community at all times and to replace negative ties with new, positive ones, regardless of where the offender is located. I have often urged that the plan to return offenders home when they are institutionalized should begin the day they step inside the institution. This can be accomplished by making every effort to uphold family ties and to bring in community liaison persons for formal planning, individual support, and a whole variety of other positive purposes, even during the institutional period. The importance of this approach is currently recognized by the Federal Bureau of Prisons, which sponsored the First Federal Convention of CURE to discuss "how families of prisoners can work together with the Federal Bureau of Prisons on strengthening the family bonds and encouraging the prisoner in his rehabilitative efforts" ("First Federal Convention," 1996, p. 8).

The reintegration model by definition implies the following:

1. The community becomes the very center of treatment in most cases.
2. Revocation of community status is used only as a last resort.
3. Confinement is for specific reasons only and then used only when absolutely necessary.

4. Offenders are given a wide range of alternatives, and every effort is made to assist them to exercise noncriminal options, rather than to keep them under narrow restraint and tell them what to do all the time.
5. Decision making is shared by the agents of the systems (probation, parole, institutional workers) and the offender as far as possible. Institutional parole boards and others who have a stake in the offender's program, including the offender him- or herself, are included in the process whenever and as far as possible.
6. While the offender is in the institution, family and community resources are involved as much as possible in visitation and in planning of prerelease, work release, and all other programs in an attempt to minimize the separation from the community and to build a "bridge back" into the community—always as far as possible in keeping with the safety needs of the community.

Reintegration is best understood when compared against other, more traditional correctional models. One important basis for comparison is each model's emphasis on individual freedom and the needs of the offender versus social order and the needs of the community. The conflict between these two basic needs of the citizenry in our constitutionally directed free society has been a recurring theme throughout the history of corrections and the administration of justice. The struggle to maintain a reasonable balance between the need of law-abiding members of the community to be protected from the impulsive and threatening behavior of others and the rights of those accused of crime or already convicted has taken place at practically every level of the justice system. This conflict becomes particularly evident at all of the points at which an offender's degree of freedom is initially decided or changed: during the investigation before arrest, at arrest, at arraignment, during the trial process, at the time of sentencing, throughout the corrections process at every level after sentencing, and at the time of release into the community after penal sanctions have been fulfilled. It surrounds issues of probation, disciplinary actions that can be carried out during institutional confinement, and, especially, parole and other forms of conditional release into the community.

An excellent classification of four correctional models that portrays their differing emphases on the needs of the community versus those of the offender was developed over two decades ago by O'Leary and Duffee (1971, p. 379). It still has great applicability today.

According to O'Leary and Duffee, the *restraint model,* exemplified by correctional practice in many secure institutional settings, seems to be minimally concerned with effecting change of any kind in either the offender or the community. It is based on a philosophical position that people change only if they want to. Consequently, few members of the staff seem to be actively engaged in trying to effect change of any kind. Punishment seems to be the principal tool of the administration, and it is prescribed not to change inmates but only to control them. The appearance of efficiency is important, and the great goal seems to be to help the organization to survive by "keeping the lid on." In this model, due process is seen as "the enemy" because it tends to interfere with the smooth, orderly routine. Any programs such as prerelease or work release are seen as tools to pacify the inmates or as nuisances because they are disruptive to the smoothness of operation.

In the *reform model,* more emphasis is placed on community standards and less emphasis on the individual offender. The primary tool to effect change in inmates is correctional compliance. Inmates are expected to become more generally conforming and not to cause the community any more inconvenience. In this system, offenders have few rights, and the privileges granted by the state can easily be taken away. The staff has complete discretion. The change agent's style might well be expressed as "Do it because you must." To have any success, this model depends on a system of rewards and punishments, the authority to use these, and an intense program of surveillance and behavioral monitoring. The positive attribute of this model is its potential for short-term success and temporary results, which makes it especially effective in times of emergency or crisis. However, it is not nearly so successful over the long term, as history clearly illustrates, because offenders spend large amounts of energy attempting to evade present controls, manipulate the situation, and resume the old familiar patterns of behavior on release.

In the *rehabilitation model,* more emphasis is placed on the individual offender and less emphasis on the community. The change agent's major focus is on the quality of the relationship with the offender, and the change agent's style might best be expressed as "Change because someone cares." For success, the change agent must want and be able to establish a meaningful relationship with the offender. This requires intense effort, time commitment, care, and concern. The model's terminology and approach come from clinical psychology. The label *sick* is used instead of *criminal,* and the vocabulary of diagnosis and prognosis and the search for a "cure" for the criminality are medical in their orientation. When used, control and punishment are presented as therapy. The therapist is seen as the ideal staff figure. The separation between treatment and custodial staff is marked because it is assumed that therapy can be conducted only by "trained professionals" and that all others function merely in a supportive role. Within the institutions, custodial personnel are expected to maintain a peaceful atmosphere and deliver inmates to the various programs in a secure fashion but not to become involved in the change process.

This style seems to work best with younger, less sophisticated offenders, and especially with those who have few meaningful relationships and who have received minimal rewards from their criminal conduct. Hardened, sophisticated offenders who have satisfied most of their needs effectively through their criminality tend to be reached much less effectively within this model.

Legal intervention is not enthusiastically encouraged and sometimes is opposed. Because staff are always seen as properly motivated and acting in the best interest of the client, it is felt that emphasis on the rights of the offender and the work of the legal profession are often counterproductive.

The *reintegration model* places a great deal of emphasis on both the offender and the community and reconciles the needs of both. It insists that every effort be made both to help the offender find ways to abide by the laws of the community and to mobilize elements of the community to make the offender's program a success. In this model, the requirements of due process and the intervention of the legal profession are not viewed as incompatible with the task of correctional change. The entire process is much more open: Decision making is more participative, and confrontation is encouraged. The change agent uses a style that encourages correctional internalization. Instead of employing an authoritarian approach and simply attempting to force conformity, he or she presents offenders with a range of law-abiding alternatives to criminal behavior and helps offenders to engage in these alternatives successfully. Offenders are encouraged to "do this because it works successfully for you." Generally, mistakes in behavior are corrected by a demonstration of their failure in meeting the goals that were designed by the offender and the correctional worker in a joint decision-making process. In contrast to the rehabilitation model, the reintegration model does not focus on inmates' feelings and relationship to staff, but these things are examined rationally to evaluate how they affect behavior and how situations affect them.

The reintegration model also reconciles the need for freedom and the need for order. Coercion and compliance mechanisms are not completely abandoned: Incarceration is used when necessary, but only for very specific reasons and as a last resort when all other enforcement mechanisms have failed. The major emphasis is on avoiding the use of compliance mechanisms as far as possible within the dictates of community safety. When confinement does have to be used, the institutions of compliance are located as close to the community of return as possible, and every effort is made to maintain ties to the community during the period of incarceration.

Probation and parole officers are located within the community as much as possible and work continually with neighborhood groups, businesses, churches, schools, and so forth on behalf of program development for the offender. Officers function as advocates, mediators, and brokers for services, not just as therapists or counselors.

Within the institutional setting, the gap between treatment and custodial staff is lessened and should be almost nonexistent. All staff members are seen as having great value for their ability to assist the offender in the change process. A teamwork approach is encouraged. Custodial workers are expected to participate as actively in the task of change as those formerly exclusively called "treatment staff." Further, it is only in the reintegration model that correctional officers are permitted to function as part of the treatment team. In the other models, they are at best seen as control staff supporting the activity of treatment specialist and at worst seen as negative, punitive people totally uninterested in the treatment program.

More than other models, the reintegration model requires a high level of professionalism among correctional officers because of its emphasis on the need to understand cultural differences, to communicate effectively, to intervene in potentially violent situations without escalating the violence, to make decisions based on objective standards and not on one's own feelings, and especially to deal sensitively and capably with an ever-younger and in many ways ever more difficult population. The attitudinal adjustment, information base, and "human skills" required to achieve this level of professional conduct are best obtained through higher education (Hahn, 1994). For this reason, the International Association of Correctional Officers has sponsored the development and promotion of a minimal curriculum that they urge be made available to all correctional officers within this country.

When properly used, reintegration helps the offender to develop more workable social values and social stamina and provides the community with a greater sense of safety. As early as 1967, the Corrections Task Force of the President's Commission on Law Enforcement and Administration of Justice endorsed such an approach when it stated that

> the task of corrections . . . includes building or rebuilding solid ties between the offender and the community, integrating or reintegrating the offender into community life—restoring family ties, obtaining employment and an education, securing in the larger sense a place for the offender in the routine

> functioning of society. This requires, not only effort directed toward changing the individual offender, which has been almost the exclusive focus of rehabilitation, but also mobilization and change of the community and its institutions. (quoted in Hahn, 1975, p. 137)

More vividly, the commission stated why such efforts were needed: "It is easier to train an aviator in a submarine than to train someone for community life in our prisons and institutions" (quoted in Hahn, 1975, p. 137).

Some of the limitations of the reintegration model are that very immature offenders simply do not have the skills to use the options when presented. The model also requires some tolerance on the part of the community and correctional administrators for some minor law violation during the testing process. The program must be carefully observed and skillfully supervised so that it is not abandoned at the first sign of minor failure but also so that it does not inflict great harm on the community by permitting dangerous behavior to take place unsanctioned.

A program of this type generally does require a longer period of time than the other styles to be truly effective. However, when it is successful, the results are much longer lasting because offenders can test various behaviors and voluntarily incorporate into their lives those that are found to work and because ongoing efforts are made to effect necessary adjustments in the community and in its service delivery.

THE "STRAINER THEORY"

The task of combining the notions of reintegration and diversion in community-based corrections and making them operational seems quite complex. However, it can be clarified by an analogy. Use of a kitchen strainer requires that the strainer be repeatedly shaken so that, in the various stages of the process, particles of varying sizes are forced through the straining net with varying degrees of facility. On the first shaking, the smallest particles go through rather easily. When the strainer is shaken again, the next smaller group goes through, and the process continues through various shakings. As the strainer is shaken more vigorously, a larger number of particles go through the screen until, at the end of the process, only a few of the largest particles remain unable to pass through. These remain in the strainer itself no matter how vigorous the straining process may be.

When we apply this analogy to the correctional process, our model of community-based corrections would propose that, at the very earliest level, the system find ways to "shake the strainer" in order to keep out of the system all of those youth whose needs can be far better met within the family, the public and private agencies, the school system, and the churches. This first "shaking" is the level of prevention. At the next level, after some misbehavior has taken place, offenders should be diverted at the police level, screened out at court intake, and thus kept, as much as possible, from having official court contact or compiling a court record. This is the level of traditional diversion.

This "strainer" process should proceed through all of the levels of the court's caseload, preventing penetration into the system at every level by using counseling, agency referral, probation, and other inventive programs designed to reduce the need for residential placement. Work programs, community service, restitution, mediation, and a whole host of other services have been developed and are functioning with great effectiveness in various juvenile courts throughout America in providing relatively nonpunitive sanctions for a large portion of the court's caseload. This is diversion in the wider sense of the least restrictive alternative in keeping with the safety needs of the community.

When residential placement is absolutely necessary, the search for the least restrictive alternative continues. Foster homes, group homes, halfway houses, wilderness programs, and a whole spectrum of noninstitutional residential placements should be used before placement in secure institutions. When the very serious or dangerous offender requires secure placement, then small, adequately staffed and funded, caring environments (which can qualify as such and still be secure) should be developed and used to prevent placement in large, punitive institutions.

At the end of a sophisticated and vigorous "shaking process," only a few particles that will not go through the screen remain in the strainer. This is a good representation of the very small number of the total caseload who will actually require secure residential placements.

At the adult level, the same analogy can be used to represent the need for diversion from the system of petty offenders and those whose behavior is much better described as obnoxious than as criminal. These require social agency services. At the next "shaking of the strainer," offenders are screened into programs of probation, house arrest, electronic monitoring, community service, and other alternative programs. Families, neighborhoods, and the entire community can be effectively brought into planned programs for these nondangerous offenders. Neighborhood councils, churches, and other interested civic groups can be invaluable in providing alternative programming. When combined with a program of community policing, intense neighborhood interest can deliver a degree of control for the offender and a sense of security to the neighborhood that traditional methods have historically failed to deliver.

When secure institutionalization is necessary, small, secure facilities should be developed and located as close as possible to the community of origin of the offender. In this way, intense reintegrative efforts can begin while the offender is in the secure setting. Family and community ties can be maintained and improved, thus building a bridge back to the community for the offender during incarceration. This provides an important motivational tool in preparing offenders for better adjustment on release in the overwhelming majority of cases.

It seems to be merely a commonsense observation that, because most offenders at the adult level and practically 100% of offenders at the juvenile level return to the community (unless they are killed or die of an illness in the institution), constant efforts should be made both in and out of secure institutions to ensure that offenders' relations with the community and functioning in the community are interrupted only when absolutely necessary. This approach is quite different from the traditional approach, which frequently has as its primary goal getting offenders out of the community and keeping them away as long as possible.

As Milton Luger (1973), one of America's finest juvenile justice administrators, summed it up, offenders should be moved away from the community only as far as their needs and the protection of society demand. But community-based corrections means that the community has a "terrible responsibility" to develop effective programming, without which the safety of the community and the needs of the offender cannot be adequately provided for. Further, a program of viable community-based corrections requires diversified facilities capable of meeting all the needs of all offender types, ranging from completely open settings through the spectrum of facilities to small, highly structured secure institutions. The development of such a program, according to Luger, is the only alternative to reliance on the "horrible and hideous bastille-type" mass custody institutions that have been so destructive in the past.

A NEW MODEL FOR CRIME CONTROL

The history of the models for crime control that have been used in this country shows that one-dimensional models are inadequate. Any adequate model for crime control planning in contemporary America must include the entire criminal justice system and all of its elements, along with very important other sources of input outside the system. Those who must be involved in all planning necessarily include

- All personnel within the criminal justice system at all levels, including police officers, court workers, probation and parole officers, and institutional personnel
- The judiciary, the prosecutors, and the members of the bar
- Governmental officials and funding authorities, without whose support no realistic program is possible
- The general public, the community at large, and particularly the many interest groups concerned about criminal justice, such as victims' and offenders' families
- The victims themselves, who up until recently have been terribly neglected, and for whom victimology studies and victims' organizations have been only the beginning of an important and much-needed continuing trend
- The offenders themselves; although in the past the entire burden of change has been seen as resting on them, they still must be included from a standpoint of accountability and assumption of responsibility

Community-based corrections is the only model of corrections that does include all these elements.

Further, any adequate model for crime control planning must address itself to all the possible areas of friction between community needs for safety and order and the rights of individuals to seek their own happiness and fulfillment. As human beings strive to satisfy their needs through their behavior, the society in which they live often seeks to limit their behavior in keeping with the needs and desires of the larger group. Such conflicts are often difficult to resolve because the behavior of the individual can easily be influenced by ignorance, disordered passions, faulty learning, poor judgment, and pressures from family and peer groups, and an almost limitless number of other external factors and because the larger society and smaller groups within it express their expectations for individual behavior in terms of laws that are marred by ignorance, prejudice, fear, vested interests, and, again, an almost limitless number of other factors. Further, these laws are enforced by imperfect human organizations and individuals, so there can be differential enforcement based on such factors as discrimination, "culture gaps," response to pressure groups, and misinterpretation of the law for personal reasons. Thus, any model that is to address successfully and realistically a situation in which a law has been enforced and an individual has been accused or convicted of its violation must be complex and eclectic enough to relate to all of the factors involved and not to ignore some at the expense of others. In any community that is selecting correctional models or establishing correctional goals, the struggle to balance individual and social interests is easily observed. It must be resolved if the planned system is to have any unity or effectiveness.

Unfortunately, all too often, the question of crime control is reduced simply to the two options of "locking up almost everybody" and "keeping almost everybody on the streets." Many people seem to be simply unwilling or unable to grasp the complexity of the task of rational criminal justice planning.

Clear and O'Leary (1982) argued that the fundamental aim of such planning is "to develop a fair system of community protection in which incapacitative and treatment measures designed to control risks are employed rationally. . . . a system constrained by the notion of desert, which fixes the range of acceptable punishment and encourages the use of such devices as restitution and community service" (p. 27). The development and management of such a system is, however, complicated, "often involving trade-offs of benefits, cost determinations and interaction effects with offenders. Correctional managers cannot take actions which jeopardize the safety of the community, but their decisions are not simple, for the best method to protect the public is not always clear" (p. 27). Three values—humaneness, knowledge utilization, and cost—have to guide their decisions so that the least restrictive alternatives are used to the greatest extent possible without significant increase in risk to the community. These are the considerations that guide an enlightened community-based corrections program as we have defined it in this book.

Instead of simply making community-based corrections programs one integral part of a comprehensive advanced correctional system, the definition of community-based corrections outlined in this book proposes that from the possibility of diversion at the beginning of the system up to the possibility of reentry at the end of the system and at all stages in between, community-based corrections should become the total operational philosophy. More than "tinkering" is required to implement this vision. "Band-Aid" approaches have been initiated countless times in recent years, but the most well-intentioned of them seem to fail, largely because there is no change in the overall philosophy and goals of the system. Despite constant protestations to the contrary, the secure mass custody institution (prison for adults and state training schools for juveniles) remains the backbone of the American correctional apparatus.

An expanded definition of community-based corrections and the impetus that it would give to a total correctional "examination of conscience" could help us to move toward a better understanding of crime and delinquency as social problems that require social answers and not just increased law enforcement. In a more rational debate, we could focus more light than heat on the topic, more intelligent planning and less emotional "kneejerk" reactivity. The ineffective notions of pure punishment and revenge could give way to an emphasis on risk control—the reduction of the probability of crime and further hurt to the community. The positive emphasis on risk control would become one of our principal considerations in sentencing. In all of the programs that followed from it, the test of effectiveness would replace the desire for "a pound of flesh," as the needs of victims and the total community would receive greater consideration. Certainly, there would be punishment—but punishment for utilitarian reasons, not just for revenge.

This notion of risk control, properly understood, could alleviate much of the concern of those who feel that community protection, accountability, and punishment can be obtained only by the use of secure institutions. As Clear and O'Leary (1982) have stated, "The erroneous belief that community supervision is something other than punishment needs to be rectified; and the design of any system of sanctions should include the option of keeping the offenders in the community. A constrained risk control approach addresses these dual purposes" (p. 21).

The continuing practice in this country of placing into very secure institutions a large number of offenders who could be far better cared for through well-planned community corrections seems to be caused by several factors. First, countless citizens are committed to pure punishment and even revenge as a correctional motive. Although this is often emphatically denied, the evidence of its existence is continually demonstrated in a variety of ways. Letters to the editor, the popularity of "get tough" speeches by politicians, and, above all, the meager correctional dollars available for anything but secure institutions all speak loudly of the widespread commitment to the underuse of community-based sanctions.

Second, we continue to rely primarily on a crime control strategy of deterrence—even though we know full well that it most often has little effect on those who are addicted to drugs, commit crimes of passion, have no stake in society, or have not been acculturated into embracing middle-class values.

Third, we seem to be committed to the "away syndrome." This is a peculiar American phenomenon in which we simply wish that all of our "problem people" would go away or, better still, be sent away so that we are sure they are gone. This thinking is applied not only to public offenders but also in many cases to mental patients, the retarded, the indigent aged, the chronically ill, illegal immigrants, and anyone else whose presence in our midst we find distasteful. Somehow, we feel secure if our social problems are "away," kept securely out of sight and handled with as little expense as possible. Certainly, common sense indicates that some offenders must be securely institutionalized for the protection of society, but we are speaking here of the needless institutionalization of a staggeringly large number who could better be handled by numerous other approaches with little threat to public safety.

Finally, the development of community-based programs has been delayed and stunted in many places because of the belief that noninstitutional corrections has been tried and found unsuccessful when really our attempts at implementing it have been a mockery. Probation with caseloads so large that it simply becomes a noninstitutional body count; poorly planned and resourced halfway houses, boot camps, and other community residential facilities; drug treatment programs that are so poorly funded and staffed, or so barren in their treatment concept, that they have no resemblance to the very successful drug treatment programs available in other communities; and a whole host of other noninstitutional corrections programs that have no real substance—all these have caused a myth to develop that community-based corrections programs do not work. Properly developed, staffed, funded, and operated, noninstitutional programs do work and have worked very well, and their successes are well documented. However, in many places, they simply have not been tried.

SUCCESS OF COMMUNITY-BASED CORRECTIONS PROGRAMS

There is much available evidence of the success of community-based corrections programs. The above-mentioned recently published RAND Corporation study by Greenwood et al. (1996) favorably compared the crime control effectiveness of several early intervention programs with that of secure incarceration. There are particularly encouraging reports of program effectiveness in the field of correctional drug treatment (Friedman, Granick, Kreisher, & Terras, 1993; Goldstein & Kalant, 1991; Sechrest & Josi, 1992). This challenging field is in many ways leading the way in producing positive program results. The Bureau of Justice Statistics (1992) recently stated that prevailing opinion is no longer as pessimistic as the "nothing works" sentiments of the 1970s.

Successful drug treatment programs show that substance abuse problems, like many of the other "lifestyle" problems presented by offenders in the correctional system in general, "do not yield to counseling only, or just to employment, or job training, or other forms of social programs. Success lies in doing many of these things in varying degrees" (Sechrest & Josi, 1992, p. 4). The recognition that recovery is a process, not an event, helps us to understand that effective approaches require several specific ingredients. The National Task Force on Correctional Substance Abuse Strategies (1991) identified the following common characteristics of successful programs:

1. Clearly defined missions and goals, admission criteria that target appropriate participants, and an assessment strategy for those seeking treatment
2. The visible support and understanding of key administrators within the agency, as well as of those line staff with whom the program must interact
3. Consistency in intervention strategies facilitated through formal and informal links with other agencies as an offender moves through the system
4. Staff who are well trained and who are given an opportunity for ongoing professional education
5. Continuous evaluation and development on the basis of both outcome studies and process data

Although these observations are confined to drug treatment programs, they are applicable to other correctional settings as well. And other treatment elements recommended by the National Task Force are similarly generalizable. These include individualized multidisciplinary treatment plans, matching of offenders with programs appropriate to their assessed needs, provision of a full range of services, prerelease treatment programming, staffing that integrates custody and treatment, the use of incentives and sanctions to increase motivation for treatment, self-help groups as an adjunct to treatment and for aftercare, targeted programs for special-needs populations, and education and treatment for relapse prevention (National Task Force, 1991). Such recommendations are supported by findings of other studies that have characterized effective programs as intensive and multifaceted, addressing the multiple problems of offenders (Gendreau, 1996; Sechrest & Josi, 1992).

The available evaluative research indicates clearly that although some programs do not work, and although a few may even do more harm than good, many community-based programs do work, and with good results. Latessa and Allen (1997) recently reported the encouraging results of evaluative research by Paul Gendreau (1995), who examined hundreds of correctional and rehabilitation programs:

> When rehabilitation programs incorporated at least some of [Gendreau's] eight principles of effective intervention, those programs reduced recidivism in the range of 25-70 percent, with the average about 50 percent. His principles of effective intervention are as follows:
>
> 1. Programs have intensive services that are behavioral in nature, that occupy 40-70 percent of the offender's time in a program and are from 3-9 months in duration. [Behavioral means using positive reinforcers to strengthen behavior, such as rewarding "doing good" with attendance at sports events, praise, and approval.] Further, behavioral strategies are essential to effective service delivery.
> 2. Behavioral programs target the criminogenic needs of high-risk offenders, such as antisocial attitudes, peer associations, and chemical dependencies.
> 3. Programs incorporate responsivity between offender, therapist, and program. Simply said, the treatment program should be delivered in a manner that facilitates the offender's learning new prosocial skills.
> 4. Program contingencies and behavioral strategies are enforced in a firm but fair manner; positive reinforcers are greater than punishers by at least 4:1.
> 5. Therapists relate to offenders in interpersonally sensitive and constructive ways and are trained and supervised accordingly. Treatment is systematically delivered by competent therapists and treaters.
> 6. Program structure and activities disrupt the delinquency network by placing offenders in situations (with people and in places) where prosocial activities predominate.
> 7. [Programs] provide relapse prevention in the community by such tactics as planning and rehearsing alternative prosocial responses, anticipating problem situations, training significant others (family and friends) to provide reinforcement for prosocial behavior, and establishing a system for booster sessions.
> 8. [Programs provide] a high level of advocacy and brokerage as long as the community agency offers appropriate services. (pp. 404-405)

More generally, Haas and Alpert (1986) identified five conditions as influencing the outcome of intervention efforts:

1. *Authority.* Rules and formal legal sanctions are clearly spelled out and enforced.
2. *Anticriminal modeling and reinforcement.* The development of prosocial and anticriminal attitudes, cognitions, and behaviors is engendered and reinforced by appropriate modeling of prosocial behavior.
3. *Problem solving.* Clients are assisted in coping with personal or social difficulties, particularly where these relate to fostering attitudes that lead them to experience prosocial behavior.
4. *Use of community resources.* The things actually needed to implement an effective program are made available.
5. *Quality of interpersonal relationships.* Relationships are characterized by empathy and the establishment of open communication and trust between the two human beings involved.

When these ingredients are present to a high degree, the probability of successful outcomes is greatly enhanced.

THE ROLE OF SECURE INSTITUTIONS IN COMMUNITY-BASED CORRECTIONS

My own definition of community-based corrections does not insist on a nonsecure environment at every level of the system. Rather, it prescribes only an environment that is the least restrictive in keeping with community safety. Thus, secure facilities are necessary for the most dangerous offenders.

It is understandable that some might have great difficulty with the idea of including small, secure facilities at the end of the criminal justice system in a concept of community-based corrections. By the traditional definitions, community-based corrections seem to exclude the notion of any secure institution outside of the community. But by including the secure institutions at the end of the system in the definition, we are forced to look at the program in the institutions and to insist that it include, as far as possible, a maximum consideration of the eventual return of almost all offenders to the community. The secure institutional environment is so destructive to the human psyche in so many ways, and so effectively lessens one's ability to function in free society, that it is absolutely necessary to incorporate reintegrative programming into the institutional setting if we are to achieve any success with our criminal justice system beyond our poor present record of achievement.

The local jail has a significant role to play in all this because it can serve as the matrix for a whole array of reintegration services. It has a place of prominence in the local system, and a large portion of its population is at a stage of optimum treatment readiness (e.g., because of first arrest or incarceration or lack of criminal sophistication); thus, the opportunity for successful intervention through service delivery is enormous.

By my definition, opportunities presented to assume such normal social roles as citizen, family member, and breadwinner are to be understood on a relative basis as opportunities to assume normal social roles *as far as possible in keeping with the setting in which the offender finds him- or herself at the present moment.* For example, if it is possible, offenders should be in their own homes under supervision or, if in a halfway house, should be going out to school or regular employment on a daily basis. If they are in secure confinement in one of the small settings at the end of the system, they should still be encouraged to plan for these roles and activities as much as possible, and efforts to bring the community to them in terms of services, visits from neighborhood people, and so forth, should be arranged as far as possible. The "direct supervision" or "new generation" jail fits eminently well into this conceptualization of maintaining ties to ordinary community living even while in secure custody.

Almost all proponents of reintegration agree that efforts should be developed to change the community by encouraging tolerance for nonconforming behavior that is not dangerous, as well as for some failure in terms of school or work experience. Similar efforts should be made in the secure institution. It is a huge job to reeducate staff in some settings to a less rigid set of expectations. Yet within the constraints of the need for institutional order and safety, much can be done to achieve this goal.

THE USE OF AUTHORITY IN COMMUNITY-BASED CORRECTIONS

It is an important task of the proponents of community-based corrections to explain that even the most "open" programs do not renounce or in any way diminish use of legitimate authority. Authority not only remains an essential component but, when used properly, can be a therapeutic ingredient of the total program.

The positive or "therapeutic" uses of authority are as follows:

1. It can be used to establish and maintain the relationship with the probation officer while the various difficulties inherent in such a relationship are successfully worked through. For example, initially, it would be impossible to get most persons into such a relationship at all if there were not some authority present. Generally, offenders are not seeking to come to the courthouse or some other formal office, nor are they looking favorably toward being forced to do things that they would prefer not to do. Therefore, in the very beginning of the program, it is absolutely necessary to use authority. Also, offenders always feel a certain amount of hostility and distrust toward the probation officer because of the strangeness of the situation and because of other things that they have seen, experienced, or heard. These difficulties need to be worked through. The relationship would probably be terminated very early if it were not for the existence of the authority.
2. Authority can be used effectively in applying the specific deterrent effect of correctional sanctions. This is especially true when we can adapt the form of the deterrence to the needs of the individual offender. For example, middle-class offenders tend to be more easily deterred by the threat of "lock-up" than persons from the streets. The latter might be much better deterred by the limitation of some privilege or from the loss of delinquent status in the peer group.
3. Authority can be used very well to instigate probationers or other offenders to initiate behaviors that they would otherwise avoid. After this initial stage, it can continue to be used to maintain that behavior until the normal process of social reward can reinforce it. For example, habitually truant children can be forced to come to school every day until effective support and services assist them to get reintegrated into the school setting and they begin to receive some social rewards. Likewise, adults with an alcohol problem can be forced into beginning attendance at an Alcoholics Anonymous Program.
4. Authority can be used to help offenders to resolve their basic authority conflicts. When it is used properly, a person with basic authority conflicts can learn that authority is not just something used to hurt or control him or her in a negative way. A probation officer or other worker can be a role model demonstrating fair, kindly, restrained, and consistent use of authority, which perhaps this person has never before witnessed.

5. Authority can be used effectively to restrain offenders from committing self-defeating or antisocial acts that would destroy or damage their progress toward adjustment or result in danger to society. Examples are the rules of probation, parole, or halfway houses that forbid association with codefendants or other persons who could be harmful to the success of the program or that prohibit the frequenting of certain places or being on the streets at certain hours of the night.
6. Authority can be used to facilitate the psychological redefinition of the offender's life experiences in terms of more acceptable values or norms. For example, "street norms" that permit an offender to steal, assault, or do many other things that go with "street life" can be redefined and "sifted out."

Authority can effectively be used in these circumstances to provide contingencies necessary for reinforcing or retraining attitudes and behavior through a process of rewards and punishments. This basic technique is available to correctional workers only because they have the authority to carry it out. Without authority, correctional workers would not be able to punish anything and in most cases would be very limited in their ability to reward.

7. Authority can be used in providing "therapeutic limits." Unsocialized, immature, unsophisticated, or suggestible offenders tend to require limits but to be unable to provide them for themselves. The presence of authority alters this situation favorably. For example, it is much easier for even a sophisticated delinquent to tell his peer group that he is not allowed to do certain things because he is on probation than for him to take a "goody stance" and lose status with the peer group.
8. Authority can be used to provide the opportunity for offenders to practice accepting authority in the small world of this relationship. Having learned this, they can begin to apply it in the larger world of free society. In most cases, offenders have had no one in their lives who set limits for them or positively exercised any authority. They have not had any practice in responding to this condition positively.
9. Authority is necessary to facilitate crisis intervention in some circumstances. Many times, only authority allows workers to gain admission to a home or to some other place such as an "after-hours joint." It enables workers to intervene in domestic situations where no stranger ordinarily could trespass, and it certainly gives them protection in doing so.

PROBATION AND PAROLE

Probation and parole are the legal auspices under which most community-based programs operate. Both involve a very grave contract between three parties: the criminal justice system, the community at large, and the offender. Simply stated, this contract promises that we will provide safety to the community and services to the offender without the need for more drastic institutional constraints. When we fail to provide these, such programs become a mockery.

The absolutely minimal task of probation and parole is to provide at least sufficient supervision to ensure compliance with the orders of the court or conditions of institutional release. If we are unable to do at least this, the whole process of sentencing and of parole hearings appears useless, if not comical. Unfortunately, in many jurisdictions today, this is the case. Overwhelming caseloads, a lack of resources, and, in many places, misunderstanding of the most effective use of personnel all contribute to a situation in which probation and parole are constantly condemned as having failed. In reality, they are not being truly implemented, and in many cases they have never really been tried.

The necessary ingredients for probation and parole to function properly within the reintegration model are as follows:

1. The community, as much as possible, becomes the center of treatment.
2. Confinement is for specific reasons only and then used only when absolutely necessary.
3. The least restrictive alternative in keeping with community safety is always the alternative of choice.
4. The offender is provided with a wide range of options within which every effort is made to assist him to engage in noncriminal behavior.
5. Decision making is shared with all persons who have any stake in the success of the program (family, neighborhood groups, churches, and, as much as possible, the offender), in keeping with community safety needs.
6. The worker must engage in nontraditional roles, the most important of which is that of a "bridge builder" who constantly supports or creates links to the community. This role includes such important specific roles as broker for services and advocate-mediator.
7. In all of these roles the worker is constantly doing two important things: mobilizing community resources and helping the offender to develop social stamina.

8. In this model, the worker should be much more visible in the community than in many of the traditional models. Consequently, the community should feel a greater sense of safety.

Unfortunately, the vast majority of officers today maintain their commitment to the more outmoded traditional approaches with which they are more comfortable. Also, many agencies simply will not allow their workers to engage in new roles or to provide new services beyond the traditional concept of "what a probation or parole officer ought to be doing." Consequently, the service delivery style that remains most frequent is either (a) a deterrence-based approach that relies almost completely on surveillance and the offender's fear of losing freedom or (b) the traditional casework approach, based on the "medical model" and using individual counseling as its primary tool. For whatever reason, neither of these approaches has been seen very successful in American corrections. Ironically, even if either approach had the potential to work, it would not work under existing time constraints, which make adequate surveillance very difficult and individual counseling practically impossible.

One of the most important and fundamental roles of the officer in a reintegration program is resource brokerage. The basic principles in such a program according to Dahl (Dahl et al., 1980) are as follows:

1. All probationers will at some point be released from supervision into our communities. Consequently, citizens have a right to expect that offenders have been given the opportunity to prepare for the responsibilities of community life.
2. Each individual is accountable for his or her own behavior. Therefore, responsible behavior is required to maintain freedom, and it is only learned by "doing." Services and programs are necessary to present opportunities to learn to make responsible choices.
3. Consumers of these services generally need the opportunity to learn new workable strategies for handling their life roles while they are under supervision. They have not learned these previously, and they cannot learn them properly in an institutional setting.
4. Programs do not change people, but they can provide appropriate opportunities for individuals to change themselves and their life situation.
5. Probation and parole are in need of innovative approaches to service delivery. Because time constraints and pressure of caseloads currently prohibit individual officers from being able to deliver all the desired

services, officers should employ all available resources to meet offenders' needs.

6. Most offenders are not pathologically ill. Therefore, the role of "therapist" is usually inappropriate. Also, only a small percentage of all officers are sufficiently trained to undertake this function, even if it were desirable.
7. The kinds of services needed by the offender to succeed in society are in fact available in the community or can be developed with community cooperation, but dedication, effort, and some ingenuity are required to access these successfully.
8. Officers must assume advocacy roles by negotiating for community-based services and ensuring that these are actually delivered. Agencies should be monitored and held accountable for service delivery and not permitted merely to perform in a "paper-shuffling" mode that enables them to look good but provides no real assistance to the offender.

Such a response is vividly described in the poem in the box, which paraphrases Jesus's words urging care for the needs of others. (The poem was given to me by a juvenile probationer in 1967. Unfortunately, the author is unknown.)

THE REFERRAL GAME

I was hungry, and you referred me to an "Appropriate Agency" and you set going a humanistic process whereby that agency and you discussed my hunger.

I was naked, and you wondered, Wasn't that perhaps immoral or unhealthy, or at best a reflection of my "deviant lifestyle"?

I was ill, and you considered me to be a problem for the "Health Profession" and determined to write up a full report for them when you returned from your vacation.

I was homeless, and you decided to attend the next meeting of the Better Housing League to learn more about the social impact of such conditions.

I was in prison, and you thought that would "teach me a lesson."

I was lonesome, and you left me alone so that you could be "objective" and maintain your "professionality"; with all the above, you have really been "professional," but I am still hungry and lonesome, and I'm freezing from the lack of the "human touch."

9. Proper utilization of community resources will enable clients to meet their needs independently when they are released from supervision because they have learned to do this during the correctional process.

The goals of a reintegrative probation and parole approach using resource brokerage according to Dahl are

1. To operate a highly structured community resource program that makes practical, effective services available to those under supervision
2. To increase the opportunities for offenders to change themselves and the conditions that brought them into the criminal justice system, such as problems of immature decision making, alcohol and drug use, lack of employment, and negative use of leisure time
3. To develop a social climate that facilitates personal change, encourages the acceptance of responsibility, and increases social problem-solving skills in the offender
4. To encourage and guide those receiving the services toward development of positive interpersonal relationships with family members and others as appropriate
5. To operate a program in such a manner that the community feels safe and comfortable with the offender's presence in the community and the involvement of probation officers in the offender's effort to successfully adjust
6. To release from supervision persons with appropriate employment, savings, and suitable housing so that they have a real chance of "making it" in open society
7. To implement a program that provides economic and social advantages to the community, such as savings on the cost of incarceration and the release of employed ex-offenders who support families, pay restitution, pay taxes, and stay off the welfare rolls
8. To decrease the probability of continued crime after release for those who have successfully completed the program because they are now legitimately satisfying their needs in positive ways (For a complete discussion of this topic see Dahl et al., 1980)

There is some reason to believe that the use of teams in delivering probation and parole services within this model has advantages over the use of individual officers because

1. Teams can handle larger caseloads uninterrupted.
2. It is possible to offer a broader range of expertise and skills.

3. Supervision is continuous despite one officer's absence.
4. Recipients of this service may find greater compatibility with one officer than with another.
5. Officers can specialize by function.
6. The team provides a mutual support network and an opportunity for accountability to the group on the part of individual officers.
7. There is greater flexibility of backgrounds and temperaments brought to each situation. Group decision making has been proven to be more effective than that of individuals acting alone.
8. The team approach seems to lend itself more easily to the use of volunteers and paraprofessionals.

Although there has been some indication (in Albuquerque and Baltimore) that the results are better than those of traditional supervision in number of contacts, time spent on contacts, achievement of goals and rating in the client's perception, research evidence of this does not seem conclusive (Petersilia & Turner, 1993, pp. 1-11). What does seem crucial to success is that individual probation officers be "eclectic"—that is, that they each be a "one-man team." Such officers would not be committed to any specific discipline or treatment style but instead would be comfortable and conversant in many areas. They would be able to function well as resource brokers but would also be comfortable in a counseling relationship with those clients for whom this was indicated. Instead of making choices principally satisfying their own needs, as based on their own background, taste, and education, they would be primarily concerned with the delivery of the type of services needed by those in their caseload. In general, they would be seen as able to deal with all the other influences that affected the behavior of the recipient of their services. Such eclectic officers would not just concentrate on the "internal pathology" of the offender.

Of course, this is not to rule out all counseling and therapies that are directed at internal pathology. Counseling can be and has been very effective, especially with young first-time offenders who have not received rich rewards from their delinquent activity and who are more verbally skilled, more anxious, and less supported by delinquent peers. But for older, more hardened, less verbal offenders who are habitually getting their needs met (and consequently being rewarded) by illegal behavior, other approaches seem to be much more effective.

Up until about the early 1970s, it was assumed that, to alter delinquent behavior, we had to assist the delinquent in bringing out the satisfying, nonaggressive, healthy behaviors that were potential but blocked from expression. Today, assisting the offender is viewed more as an educational and pedagogic problem than as a therapeutic problem. The assumption is that the individual is lacking, or at best very weak, in the necessary skills for effective social living and satisfying interpersonal functioning. When this concept is applied, the challenge is to deliberately teach new and desirable behaviors in what amounts to a relationship between a trainee and a skills trainer.

Such interpersonal skills training (how to communicate effectively, how to express anger without violence, etc.) can be directly delivered by a skilled probation or parole officer or by another correctional worker, if time and caseload permit, but it often must be obtained from community agencies outside the justice system. If offenders have never learned as children to communicate their frustrations verbally, they will tend to strike out physically at persons who annoy them. In social skills and effective communication training sessions, they are taught to use alternative verbal skills and nonviolent problem-solving methods. Such programs lessen any threat that offenders might present to society and more effectively fulfill the goals of a good correctional program than other, more traditional approaches that do not really deal with the root cause of the problem.

Probation is the condition under which the broadest variety of positive interventions can be delivered. However, many of these services do not have to be housed within the traditional probation department. The settings housing such services can themselves take on an almost infinite variety of shapes and forms. Some of the most frequently used are halfway houses, reintegration centers, community corrections centers, alcohol detoxification units, drug abuse centers, and restitution houses. In many places, community-based programs are integrated into enlightened and progressive jail programs that successfully satisfy expectations of accountability and punishment while minimizing the amount of isolation from the community and the negative effects of imprisonment.

Whether a halfway house is "halfway in" or "halfway out," and whether a community corrections center is more highly structured or practically indistinguishable from a reintegration center, and whether some of the programs in a reintegration center could more appropriately be called efforts at resocialization, all of these settings can and in many cases do implement a variety of program elements and use many therapeutic ingredients. Many of them are currently operating in a very eclectic fashion already. The wide variety of programs already in existence and the overlap in program elements and methodologies make it virtually impossible to establish set criteria as to what kind of characteristics or how many of each define a facility bearing a certain specific name (see Hahn, 1975).

It is of fundamental importance to the success of planning and operating any of the various types of alternative facilities that two major pitfalls be avoided. The first is the tendency merely to move institutional practice and programs into smaller units in the community without a change in program emphasis and staff retraining. Program and staff must be geared toward achieving the commitment of participants to the goals of the program. Otherwise, once the coercive and restraint mechanisms of the institution have been abandoned, there will be no controls over offenders' behavior.

There are only two possible ways to control behavior in the correctional setting. One way is coercion ("I do it because I must"). The other way is commitment ("I do it because I see that it works for me" or "I enjoy it"). The traditional penal methods and many of the established programs associated with them are totally coercive and are not successful in preparing offenders to make responsible decisions outside of the coercive atmosphere of the penal institution. Programs must be geared to support the inmate involvement and participation in the decision-making process that produce commitment.

Second, the mere placement of offenders in open, nonsecure settings does not guarantee that they will be able to instantly handle such newfound responsibility without a large amount of assistance and support. There is no assurance that the participants, if the program does not succeed in getting their involvement, will remain crime free or, for that matter, even be good neighbors in their new surroundings. The old wishful thinking that people given an alternative placement rather than incarceration will be so grateful that they will make an instant positive adjustment simply does not stand the test of reality.

When properly planned and implemented, the advantages of community-based programs are many:

1. The participants are constantly confronted with real-life choices because the regimented order of the institution is removed. They are exposed to a wide variety of situations calling for realistic decision making each day. Success or failure depends on the decisions that they personally make. The forced conformity and decisions made from above in the institution are replaced by the need to develop good judgment and decision-making skills.
2. Community life constantly "holds up a mirror" to participants in which they must recognize their real motives and actual values based on the behavior they exhibit in real-life situations. They can no longer use the excuse, "I never had the chance to decide these things."

3. Community living provides built-in ego-supportive experiences, ranging from the more normal lifestyle itself through such special circumstances as the opportunities to do volunteer work or in other ways be useful and appreciated in the community.
4. The individual rights of the offenders are much more easily safeguarded in such settings. Civil and criminal actions, class action suits, and grand jury investigations are considerably fewer in open programs than within the secure institutions.
5. By their very nature, community-based programs tend to nudge the citizens of the community toward recognizing that they have a definite role to play in restoring offenders to useful citizenship. The offenders are no longer "away" and out of sight, so community responsibility cannot be ignored.

In such progressive settings, correctional workers much more easily develop new roles as "brokers for services," "connecters," and "advocate mediators." In doing so, they are able to realize much more fully their own professional potential.

One of the secrets of success of such program operations lies in the area of offender and staff selection, combined with program and staff development. Facilities that are poorly conceived, poorly programmed, inadequately staffed, and not extremely careful in the selection of participants can fail miserably. Unfortunately, history shows us many examples of so-called community-based programs that lack accountability and are totally unrealistic in their conception or their implementation. Such facilities notoriously have provided only the "human warehousing" that was part of the institutional program or have deteriorated into "delinquent subcultures" with much new offending on the part of participants. Such failure results in great harm to the community, which does not receive the degree of safety it longs for; to the offender, who does not receive the realistic program directed at a level to satisfy his or her real needs; and, perhaps most of all, to progressive corrections because the outraged citizens will eventually conclude that such facilities simply "do not work."

For this reason, community-based programs must be accountable. One of the best discussions of this accountability was developed and presented by Joseph Rowan (1978), who has been a consultant to hundreds of correctional facilities over the past 30 years. Although the following questions are designed for juvenile facilities, they have much applicability to adult facilities also.

- Program Accountability
  1. Is there really an active program, or does it exist in name or on paper only?
  2. Is it year-round and around the clock?
  3. Is it planned realistically, are staff involved in planning it, and are there adequate staff to carry it out?
  4. Does it include all of the necessary elements, such as education, recreation, medical care, and especially the use of volunteers?
  5. Are parents involved in the program as much as possible?
  6. Is the program preoccupied with security? (This does not mean that security is not important, but is there a ridiculous overemphasis of it at the cost of the program?)
  7. Is the program evaluated regularly?
  8. Is any element of the program ever discontinued because it is thought to be noneffective?

- Personal Accountability
  1. What are the qualifications of staff? (A large number of juvenile court personnel in this country are on the patronage system, yet most police are on a merit system.)
  2. Are there adequate background checks of employees?
  3. Is there proper preservice and inservice training? (Requirements for police and adult prisons are becoming ever stricter; why should juvenile programs be less?)
  4. Are we paying adequate salaries to get good people? (Police salaries are much higher in almost all jurisdictions.)
  5. What efforts are made to get public support and even necessary laws supporting increased training or salary levels?

- Structural Accountability
  1. Does the structure actually support programming, or at least allow for it, or is it so bad that it inhibits program development and implementation?
  2. Is it an independent structure, or is it attempting to function as part of a larger building such as a hospital, courthouse, or jail?
  3. Is it subject to inspection for fire safety, security, health, ventilation?

- Treatment Accountability
  1. Even though we say, "We're here to help you," do the children constantly sense from our inaction or neglect that this is a lie?

- Philosophical Accountability
  1. Philosophy is more important than skills. A "we care" philosophy of disciplined treatment, as opposed to a "lock-em up—we're in control" philosophy, is essential. Staff with the wrong philosophy will do damage no matter how good their skills are. Persons with the proper philosophy will have basic honesty, healthy role model ability, ability to provide emotional support, ability to do healthy limit setting, and genuine empathy and concern. The presence of a "positive caring environment" is essential for treatment. The opposite, a "negative-punitive environment," makes treatment impossible.

Within residential community-based facilities, all sorts of possible services are emphasized. These include housing, vocational training and/or placement, remedial or continuing education, a stable environment, and cultural enrichment. They can also include intervention techniques, such as communication skills training, encounter groups, and self-awareness experiences. When these strategies are properly planned, staffed, implemented, and evaluated, they present very positive potential interventions into the lives and behavior of the offender group.

INTERMEDIATE SANCTIONS

A well-developed program of positive intervention would include not only various diversionary programs before adjudication at either the juvenile or adult level and proactive jail programs while in custody, but traditional probation and any or all of the above-mentioned community-based facilities after adjudication. It would also include an array of the more recently developed programs commonly called *intermediate sanctions.* These sanctions, when added to the more traditional ones, provide the opportunity to fill any gaps in a continuum of sanctions before the use of secure facilities at the end of the system. Such intermediate sanctions generally include intensive probation supervision (including electronic monitoring), "boot camps" (also known as *shock incarceration programs*), fines, community service programs, and restitution.

Intermediate sanctions were defined by the U.S. Department of Justice (1990) as punishment options that are considered on a continuum to fall between traditional probation and traditional incarceration. Attorney General Richard Thornburgh (1989) expressed the rationale for the use of such sanctions:

> We . . . know that there are many for whom incarceration is not appropriate. But is simple probation sufficient? Particularly when probation officers are carrying caseloads far beyond what is manageable? We need to fill the gap between simple probation and prison. We need intermediate steps, intermediate punishments.
>
> This concept appeals in both principle and practice. In principle, if we recognize gradations in the seriousness of criminal behavior, then we should have gradations in sanctions as well. That's why we need a portfolio of intermediate punishments that are available, independent of whether our correctional facilities are full or empty, or whether our correctional budgets are lush or lean, or whether our offender populations are increasing or declining.

Intensive supervision has an almost infinite variety of styles and forms, some of which include electronic monitoring and some do not. Almost all of the states have within some of their jurisdictions some form of this program. Reports of success vary greatly.

Boot camps also differ widely in their development and implementation. Some are much more highly structured than others. Some include drug treatment and some do not. Many have an educational component, but some do not. Some form of this "shock incarceration" concept can be found in almost all of the states at either the adult or the juvenile level.

The use of fines has been extended to many areas of law violation, including juvenile offenses in some jurisdictions, and has come to include both traditional fines and the newer "day fines" (fines proportionate to the offender's earnings). Some variation of fines is used almost universally.

Community service programs, implemented at both the adult and the juvenile level, are widely used and have developed from simple "work programs" to include sophisticated concepts such as services in hospitals, to the blind, and in many other areas commonly deemed to be contributions to the community. Some variety of these can be found throughout the country. They are almost universally used in major metropolitan area systems.

Restitution programs have a long history and are being used more frequently than ever in recent years. These can include simple monetary payments or, as has been developed in many places, personal service to victims or the community. The use of restitution is extremely widespread. (For more extensive descriptions of these options, see Chapter 5.)

From all of the above, it is obvious that there are real opportunities to develop and use many sanctions long before incarceration is necessary. The problem is in the system's willingness to use them. Dispositions in juvenile courts and sentences in adult courts simply have not caught up with the array of services and programs available nor has the allotment of resources. A major portion of correctional budgets continues to pour into the secure facilities at the end of the system, even though economies and efficiencies can be better attained by a revised allocation of available funds.

CONCLUSION

The concepts of community-based corrections are in place and provable. Successful programs exist throughout the country, and pilot projects and evaluation research have verified that positive intervention can be implemented at every stage of the causal chain, and in the correctional process after the commission of offenses. As the American Correctional Association (1991) has stated,

> Community corrections is a viable alternative which requires diversified programs capable of meeting all the needs of varied type offenders in a non-institutional type setting, emphasizing due process and the development of service delivery systems to divert the maximum number of offenders.
>
> Provisions through community corrections allow more effective and economical reintegration of offenders into normal community roles for a great number of juvenile and adult offenders; a more selected use of institutionalization by the court (reserving this sentencing alternative for dangerous and persistent offenders); and an increased opportunity for offenders to provide family support.
>
> Gains to local and state governments are recognized in greater fiscal savings by provisions for the individual to contribute to the tax-base through his continued employment. Additionally, already existing services established in the community can be utilized by easily accessible referrals from the community corrections staff. (p. 13)

Anthony Travisono (1990), executive director of the American Correctional Association, reaffirmed this position of the association: "Today, 1 out of every 24 American males is under correctional supervision. How many more will we need to have in our custody before new prevention efforts are developed and carried out? . . . Our huge budgets need to be successfully reallocated to community programs. Somebody out there knows how to do this. So let's find who has the key and stop this madness" (p. 1). This eloquent voice of the American Correctional Association has been preceded and echoed by enlightened community leaders, authors and researchers, church officials of numerous denominations, and committees of the United Nations for over 20 years.

Probably the ultimate argument is the one of simple common sense. We cannot train people to swim successfully by tying them hand and foot and placing them on the side of the pool. To learn to swim, they must be in the water. It would seem logical to apply the same cause-and-effect kind of thinking to the problem of successful community living. To learn to live successfully in the community, one must live in the community. Of course, this is not intended to obviate the equally commonsense axiom that every community has the right to defend itself in every way possible from the predatory behavior of the dangerous few. Consequently, we can never eliminate all secure institutionalization, but we certainly can prevent its need in many cases, minimize its use to a "necessity only" basis, and work for the most successful return of the overwhelming majority of those who are institutionalized, given that they *will* return to our community, ready or not.

In all of this, we must exercise great caution so that none of the community-based programs are used to "widen the net." In many places, examples can be found of persons placed in various programs who would have been processed much less formally if these programs had not been available. This is a perversion of the entire concept of community-based corrections that communities cannot afford. At the other extreme, we must never place persons in a lesser degree of control than their real and present danger to society demands. What is required is a rational approach, based on objective standards and free of emotional reactions, prejudice, and personal preference.

True criminal justice professionals must never be guided by public opinion in planning facilities and programs. We must share our knowledge and concern and thus shape public opinion. If we do this, the public can be assisted to understand and support a rational approach to crime control.

Properly presented and understood, community-based corrections is certainly not "leniency" or a "soft" approach to crime control. It is certainly much more than just "probation and parole and a few halfway houses," which the public all too often interprets as interchangeable terms for high recidivism and failure. What is it, then? It is nothing less than our best opportunity to incorporate the legitimate public desire for safety and offender accountability with community participation, positive programming, and individual competency development in a setting of controlled risk and ongoing effectiveness evaluation.

Community-based corrections cannot be achieved as simply a band-aid on the existing system. Nor can it be wished or hyped into existence by those who find it expedient to give lip service to the need for change but who remain committed to the failed concepts and practices that have brought us the overcrowding and abuse of the present system. Community-based corrections requires proper understanding, careful development, hard work, and true commitment to its concepts and goals. When this is achieved, community-based corrections can, along with community policing, serve as a pillar supporting the edifice of a new criminal justice system.

5

Restorative Justice

WHAT IS RESTORATIVE JUSTICE?

Many professionals and scholars have been urging us to recognize that an effective crime control policy requires not only an effective criminal justice system but a partnership for crime control with all segments of the community. Community policing has facilitated such partnerships. But the idea of finding out what the community wants and giving it to them extends far beyond community policing. It involves returning to the ancient view that redefines crime more as an injury to the victim and the community than as an injury to the government. It views criminal justice as involving the victim, the offender, and the entire community in its processes. Above all, it views the proper response to crime as "community building." Everything that is done should be designed to restore the fabric of the community. The intervention of the criminal justice system should be seen as an "opportunity to do fabric repair" (Bazemore, 1995).

This new model, commonly referred to as *restorative justice,* has been discussed in detail by Bazemore and Umbreit (1994b). According to their definition,

> While retributive justice is focused on determining guilt and delivering appropriate punishment (just deserts) through an adversarial process, restorative justice is concerned with the broader relationship between offender, victim and the community. . . . Restorative justice differs most clearly from retributive justice in its view of crime as more than simply law breaking—or a violation of government authority. Rather, in contrast to both retributive justice and the individual treatment model, what is most significant about

> criminal behavior is the injury to victims, communities and offenders that is its result. (pp. 13-14)

Effective restorative justice addresses itself to these injuries and to all of the injured parties. The focus of judicial proceedings is no longer only to the offender, and the state is no longer the only party that addresses the problem. In this model, the community is effectively involved in deciding how to deal with the offender. It must decide how much punishment is required and what can be done to ensure that the offender is reintegrated into the community if this is at all possible.

The concept that the community must be viewed as the ultimate "customer" and as a true partner in the production of justice is probably the first and major aspect of restorative justice that sets it apart from the traditional justice system. Of course, we must always remember that the role of the state is to safeguard the interest of social and distributive justice through its criminal law. Consequently, its use of punishment is aimed at maintaining a just and viable society. This is the Anglo-Saxon tradition, and all efforts to reform the justice system must recognize it. However, retaining this tradition in no way prohibits efforts to empower communities to contribute more fully to the rule of law as it affects them.

Another significant distinguishing feature of the restorative approach is its tendency to define justice in more human and humane terms. This has been elaborated upon by Fabian (1995):

> Whereas retributive justice defines crime as a violation of the state, restorative justice defines crime as the violation of one person by another. Whereas retributive justice relies upon a technical process of legal rules, restorative justice relies upon the amendment of relationships. Whereas retributive justice replaces one social injury with another, restorative justice focuses on repairing social injury. Whereas retributive justice defines accountability as taking punishment, restorative justice defines accountability as understanding the impact of one's action, and participating in making amends for that action. And whereas retributive justice includes a debt owed to state and society in the abstract, restorative justice calls for recognition of debt to the victim and immediate community. In sum, a retributive system focuses on justice through guilt, punishment and vengeance; a restorative system focuses on justice through enablement, empowerment and real accountability. (p. 1)

Still other distinctions between the two paradigms include a focus on a problem-solving, "forward-looking" approach to crime rather than a concentration on establishing blame or looking backward to the act committed; a change from an adversarial relationship to one of cooperation and partnership; and a view of the community as actively involved in the entire "repair" process, as opposed to simply standing on the sidelines and watching the criminal justice process unfold.

Judge Barry Stuart (1996a) compared the restorative justice model to a "family model" in that the health of the community, like that of a family, is directly related to the degree to which members make the decisions that govern the life and quality of the relationship. When a community or a family determines how to deal with an offending member effectively, conflict is resolved, and all of the participants can again make the group strong, sometimes stronger than before. Some control of the process must be given to the victims and to interested community members, but this must not be an opportunity for victims then simply to inflict revenge on the offender. There must be equity in relating to both victim and offender. Thus, restorative justice is concerned with "balanc[ing] the needs of three 'customers' of the justice system": victim, offender, and community (Bazemore & Umbreit, 1994b, p. 14).

Four principles of restorative justice have been outlined by Carey (1996):

1. Hold the offender directly accountable to the individual victim and the specific community affected by the criminal act.
2. Require the offender to take direct responsibility to "make things whole again" to the degree that this is possible.
3. Provide the victims purposeful access to the courts and correctional processes, which allows them to assist in shaping offender obligations.
4. Encourage the community to become directly involved in supporting victims, holding offenders accountable, and providing opportunities for offenders to reintegrate into the community. (p. 153)

Programs including these principles are in operation in Australia, New Zealand, and much of Europe and the United States. Today, there are at least 175 programs in North America, and there are even more in Europe.

The commonsense basis of the principles of restorative justice was pointed out recently in a folksy but wise commentary. In an article entitled "Mamma Knows Best," Ken Breivik (1995) suggested that much of the "new" approach is not so new at all. He stated that three elements in his mother's correctional program for him as a child could well be applied to contemporary planning:

Punishment was swift and certain, mother had an arsenal of punishments at her disposal (a range of sanctions), and he was always made to apologize and to make amends if his crime was directed at any other persons or their property.

GOALS AND EVALUATION OF RESTORATIVE JUSTICE PROGRAMS

The goals of restorative justice programs are succinctly set forth in Carey's (1996) suggested changes to the wording of all Community Corrections Acts (in 25 states as of 1995) to transform them into Restorative Justice Acts:

> The purpose of correctional intervention shall be to repair harm and injury caused by crime. This objective will be administered by addressing the following goals:
>
> - Offender: public safety, accountability, competency development.
> - Victim: input, communication, restoration.
> - Community: awareness, ownership, restoration.
>
> The offender, victim and community shall have the opportunity for direct, distinct and equal participation in the criminal justice process, whereby the criminal justice system serves as facilitator in accomplishing these objectives. (p. 154)

The state of Vermont (Vermont Department of Corrections, 1995b) has expressed a commitment to similar goals in its statement of the desired outcomes of a reparative sentence for offenders specifically:

1. Restore and make whole the victims.
2. Make amends to the community.
3. Learn about the impact of crime.
4. Learn ways to avoid re-offending.

Goals are also set forth in Pranis's (1996) list of various aspects of the response to crime that restorative justice aims to improve:

1. Services and support for victims
2. Victim opportunity for involvement in decision making
3. Offender encouragement to take responsibility
4. Offender involvement in repairing the harm

5. Community member involvement in decision making
6. The use of processes which build connections among community members (p. 6)

Certainly, successful programs should assist in reducing crime and should also produce at least a "feeling of justice" for the victims, the offenders, and all others concerned. Offenders must feel that they are being held accountable, and the community must be in agreement that this is in fact taking place. Offenders must experience "shaming" for what they have done, but as soon as the shaming phase is finished, their reintegration into the community must be emphasized.

Market research done by the Vermont Department of Corrections (1995b) in preparation for developing its restorative justice program indicates that this approach speaks to what the public wants from a justice program: "The public wants offender accountability, public service, restitution, an apology from the offender, offender treatment to reduce the likelihood that offenders will continue to commit crimes; the public wants to be involved in the criminal justice system; and the public wants to be safe from violent criminals" (p. 6).

As with all human endeavors, "the proof of the pudding is in the eating." How can we test the extent to which restorative justice programs fulfill these goals? In 1990, Howard Zehr published a "yardstick" for testing the effectiveness of restorative justice:

A. Do victims experience justice?
   1. Do they have sufficient opportunity to tell their truth to responsive listeners?
   2. Do they receive needed compensation or restitution?
   3. Is the injustice adequately acknowledged by all concerned?
   4. Are they sufficiently protected against further violation?
   5. Does the outcome adequately reflect the severity of the offense?
   6. Do they receive adequate information about the crime, the offender, and the legal process?
   7. Do they have a voice in the legal process?
   8. Is the experience of justice adequately public?
   9. Do victims receive adequate support from others?
   10. Do victims' families receive adequate assistance and support?
   11. Are other needs, material, psychological, and spiritual, being addressed?

B. Do offenders experience justice?
   1. Are offenders encouraged to understand and take responsibility for what they have done?
   2. Are misattributions challenged?
   3. Are offenders given encouragement and opportunities to make things right?
   4. Are offenders given opportunities to participate in the process?
   5. Are offenders encouraged to change their behavior?
   6. Is there a mechanism for monitoring or verifying changes?
   7. Are offenders' needs being addressed?
   8. Do offenders' families receive support and assistance?

C. Is the victim-offender relationship addressed?
   1. Is there an opportunity for victims and offenders to meet, if appropriate?
   2. Is there an opportunity for victims and offenders to exchange information about the event and about one another?

D. Are community concerns being taken into account?
   1. Are the process and outcome sufficiently public?
   2. Is community protection being addressed?
   3. Is there a need for restitution or a symbolic action to the community?
   4. Is the community represented in some way in the legal process?

E. Is the future addressed?
   1. Are there provisions for solving the problem which led to this event?
   2. Are there provisions for solving problems caused by this event?
   3. Have future intentions been addressed?
   4. Are there provisions for monitoring and verifying outcomes and for problem-solving? (pp. 230-231)

SCOPE OF RESTORATIVE JUSTICE

The Role of Restorative Justice in Secure Institutions

Although specific restorative justice programs tend to be most frequently victim-offender mediation, restitution, work programs, and other programs generally aimed at the nondangerous offender, the restorative justice paradigm is *not* limited to working with offenders in the open community. Just as our definition of community-based corrections extends its philosophy and goals into even secure institutions (see Chapter 4 of this book), so the principles of victim restoration and the need for offenders to take responsibility for their actions remain overriding concerns even when offenders need to be securely incarcerated. Carey (1996) argued that

> restorative justice initiatives involve all offenders, not just those deemed to be non-dangerous. Many interventions are appropriate even when personal crime is committed. The offender can engage in victim conferencing, restitution and restorative gestures from a jail or prison cell. The community response is even more crucial under such harmful conditions of violent crime. (p. 153)

Kay Pranis (1996) similarly stated that

> the concepts of restorative justice are not limited to offenders in the community. Although most corrections professionals recognize the necessity of secure custody for serious violent offenders, even these cases lend themselves to the application of restorative principles.
>
> Offenders in secure custody can still participate in community service through projects such as bulk mailing assistance. If offenders in custody are provided work opportunities, they can pay off their restitution. Victim-impact panels and victim empathy classes are perhaps even more important for offenders in prison. (p. 6)

The general axiom of progressive community-based corrections, that punishment for crime should interfere as little as possible with the possibility of reintegration into the community and the pursuit of noncriminal behavior, is very much part of restorative justice. When, at the end of the correctional process, secure incarceration is necessary, prisoners must be given as much opportunity as possible to exercise noncriminal options and engage in productive activities, in keeping with safety and security needs. The small, secure facilities located at the end of the correctional system, and used only when absolutely necessary, are simply one type of services in a whole array of services and a necessary component of any system of restorative justice.

Tools of Restorative Justice Programs

One eloquent spokesperson on behalf of restorative justice, Joe Lehman, Commissioner of the Department of Corrections in the state of Washington, spoke in an interview of a "range of programs and sanctions that could be tailored to individual offenders based on the harm they did, their circumstances, the situation of the offense, as well as the opportunity to influence their behavior" (quoted in "The Commish's Dream System," 1993, p. 8). When the journalist asked him, "If you could build your own correction system from scratch, what would it look like?" Lehman responded, "My system would respect the complexity of the problem" (p. 8). Restorative justice, in contrast to the simplistic models underlying "one size fits all" programs, emphasizes and allows for flexibility and a wide variety of options for dealing with offenders.

Mediation

Bazemore and Umbreit (see, e.g., Bazemore & Day, 1997; Bazemore & Umbreit, 1994a; Umbreit & Coates, 1993) have been outstanding in their research and their advocacy efforts promoting restorative justice. They have found that victim-offender mediation is a realistic sanction that often gives some degree of satisfaction to both victim and offender.

Mediation (along with several other program elements, such as restitution and community service) is an essential part of a national movement, led by the Office of Juvenile Justice and Delinquency Prevention (OJJDP), to redirect the thrust of the juvenile justice system through its Balanced and Restorative Justice Initiative. (Gordon Bazemore is the principal investigator for this project.) The use of mediation in juvenile justice is increasing, and the cases handled in this way are numbered in the thousands, with considerable success being reported.

A study by Umbreit (1994) reported that as of February 1994, 3,142 cases had been referred to four mediation programs (the Victim Offender Mediation Program in Albuquerque, New Mexico; the Center for Victim Offender Mediation in Minneapolis, St. Paul; the Victim Offender Reconciliation Program in Oakland, California; and the Travis County Juvenile Court and the Local Dispute Resolution Center in Austin, Texas). Eighty-three percent of the cases involved property crimes and 17% involved crimes of violence.

Mediation in juvenile proceedings received strong support from officials, judges, probation staff, and others involved in the justice process. It resulted in very high levels of satisfaction (for 79% of victims and 87% of offenders) and perceptions of the justice system's fairness (for 83% of victims and 89% of offenders). The process had a strong effect for both victims and juvenile offenders in humanizing the system. It also reduced fear and anxiety among victims. It was perceived to be voluntary by the vast majority of offenders (81%) and victims (93%) who participated.

Mediation had a significant impact on the likelihood that offenders would complete their restitution obligations (81% of offenders with mediation versus 58% without). Juvenile offenders did not perceive mediation as a less demanding response to their behavior. Rather, they saw it as holding them accountable for their crimes. Offenders in mediation programs had committed considerably fewer and less serious additional crimes at a 1-year follow-up than similar offenders not in mediation. (This finding, though consistent with two recent English studies, was not statistically significant because the size of the program was too small at the time.)

The American Bar Association has formally endorsed the use of victim-offender mediation (Umbreit, 1994). Although most of the mediation programs in the United States still operate in the juvenile justice systems, an increasing number of programs are being implemented at the adult level. And according to Umbreit (1996), although most offenses going to mediation are minor assaults and property crimes, "In recent years, this vision has even been applied in a small but growing number of serious violent crimes (including homicide), often at the request of victims who are more interested in gaining a greater sense of closure and peace than in seeking harsher punishments" (p. 11).

Mediation programs are in operation in at least 13 countries, and in two countries, Austria and New Zealand, victim-offender mediation is available in all jurisdictions (Umbreit, 1996).

In the United States, one exemplary program is being conducted at the Pennsylvania State Correctional Institute in Graterford, Pennsylvania. The Graterford Victim-Offender Reconciliation Project seeks healing and restoration for the victims of serious crime. It is designed to

- Encourage inmate participants to take personal responsibility for past crimes
- Enable inmates to learn the actual consequences of crime for victims
- Help all participants understand crime in a context of restorative justice
- Enable victims and offenders to interact in an educational setting
- Help inmates and victims move toward mutual understanding and healing (*Justice for All,* 1993)

In a similar vein, in New York City, Crime Victims United involves victims of crime in a jail program to give victims a chance to voice their hurt and increase offenders' understanding of the impact of their behavior while they are incarcerated in the local jail.

Intermediate Sanctions

Although all community initiatives generally include the use of traditional restraint mechanisms, such as jail and prison, when absolutely necessary, the options most often exercised are those currently referred to as *intermediate sanctions.* As discussed in Chapter 4, intermediate sanctions, according to the Office of Justice Programs (1990), are punishment options that are considered on a continuum to fall between traditional probation and traditional incarceration. These sanctions are already very popular in the traditional justice system, having been developed primarily in response to jail and prison overcrowding. Such options are especially fitted to the concept of restorative justice and its goals.

Intensive Supervision. Among the most frequently used of these sentencing options is intensive supervision. Almost all of the states and large metropolitan area courts have some variety of these programs in place. Increased supervision and surveillance are usually achieved through reduced caseloads, an increased number of contacts per month, and a range of mandated activities for participating offenders (including work or vocational training, drug testing, curfew, and community service).

These programs vary widely as to number and type of contacts per month, caseload size, type of surveillance conducted and services offered, staffing (whether by specially trained officers or regular probation officers), and use of a team approach. They also vary in requirements for intake into the program and mechanism of placement (e.g., judicial sentencing or the decision of a prison release board, a parole board, or a probation agency).

Programs of intensive supervision lend themselves particularly well to use within the framework of restorative justice. Programs to restore victims to "wholeness," opportunities for offenders to "mend their ways," and the availability of intimate knowledge about offenders' whereabouts and behavior are all readily attainable within this framework.

The success of intensive supervision programs depends to a great degree on the acceptance and involvement of the local community. Petersilia (1990) concluded from a study of such programs that "unless the community recognizes or accepts the premise that a change in corrections is needed, is affordable, and does not conflict with its sentiments regarding just punishment, an innovative project has little hope of surviving, much less succeeding" (p. 144).

"Day Fines" or "Means Fines." Another frequently used intermediate sanction is "day fines" or "means fines." These fines are figured as multiples of an offender's daily income and set in proportion to the offender's means to pay.

In general, fines have not been used to a great degree in criminal cases in the United States because they have been seen as working against the principle of proportionality in sentencing. To a rich person, a fine of $5,000 might be minimal, but to a poor person it could be an overwhelming amount.

Day fines were first instituted in Europe many years ago and are now widely used in both West Germany and Scandinavia. The European programs tend to have the judge first decide the number of "day fine units" in each case, based on the nature and severity of the crime. Then the monetary value of each day fine unit is determined, primarily on the basis of the offender's income, but with some differences in computation in various jurisdictions. These fines can be truly individualized, as, for example, in Sweden, where a day fine is 1/1,000th of the individual's annual income, with deductions made for taxes, dependents, and major debts. The idea in this program is essentially to deprive offenders of disposable income over and above their basic living expenses. However, in Germany, a day fine is described as an offender's net income for one day, with no deduction for family maintenance. The idea is that the day fine represents the net income that the offender would have lost if he or she had been incarcerated for one day. (Occasionally, such fines are adjusted to reflect individual circumstances, but only in exceptional cases.)

In the United States, the Staten Island Day Fine Program provides for consideration of the seriousness of the crime as well as the offender's daily income and number of dependents. In practice, judges are given detailed presentence reports and information about offenders' financial status. They also use wide discretion because "the underground economy—be it from off-the-books employment or criminal gains—supports a substantial proportion of those who come before the criminal courts" (Greene, 1992, p. 29). It is important to know in this situation if an offender who is on welfare is making $30,000 a year selling drugs on the side.

"Day fines" fit easily into the restorative justice model for a number of reasons. They can be used as an alternative to removing the offender from the community and can be tailored to his or her means so as not to be excessively punitive or destructive to his or her family. They can be used as part of the accountability element within the restorative justice model, and the input of the community can be invaluable in planning the program.

Of course, it is always necessary to observe caution in employing economic sanctions, not only to avoid injustice and overly repressive policies, but also to prevent possible negative impact on the agency in charge of collection. For example, offenders who fall behind in their payments can consume an excessive amount of community corrections agency time. At worst, the agency emphasis can change from community corrections to monetary collection.

Some critics have argued that the dominant goal of many economic sanctions is to raise revenue for the government from the very vulnerable group of criminal defendants. Harland (1992) therefore suggested that the appropriateness of economic sanctioning policy and practice be gauged on the basis of adherence to three principal system goals:

1. *Compensation*—exacting compensation/reparation from offenders for the cost of their crimes to victims, the criminal justice system, and the community
2. *Prevention*—Promoting public safety and reduction of further crime (general deterrence) or recidivism (specific deterrence, rehabilitation, incapacitation)
3. *Retribution*—Inflicting painful consequences not to achieve any socially utilitarian aim, but to satisfy the principle that morally, offenders simply deserve to be punished for their wrongdoing (p. 6)

One program that the National Institute of Corrections heralds as an example of success is the Maricopa County, Arizona, Day Fine Demonstration Project. This is a means-based financial sentencing program that began on April 15, 1991 (with the pilot period ending August 31, 1992).

Fines range from $60 for a Class II misdemeanor committed by a low-income person to $12,000 for a Class III felony committed by a high-income person. In actual practice, the fines average from $900 to $1,000.

When the fine is paid in full, the offender's probation is terminated. It is reported that since the beginning of the program, more than 250 defendants have been sentenced, and more than half have successfully completed the program. The collection rate for active cases has consistently exceeded 95%, with a compliance rate between 85% and 90% for all offenders sentenced. Concerns that the program would target white, male, white-collar offenders have been proven false. Probationers in the program are very similar to the general probation population, with women slightly overrepresented and white-collar offenders making up only 2% of the caseload. Of those sentenced, 35% were unemployed before sentencing, and only 16% of the employed offenders had a weekly income of more than $250.

The results have been termed so successful that the program was ordered to continue and was expanded to include all criminal divisions ("Programs in Action," 1992, pp. 14, 15).

Restitution. Another frequently used economic sanction is restitution. Generally speaking, restitution can be seen as repayment to a crime victim by the offender with money or services. Restitution is a very appealing sanction to the general public because it is directly related to the crime and intuitively seems fair.

Restitution can be and is used at almost any point in the criminal justice process: before trial or sentencing, during or after incarceration, or as part of an alternative to incarceration. In any of these uses, it can fit very well within the restorative justice concept because of its ability to hold the offender to real accountability and its potential for restoring victims to "wholeness."

Restitution is a very early development in the history of criminal justice. From antiquity, private vengeance was succeeded by collective vengeance and moved toward the process of negotiation and composition (payment by the offender to the victim). This process was eventually institutionalized when monarchs and the nobility acted as mediators and took a percentage of the financial awards for themselves. Government eventually took over the entire criminal justice process, at which time restitution practically disappeared from the criminal law. It only resurfaced in the United States in the 1960s in California. It gained increased usage during the 1970s, when various states began writing it into their criminal codes in an effort to relieve overcrowded prison systems.

Given that the overwhelming majority of offenders are unable to pay damages, some issues need to be raised concerning restitution:

1. Could low-income offenders end up bearing the brunt of "symbolic restitution" programs requiring enforced personal services or, in the worst-case scenario, receive harsher sentences based on their inability to pay damages?
2. Could the justice system end up taking the role of "squeezing every penny" out of already impoverished persons who find their way into the criminal justice system?

3. At what point does someone's ability to pay no longer exempt him or her from facing other consequences in the criminal justice process?
4. Is restitution most often used as a real alternative to incarceration, or is it simply a new tool in the process that can be used to place an additional burden on many who, without it, would have been diverted from the process very early or have received only probation?

These and other questions highlight potentials for abuse that must be prevented in the planning and development of restitution programs.

Restitution programs, like other intermediate sanctions, function best in the context of community involvement because the means of offenders, their willingness to cooperate with the program, and all the circumstances of their economic environment are better known and better able to be dealt with.

When well developed and administered, restitution programs have great potential for success. A study by Butts and Snyder (cited in "NCJJ Study," 1992) showed that even when used within the traditional criminal justice system, they were reported as being "consistently associated with lower recidivism compared to probation alone. In many areas the results were statistically significant, and even in the categories where the numbers were too small to be statistically significant, the differences were in the direction of favoring restitution" ("NCJJ Study," 1992, p. 5).

Some jurisdictions have formalized restitution programs by the establishment of "restitution centers." In these centers, restitution is combined with other programs thought to be beneficial so as to provide a structured environment for the offender. One example of such a program, cited as successful by the National Institute of Corrections, is the South Carolina Restitution Centers. These centers were designed to be used as alternatives to prison so that prison spaces could be reserved for violent and repeat offenders. At the time that the federal report was written, there were two centers, with additional centers planned for the state's larger metropolitan areas in the near future. These are described as

> strictly supervised residential environments for non-violent offenders. Residents are required to maintain employment and perform unpaid public service work during their off hours. They turn their paychecks over to the restitution center staff, who apply the funds toward their financial obligations, including restitution, fines, child support, taxes and expenses for room and board at the center. Since most residents have never held a steady job and have a history of either alcohol or drug abuse, low education levels and unstable residences, they are required to participate in programs designed to

> deal with these problems. . . . The restitution centers have been termed one of the most effective programs in addressing the issues driving community corrections. They have been consistently successful in meeting the program's stated goals. ("Programs in Action," 1992, pp. 10-11)

Community Service Programs (Work Programs). Closely linked to restitution is another economic sanction, community service. This is a program of court-ordered unpaid work done by offenders in service to the community at institutions, parks, hospitals, and other public and private nonprofit agencies. Typical tasks include cleaning of public parks or highways, maintenance work at hospital or nursing homes, and clerical tasks in public agencies. Such work is often assigned in conjunction with restitution or as "symbolic restitution," although it is also frequently assigned as an independent sanction.

Community service fits well into the restorative justice model because of its potential for repairing the damage to the community fabric resulting from crime. It can be used to restore victims to wholeness, to hold offenders accountable, and to add life-learning and ego-building experiences in areas where offenders have severe lacks.

Community service is frequently used as a sanction or a condition of probation for low-income offenders who are unable to pay a fine or make restitution. However, it is also frequently used as an additional punishment for white-collar offenders, along with a heavy fine, as an alternative to imprisonment, as long as these offenders are seen as posing no risk to public safety. It is used very frequently within juvenile corrections and is often referred to in that setting as "work therapy." At present, there are hundreds (over 600 juvenile and 300 adult) of these programs in practically all states and major metropolitan areas of this country.

The hours of service required are generally based on two primary factors, the severity of the offense and (in juvenile proceedings) the age of the offender. Differing philosophies of judges and court staff also influence assignments. Various additions to and subtractions from the hours may be made due to aggravating, mitigating, or other circumstances, in adherence to the "principle of proportionality" (Rubin, 1986, p. 3).

Bazemore and Maloney (1994) listed six principles that can guide probation departments in designing projects capable of exploiting the full potential of community service as an intervention:

1. Ensure that the service meets a clearly defined need and that this need is obvious to offenders.

2. The service activities should at least symbolically link offender with offense and victims, and, whenever possible, community service should be performed in the offender's neighborhood.
3. The activity should bring the offender and conventional adults together.
4. Probation staff and community service supervisors should view offenders as resources and focus on outcomes.
5. Involve offenders in planning and executing projects.
6. Provide for a sense of accomplishment, closure and community recognition. (p. 30)

These principles are soundly based in restorative justice concepts and should be put into practice in development of service programs.

According to Bazemore and Maloney (1994), the second principle presents a challenge to those who develop service programs:

> Perhaps most important from a restorative justice perspective is that the service, to the greatest extent possible, be victim driven. The victim should have primary input into the service activity. When they are not available for this, then community organizations which have suffered directly or represent the interest of those who have suffered could be asked to determine an appropriate and relative service requirement. (pp. 28-29)

In linking community service programs even more clearly to restorative justice goals, the authors suggested that "more carefully conceived community service interventions could be tailored to meet rehabilitative and reparative objectives, which previously brought support and enthusiasm for these sanctions and programs in community corrections" (p. 24). In support of their position, they quoted Hudson et al., who argued in 1980 that

> community sanctions may be more rehabilitative than other correctional measures because they are rationally related to the amount of damage done, require specific sanctions which allow the offender to clearly know when requirements are completed, require the offender's active involvement, provide a socially appropriate and concrete way of expressing guilt, and create a situation in which an offender is likely to elicit a positive response from other persons. (quoted in Bazemore & Maloney, 1994, p. 25)

When properly planned, developed, and implemented, community service programs have met with considerable success. One such program, called "Pay Back," in St. Louis County, Missouri, received the Missouri Juvenile Justice

Association Award for Excellence in 1993 and the Corrigan-Weisman Special Partnership Award of the St. Louis County Juvenile Justice Association for outstanding programming for youths in 1992.

"Pay Back" provides juvenile offenders an opportunity to be accountable for their delinquent behavior. Its goals, as listed in its mission statement, are "to restore the wrong-doers' respect for the law, to awaken their sense of personal responsibility, and to instill good work habits and job skills, which enhance their future, so first offenders do not become habitual offenders" and "to compensate the victims for their loss with money earned by the youths who committed the crime" (National Consortium, 1995, cover page).

In the exemplary "Building Bridges" program in Montgomery County, Ohio, which has been in operation for over a decade, almost totally funded by the private sector, hundreds of youth are placed in constructive community service activities in hospitals, institutions, and public agencies. Under the leadership of Michael Pratt, liaison is maintained with many business leaders. Bank presidents, corporation executives, and a veritable "who's who" of commerce and industry serve on the board and actively engage in fundraising activities in support of this unique effort. The program has even brought in an All Star major league baseball player, George Foster, who lends his name and active support to the small residential aspect of the program, the George Foster House (Montgomery County, 1995).

Community Justice Services

Just as community policing, community corrections, and community sentencing are becoming more common in this country, so we are starting to witness the emergence of community prosecution and community defense.

According to Boland (1996),

> More than anything else, community prosecution is an organizational response to the grassroots public safety demands of neighborhoods, as expressed in highly concrete terms by the people who live in them. They identify immediate, specific crime problems they want addressed and that the incident based 911 system is ill-suited to handle. The typical problems involve quality of life and disorder offenses, although in high crime areas, these issues are overtaken by more serious crime. (p. 35)

Community prosecution is a radical departure from conventional notions of dealing with crime that is arising from outside existing organizational structures. For example, in Multnomah County (Portland) Oregon, it was felt that citizens would demand more traditional prosecutorial services if given the opportunity; but when a special prosecutor program was tried in the Lloyd District, it was learned very quickly that people's concerns were much more immediate and "down to earth." The citizens were demanding prosecutorial emphasis on prostitution, public drinking, drug use, vandalism, littering, garbage accumulation, and thefts from automobiles. From this list of offenses, only one, thefts from automobiles, even appears in official police counts of crime. Yet according to the "broken windows theory," which has now received considerable research support (see Skogan, 1990), "Serious crime flourishes in areas where disorderly behavior goes unchecked" (Wilson & Kelling, 1982, p. 34). The Lloyd District citizens were expressing valid concerns in their request for prosecutorial emphasis.

As a result, the Neighborhood District Attorney (NDA) Program (the name was changed from "Neighborhood Prosecutor") now works with citizens and police to develop programs to address the kind of disorder that causes neighborhood decay. The NDA works very similarly to community policing programs in that it is proactive rather than reactive and concerns itself with identifying and solving problems rather than simply responding after the fact to crime reports.

Extending far beyond case-by-case prosecution of offenders, the new program involves a multifaceted approach that is heavily dependent on community initiative. It requires trying everything within reason, monitoring what happens, dropping what does not work, and adjusting tactics as the situation unfolds (Boland, 1996).

A departure from traditional procedure that is equally innovative is seen in programs of "community defense." Public defenders, who have traditionally been seen as merely another link in the offender processing chain, now see themselves as "community defenders." Their new roles are described by Stone (1996) in his report on the Neighborhood Defensive Service (NDS) of Harlem. This experiment was designed to test new ways of using public defenders in solving problems of justice in the community while still providing high-quality representation within the boundaries of cost affordable by government.

Basically, NDS differs from traditional public defender programs in that it is based in the community rather than the courthouse. Within the community, neighborhood residents are encouraged to call the office at any time just as affluent citizens call their private attorneys. Not only has this change given public defenders a head start on preparing legal defenses, but it has "created a whole different attorney client relationship that continues to pay dividends long after the case is over. It is the public defender's equivalent of a community police officer exchanging the 911 queue for a neighborhood beat" (Stone, 1996, pp. 41-42).

This program turned the priorities of public defenders upside down, so that top priority was given to advocating and conducting thorough investigations for clients at the very beginning of their cases, often even before arrest. Priority was also given to helping former clients to avoid problems while on probation or parole. The lawyers began to mediate disputes between neighbors. They became involved in other matters resulting from a person's entry into the criminal justice process, such as loss of custody of children, evictions, and claims of police misconduct.

Though some of the early evaluation results are mixed, such as the failure of NDS to significantly reduce detention decisions at the initial bail hearing or to speed time to disposition, NDS did show real cost-effectiveness in its impact on sentencing. And perhaps more important, "The lesson that emerges from the last five years of work in Harlem is that people expect both safety and justice and do not want to sacrifice one for the other. Community justice services of every kind represent the best hope of delivering both" (Stone, 1996, p. 45).

According to Stone,

> Community justice services . . . aim to identify and solve the problems that foster crime and injustice. The transformation from machine to service is most advanced in police departments, although it is also underway in prosecution, court management, and corrections. For defendants, if the change means new opportunities to solve structural problems that have compromised public defense for the past thirty years, the community justice movement may be the best thing to come along since the Supreme Court, in "Gideon versus Wainwright," recognized indigent defendants' right to counsel. (p. 41)

COMPREHENSIVE RESTORATIVE JUSTICE PROGRAMS AT THE STATE AND LOCAL LEVEL

The Vermont Department of Corrections (1995a) is currently engaged in a comprehensive restructuring to provide the criminal justice system of the state with two separate service tracks:

1. A range of reparative sanctions designed for criminal defendants who commit crimes of lower severity. This includes a community reparation sanction (reparative probation), a supervised community sentence sanction, and a community service camp incarcerative sanction.
2. A separate range of risk management sanctions and controls designed for criminal defendants who commit violent and more serious crimes and constitute a risk to the public. This track includes an intensive probation program, a day treatment program, and a program of incarceration.

In reparative probation, offenders meet with panels of citizens (community reparative boards) to work out the program for their probation, which often includes some form of mediation and offender restitution to victims. The boards also supervise community service (Pranis, 1996).

The Department of Corrections in Minnesota has established a Division of Restorative Justice and is using mediation and related programs in hundreds of cases. Many local jurisdictions in Minnesota also have various program elements in full operation. For example, as Pranis (1996) reported, Bemidji, Minnesota, is piloting a program in which a community intervention team meets with offenders to discuss how their behavior affects the community and what the community expects from the offenders. Offenders report their progress in 3- and 6-month follow-up sessions.

Other states are seeing a rapid development of restorative justice programs in local jurisdictions. In 1995, the Justice Fellowship Arizona Task Force received $3.4 million to fund programs in 12 of Arizona's 15 counties under the state's Community Punishment Act, passed in 1988. The money will fund such programs as a transition center, an outpatient drug abuse program, and an electronically monitored house arrest program.

In Oregon, Deschutes County operates multiple programs and is a national leader in the restorative corrections movement at the local level. Dennis M. Maloney, Director of the Community Corrections Department, has written and offered training programs throughout the country based on their experience.

At the local level in adult criminal justice, an outstanding program has been put in place in Genesee County, New York. Called "Genesee Justice," it provides an extensive range of restorative justice measures and extends its mediation efforts far beyond the minor caseload (Genesee County, 1994). Programs include community service, community reparations, reconciliation, victim assistance, and presentenced diversion in the restorative track, as well as jail incarceration for risk management when indicated. Meeting with consistent success with lesser cases, the program now includes about 20% felons in the restorative track. A criminal justice community coordinating council has succeeded in developing so many effective programs that the county jail operates at far below capacity and even produces revenues for taxpayers by renting space to other localities (Genesee County, 1995).

The importance of neighborhood expression of prosocial values and cohesion was found to be a powerful force to counter the presence of criminogenic factors in high-risk areas. Neighborhoods with high rates of poverty, unemployment, single-parent families, and social discrimination were found to have lower rates of violent crime than might be predicted from those indicators if a high level of "collective efficacy" (the willingness of neighbors to intervene positively to curtail truancy, graffiti, and street-corner "hanging out") was present (Sampson, Raudenbush, & Earls, 1997).

One pioneering program that is attempting to meet the culturally diverse needs of Native Americans is the "Circle Sentencing" program initiated by Judge Barry D. Stuart of the Territorial Court of Yukon, Alaska. Based on the traditional justice processes of the tribal communities, the program assembles community members to speak with each other and the offender and thereby to arrive at sentencing recommendations. Each offender is encouraged to take responsibility and to act for him- or herself in a process that treats him or her like a person who is cared for. Circle Sentencing aims primarily to achieve real changes in the behavior, attitudes, lifestyle, and conditions of all parties and in the well-being of the immediate personal and geographic communities affected by the crime (Stuart, 1996b). As one Native American participant commented,

> We need to find peace within our lives, in our families, in our communities. We need to make real differences in the way people act and in the way they treat others. . . . Yes, they [offenders] need to take responsibility, even go to jail if need be, but making all these decisions as a community means doing it in a good way—as a community, families, elders, everyone taking a part. (Rose Couch, quoted in Stuart, 1996b, p. 1)

Judge Stuart (1996b) cautioned that

> Circle Sentencing offers no new or miracle cures. It is one means of empowering communities and people affected by crime to participate in responses to crime and the attendant social problems. Many cases are more appropriately processed with less community and less formal justice system

> resources. Other cases are more appropriately processed through the formal justice system without active involvement of the community. I do not believe that any one system can ensure an effective response to the diverse circumstances surrounding crime and criminals. (p. 1)

Reaching far beyond the goals of the criminal justice system to incorporate a vision of the total good of the community as the proper object of the process is an integral part of the Circle Sentencing approach. According to Stuart (1996b), "Circles view crime holistically; pulling together health, education, social service and economic resources to redress the underlying problems of crime. By enhancing the working relationships among all participants, by empowering families and communities, Circles strive to promote the overall well-being of communities" (p. 4).

Stuart makes it clear that Circle Sentencing should not constitute the whole community justice process and that each community must have a range of options, of which Circle Sentencing would be simply one. In his approach, a community justice committee receives input from schools, the police, the community at large, the courts, the victims, and the offender. It then can use the strengths of all community resources, including families and social agencies, victim support groups, the elders, the victim, and the offender, in determining the program that would best suit the individual situation. At this point, a diversion or sentencing circle might be arranged, a mediation might be set up, or the offender might be referred to the traditional court system. This approach seems to address the needs of the indigenous population group being served within the framework of a total community justice approach that incorporates many of the best efforts of restorative justice in its concept and its application.

In general, such restorative justice approaches to sentencing have had very positive effects on the judges using them as well. Jeremy Travis, director of the National Institute of Justice, commented on this phenomenon:

> Judges who sit in drug courts say this has been the most rewarding experience of their career. Some of them have hundreds or thousands of drug cases, but they say that not until they sat in the drug court and watched how their judicial authority could be used to move people beyond their addiction, and witness the birth of drug free babies of defendants under their supervision, have they felt that they have made a positive difference in the lives of people.
>
> What if the whole criminal justice system took this approach and extended it even beyond its boundaries? (p. 4)

CONCLUSION

Just as community-based corrections encompasses more than halfway houses and diversion programs, and just as community policing encompasses more than foot patrols and neighborhood watches, so restorative justice encompasses more than mediation and restitution programs. It is a total philosophy of criminal justice aimed at involving the community in repair of harm done to victims and to the community at large, as well as encouraging offender accountability and the responsible involvement of offenders in community life. As such, its principles and strategies can be combined with those of community-based corrections and community policing to create multifaceted programs that enlist the contributions of police, corrections, courts, community service agencies, and neighborhood groups and individuals.

This is not a new approach, but a return to a vision of community that existed for many years in this country, "back when beat cops pounded the pavement; social workers, public health nurses, probation and parole officers also made home visits; and truant officers scoured the streets looking for kids playing hookey" (Gregoire, 1996, p. 2). Although such cooperative efforts declined as more modern means of communication, mechanization, and perhaps a mistaken view of professionalism took their toll, they are once again developing and are already in place in many locations throughout the country. For example, the Office of Juvenile Justice and Delinquency Prevention (Kracke, 1996) has reported that the Office of Community Partnerships, in collaboration with the Blue Hill Avenue Coalition (a community coalition comprising more than 70 public and private agencies) will establish

> a total support network of neighborhood residents and youth, community-based service providers, schools, churches, housing authorities, probation, police and corrections to address the multiple service need of juvenile offenders and those at risk of delinquency, as well as their families. This network builds on existing resources, organizes community planning, and integrates community service systems. A unique aspect of Boston's program is increased local administrative control and decision-making through neighborhood governance boards established in each of the three target areas. (p. 1)

Similar "safe futures" programs are planned or in various stages of development in Contra Costa, California; Seattle, Washington; St. Louis, Missouri; Imperial County, California; and Ft. Belknap, Montana. In all of these locations, the programs are truly multifaceted, multiagency, and closely tied to the local community (Kracke, 1996).

At the federal level, the Office of Justice Programs has funded 76 communities across the country with "Weed and Seed" programs, designed to be neighborhood-based, multiagency approaches to law enforcement and community revitalization in high-crime areas (National Institute of Justice, 1996).

Project PACT (Pulling America's Communities Together) builds on the "Weed and Seed" strategy. Its goal is to empower local communities to address youth violence by developing broader based, coordinated antiviolence strategies that incorporate the resources of federal, state, and local government agencies, law enforcement, schools, businesses, and community organizations. The four PACT sites are Atlanta, Denver, Washington, D.C., and the state of Nebraska (National Institute of Justice, 1996).

Much of the success of such programs is based on the ability and willingness of the criminal justice system to recognize and support community initiatives in its area. As Stuart (1995) argued,

> The formal justice system must welcome and support these initiatives. There is much that officials in the formal justice system can do to help, or hinder. In the past, for a variety of reasons, the criminal justice system has either absorbed and professionalized community initiatives, or has hindered or ignored these initiatives, causing them to wither away. Community initiatives lack the extensive resources society pours into formal processes and cannot compete to survive without resources and support from justice agencies.
>
> Investigating crime, prosecuting, trying difficult cases, or cases the community cannot handle, constitutes the work that formal justice systems are superbly able to do. Helping the community do what it can do best, genuinely, earnestly exploring the potential of what partnerships between community and justice resources can achieve, will enable justice agencies to be more successful in doing the work they are best suited to handle. Refusing to admit our inadequacies, ignoring opportunities to construct new partnerships with communities, manifests a dangerous arrogance capable of destroying what little public credibility we have left, and ultimately may undermine the value we can contribute to the well-being of individuals and communities. We have a role, an important role, but not the dominant role we have acquired by assuming too much exclusive responsibility for social issues within communities. (pp. 1-2)

At first, community members are likely to react with surprise when the criminal justice system reaches beyond its bounds. In New York City, for example, when some of the very first police officers who were sent out knocking on doors to get citizens' opinions of their desires for law enforcement, calls came into central headquarters reporting that there were people impersonating police officers knocking on their doors. Similarly, in Portland, Oregon, when the district attorney went out into the neighborhood, citizens began asking what he was investigating and why he was out there when "no one had been arrested yet." But once they begin to recognize the possibilities of community and justice system cooperation, they often respond with enthusiasm and creative solutions. Criminal justice professionals at every level—police, corrections, and the courts—have frequently marveled at the results when "communities come alive" and marshal their forces to cope with crime in new, different, and exciting ways. For example, in New York, when the Midtown Community Court consulted the community about how to handle quality-of-life offenses, the community recommended and obtained changes to make sentences immediate, visible, and proportionate and to provide a courtroom setting in which justice was personalized and outcomes were individualized (Travis, 1996).

The recognition of the need for a multifaceted approach to the crime problem is shared by many proponents of community-based efforts. Community corrections, community sentencing, community prosecution, and community policing, when well planned and administered, all allow for the need for use of some of the more traditional methods in some circumstances.

A search for "balance" is highlighted in the works of most of the best advocates for all elements of the restorative justice approach. In acknowledging the need for use of more traditional methods at times, they nevertheless retain the belief that communities must be more heavily involved and given much greater responsibility in the quest for justice. As Stuart (1996b) argued,

> Yes, we use jails too much—but equally we use police, lawyers and judges too much. The excessive use of jails is directly connected to the excessive reliance upon justice professionals. We need a better balance, a balance that can only be achieved by transferring back to families and communities much of the responsibility appropriated by government in the past century. (p. 4)

Epilogue

THE NEED FOR A NEW PHILOSOPHY OF CRIMINAL JUSTICE PLANNING

For many years, debate on criminal justice planning has been characterized by an extreme polarization of viewpoints. On the one side are those who loudly proclaim that the answer to crime is simply to be "tough"—that is, to be insensitive to the "niceties" presented by human need and the law itself. In enforcement, in the courts, and in corrections, being "tough" means ignoring offenders' individuality and specific problems, dehumanizing offenders, at times even countenancing the commission of crimes against offenders, and, above all, keeping offenders grouped, labeled, and "untouched by human hands."

On the other side, equally as tragic, are the misguided and misinformed who say that there is no danger to society in anyone's conduct, that all law and discipline are outdated, that no one should ever be locked up, and that we need only "be nice" to even the most dangerous offender to keep everyone safe from harm.

Between these two extremes, few people have insisted on and consistently fought for the necessary, commonsense view that certainly there are dangerous offenders from whom society must defend itself but that this fact alone does not justify the senseless treadmill leading to institutionalization of the confused, the inadequate, the uneducated, and, in general, the poor, all of whom have found their way by default into the jails and penitentiaries of this country because alternatives to meet their needs have never been developed. Nor does it justify the atmosphere of hatred and revenge that has permeated the system in many ways during our commitment to retributive justice.

Careful observation of the workings of the criminal justice system also reveals serious structural and functional flaws. Indeed, the system really is more of a "nonsystem." Applying almost any model of systems analysis to criminal justice quickly reveals little agreement on the input, the product, or the process. In addition, the lack of effective communication between the parts and the actual competition for tax dollars and the approval of the public make this "system" more closely resemble a three-ring circus (see Hahn, 1975). As Smith (1996b) argued,

> What is the criminal justice system to which so many look for effective crime policy? It is not a system at all. It is a sequence of autonomous agencies and activities, each one generating a caseload for another, and each one bidding to the public purse for adequate resources to deal with its caseload. Each bid for more resources is presented as a promise for more public safety, however implausible that promise might be. (p. 5)

Much of the polarization of debate on criminal justice is due to the lack of a unifying philosophy concerning the system's long-term goals and objectives. Differing goals of retribution, deterrence, incapacitation, and rehabilitation create differing operating policies.

Although generally one can say that most prosecutors tend to be much more supportive of a punishment response and that most probation and parole officers tend to be committed more to rehabilitation or reintegration, there are notable exceptions to these tendencies in almost every area of the country. The same is true regarding the philosophical leanings of judges, correctional workers, and all of the other players in the criminal justice system. Even within specific divisions of the system, it is impossible to find a unifying philosophical principle. As a result, public outcry and legislative demand for changes and improvements result mainly in "tinkering" without radical reconstruction.

There is almost universal dissatisfaction among all players in the system, as Carey (1996) pointed out:

> Despite improvements, a great deal of dissatisfaction remains. Offenders do not feel obligated to make amends because they say justice was not done unto them. Victims often are re-victimized by the system, despite policy and practice gains on behalf of victims in recent years. Furthermore, their role often is one of interested but passive players who are bounced about from one bureaucratic procedure to another. The community continues to voice a lack of confidence in the criminal justice system, often claiming that justice

> is not being done. Criminal justice professionals themselves often are cynical about the trappings of the system that appears more preoccupied with case processing efficiencies and due process procedures than with more preferred outcomes.
>
> If so many hard working, highly skilled professionals, legislators and citizens are frustrated with the workings of the criminal justice system, then perhaps it is time to review the underpinnings by which the current system operates. The practices of the very system we have constructed are preventing it from obtaining its goal. (p. 152)

Because the crime rate is much more dependent on demographics (the percentage of the population currently in the most "crime-prone" age range) than on any crime control policy, because probably 10% or less of all crime ever comes to the attention of the criminal justice system, and because more and more prisons are being built and citizens are being incarcerated at an enormous financial cost, the failure of the "war on crime" approach to criminal justice planning has produced increasing demand for a more rational criminal justice policy in this country. The lack of a unifying philosophy in the criminal justice system, the cries of victims who feel neglected or abused in the criminal justice process, citizen concern about expenditures for an ever-increasing prison complex, and the general dissatisfaction among the public as to the amount of protection from crime it is receiving all fuel the demand for major systemic change.

Despite the inflammatory rhetoric and public posturing of politicians who continue to loudly insist that "more of the same" will produce the solution to all of these problems, there is general unrest among the citizenry and in professional circles, and demand for a radically different approach continues to escalate. This growing momentum for change was well described by Barajas (1996):

> A revolution is occurring in criminal justice. A quiet, grassroots, seemingly unobtrusive, but truly revolutionary movement is changing the nature, the very fabric of our work. . . . What is occurring is more than innovative, but truly inventive. [A] "paradigm shift" is changing the focus of the work of criminal justice away from the offender toward the community and victims.
>
> The call for a new paradigm is being spearheaded by citizens and victims who feel left out of the criminal justice process. Citizens might not articulate their frustrations in terms of a need for a paradigm shift, but at the heart of their anger and dissatisfaction is the feeling that the criminal justice system does not represent their interest. (p. 32)

This "paradigm shift" is exemplified in the movements toward community policing, community-based corrections, and restorative justice. It is a much more radical change than simply the development or addition of a new theory; it demands, as DiIulio (1993) recently observed, that we engage with realities that have previously been deemphasized or ignored (such as the ineffectiveness of traditional responses to crime) and change the entire way in which we think about a given subject. It also demands that we not only institute new policies and programs but rethink our goals and develop new ways to measure our performance. The traditional notion of simply "counting" our activities (response time, number of arrests, numbers receiving correctional services, etc.) must give way to a much greater concern about results of our activities. And even this evaluation based on results needs to be rethought in its very substance. Most evaluative research in criminal justice today measures things that are done "to" or "for" offenders. The rehabilitation step is the primary focus, and because low recidivism is the principal measure of success, competition with other work purposes is perpetuated. The development of the new paradigm involves designing a criminal justice system that has noncompeting goals and thus encourages cooperation among all parties and agencies involved (Barajas, 1996).

THE NEED FOR PROVISION OF SOCIAL SUPPORT

The necessity of social support in prevention and control of crime cannot be overemphasized, and any proactive model relating to crime must rely on it. This fact was addressed by Francis T. Cullen in his presidential address to the Academy of Criminal Justice Sciences in 1994. Cullen set out 14 assumptions relating to the effect of "social support" on crime causality:

1. "America has higher rates of serious crime than other industrialized nations because it is a less supportive society" (p. 531).
2. "The less social support there is in the community, the higher the crime rate will be" (p. 534).
3. "The more support the family provides, the less likely it is that a person will engage in crime" (p. 538).
4. "The more social support in a person's social network, the less crime will occur" (p. 540).

5. "Social support lessens the effects of exposure to criminogenic strains" (p. 541).
6. "Across the life-cycle, social support increases the likelihood that offenders will turn away from a criminal pathway" (p. 542).
7. "Anticipation of a lack of social support increases criminal involvement" (p. 543).
8. "Giving social support lessens involvement in crime" (p. 544).
9. Crime is less likely when social support for conformity exceeds social support for crime" (p. 544).
10. "Social support is often a precondition for effective social control" (p. 545).
11. "A supportive correctional system lessens crime" (p. 546).
12. "Social support leads to more effective policing" (p. 548).
13. "Social support lessens criminal victimization" (p. 549).
14. "Social support lessens the pain of criminal victimization" (p. 550).

These principles are of fundamental importance to the entire concept of restorative justice at every level of implementation. They are applied in community policing when sensitive officers counsel children, refer families to agency services, steer people to job opportunities, and talk regularly with neighborhood groups; in community prosecution when neighborhood relationships are formed before any formal legal action; in community defense when legal services are made available to local residents on much the same basis as for affluent citizens retaining private counsel; and certainly in community sentencing and corrections when every effort is made to keep the offender involved in the community and all lines of support are encouraged.

The efficacy of social support and the ability to provide it in even the most difficult of circumstances are well seen in a special effort of the correctional services of Canada, where at the "end of the system," in the women's prison, every effort is made so that "federally sentenced women will live in a way that mirrors, as closely as possible, life in the community. . . . Federally sentenced women will be encouraged to make informed decisions about their present living condition in the facility and their future plans in the community" (Construction Policy, 1992, p. 6).

In explaining this enlightened program, J. Louis Theoret (1994), Community Liaison for the Correctional Services of Canada, cited such ingredients of the program as the development of small "townhouse" prisons, instead of more mass custody institutions, that are close to communities of origin and can house a wide range of offenders. Also, facility planning ensures that Native American inmates live in "lodges" rather than in the more formal prison structure and that a "round building for healing" is the architectural style, in keeping with the Native American culture. Correctional officers are referred to as "aunts," and the warden is called by the indigenous language equivalent of "Mother." For a group of prisoners whose native culture presents little or no concept of incarceration or of many other correctional programs, such efforts at providing social support are invaluable and contribute greatly to the success of any correctional efforts on behalf of this group of women.

The need to provide social support informs all aspects of restorative justice and relates to all those involved in the justice process. Work with troubled families, attention to children in their own homes and in foster care, formation of neighborhood groups, provision of educational and vocational opportunities, changes in the roles of personnel in the criminal justice system, correctional programs in the community and in the institution—all these and countless other efforts contribute to the provision of social support and thus fit well in the restorative justice model.

Many state and local governments are recognizing the importance of social support in program development and enabling legislation. For example, the state of Washington, in 1995, under the leadership of Attorney General Christine O. Gregoire, passed a series of bills that implemented improved ways to work with troubled families, shortened the length of time children stay in foster care, made dramatic changes in the runaway laws, and substantially improved the tools available for dealing with youth in crisis.

At the federal level, the Federal Bureau of Prisons has become interested in efforts to strengthen family bonds and to provide the social support that could encourage federal prisoners in their rehabilitative efforts. The first federal convention of the prison chapter of CURE in 1996 represented the first time that the bureau had formally had a dialogue with the families of federal prisoners, and the group was addressed by an assistant director of the bureau ("First Federal Convention," 1996).

The recognition of the need for social support in the prevention and control of crime and its conformity with the restorative justice concept that we need to "mend the torn community fabric and promote healing" as a basic response to crime present a real ray of hope in the bleakness of America's traditional approach to crime in the age of the "get tough" policy.

The rhetoric of the "war on crime" seems to promote division and gives us permission to hate our fellow citizens. It is a morally bankrupt concept that has also been proven to be far too costly and to be ineffective as a means of crime control.

Perhaps the "war on crime" mentality can begin to be replaced with the concept of "community healing," in which the causes of crime are addressed effectively along with the needs of the victims and all others affected by disruptive behavior, and in which offenders are seen as members of the community who need to be reintegrated into it as soon as possible (in keeping with community safety) after shaming and accountability have been satisfied. Of course, this drastic change in the overall thrust of crime control has large philosophical and ethical dimensions.

Fyodor Dostoyevsky cautioned us that the morality of any society can be gauged by the way in which it treats the persons who offend it by breaking its laws. Alexis DeTocqueville warned that America is great because its citizens are good and that it will stop being great when its citizens stop being good. Both of these ethical admonitions have implications for the selection of models for criminal justice planning in our country.

Concepts such as community healing, sensitivity to individual needs of citizens, concern about making neighborhoods better places for residents, and the many other basic principles underlying community initiatives in a restorative justice model lend themselves much more readily to the fulfillment of the traditional virtues, such as justice itself, along with compassion and mercy. When these virtues can be practiced within the justice system without compromising community safety, such a system has approached a "moral high ground" much more effectively than one based on the hostile, insensitive "war on crime" mentality and its purely reactive response to the complex problem of crime in our society.

A criminal justice system that emphasizes a simplistic, "pure punishment" response to crime is in many ways ineffective and often unjust. A policy that permits and even encourages the highest likelihood of severe punishment for those already most severely punished and the rejection of those already most rejected cannot provide the protection that is so longed for or the justice that is idealized.

The children of violence who rape, rob, and destroy; the "unattached children" who can hurt with impunity because no one has ever bonded them into loving relationships; the children who "cannot think beyond lunch" because their tolerance of frustration is so low and their need for instant gratification so high; those whose human worth has never been established for them; those who have never learned to read and write in our public school systems; those who have never learned the dignity of work; those whose belief in causes or persons higher than themselves has never been developed—these people cannot be threatened or punished into being caring and productive citizens.

THE NEED FOR ETHICS IN CRIME CONTROL POLICY

As Dr. Sam Souryal (1994), Professor of Corrections at Sam Houston University, has consistently and eloquently stated, a professional approach without basic goodness spawns insensitivity and arrogance. And I would add that when it is divorced from intimate community contact and it ignores or rejects input of the affected citizens, it is counterproductive at best, and when accompanied by an ethnocentric mind-set that ignores cultural diversity, it can be very dangerous.

Recent events bear out the truth of this statement. Civil disorder and the breakdown of the rule of law in many minority communities and the refusal of a jury to convict in a recent celebrated murder case because of their basic distrust of the local police department give eloquent testimony to the need for a "feeling of fairness" and a sense of empowerment in communities if the rule of law is to be effective.

The input of victims into sentencing and parole release hearings and the involvement of neighborhood groups in planning community sanctions are just a few examples of programs that can uphold both offender accountability and community safety. Occasional cases in which undeserved "leniency" does result usually call forth outrage from community members, who are the first to sense the inappropriateness of the action. Of course, numerous examples of the disregard for community safety in disposition of cases can also be found in the traditional justice system when judges act on totally personal motives or from their own emotional or character defects in releasing dangerous offenders, or prosecutors plea-bargain with dangerous offenders to obtain conviction of others of greater notoriety or more serious involvement in crime.

An ethical approach to crime control would also be a rational approach. It would advocate a constructive program at every point of the system and insist on protection of the innocent, while providing for the accountability of the offender; the recognition of the damage done to others in an effort to repair it; necessary "shaming" of the offender's behavior to uphold community standards; and an effort, as far as allowed by the needs of community safety, to reintegrate the offender after shaming and punishment have taken place. Such a program would include the essential ingredients of a balanced approach: emphasis on community safety, accountability, and competency development (see Bazemore & Umbreit, 1994a).

An ethical approach to crime control has as little to do with the "toughness" of a "pure punishment" response as it does with leniency. The present predominantly "get tough policy" advocates locking up more and more people for longer and longer times, "throwing the keys away," and making offenders increasingly miserable by adding an ever-escalating level of deprivation and humiliation to their confinement. It has failed miserably for at least 20 years and does not give a major emphasis to the needs of victims or communities.

An ethical approach to crime control has nothing to do with the position taken by some "moral anarchists" that everyone is born good and will get better and better if society just gets out of their way. Such a belief is horribly dangerous and destructive and contributes nothing to community safety or to the general good of neighborhoods or individuals.

Restorative justice, if properly conceptualized and implemented, demands great concern about community safety and the requirements of justice, but implicit in it is the importance of the virtues of kindness, mercy, and forgiveness. These virtues—surprisingly to many who do not fully understand them do not lead to inordinate "leniency" or "softness on crime." They do tend to remove the hatred for the criminal offender and emphasize the hatred of the offense, and they emphasize the need to do something constructive about the crime problem.

An outstanding example of this is found in a recent statement of the father of a young woman brutally strangled in her Chicago apartment in 1994. The grieving father, Gordon Rondeau, said in a recent interview:

> People ask me how much hate I have for the perpetrator; they want to know my feelings about the death penalty, and on and on.
>
> While my emotional side causes me to have strong feelings about both, my rational side has me believing that these issues are wholly irrelevant to the problem of crime in these United States.
>
> We must find a way to turn off the production mechanism—by understanding the factors that cause so many to resort to lives of crime. Otherwise, we are committing ourselves and our children to an existence in a society where the crime problem, as bad as it is today, can only get worse. (Rondeau, 1995, p. A19)

More recently, both parents stated:

> Politicians who focus only on punishments are cheating Americans out of the solutions that could have prevented Renee's death and so many others.
>
> We must challenge our political leaders to act now. We must call on politicians to skip the sound bites and tell voters what they'll do to boost the investments in children that are our most powerful weapons against crime.
>
> We need to vote for candidates who are ready to fight crime not only from the back end—after someone has been hurt—but also from the front end, by investing in today's children. Anything else is too little, too late. (Rondeau & Rondeau, 1996, p. A21)

Although many would say that these parents are so exceptional that their positive attitude in this terrible circumstance has little bearing on "the real world," the importance of forgiveness is being more widely recognized, along with its ramifications for criminal justice. For example, there is now a national organization, Families of Murder Victims for Reconciliation, and, under different auspices, a National Conference on Forgiveness was held in April 1995. This conference, designed to "focus on ideas and methods for forgiving people who have inflicted deep hurt" (National Conference, 1995), included an important section on "forgiveness in the criminal justice system." Led by a prominent law school professor, Walter Dickey, it was well attended by professionals, educators, and others.

Of course, there are many who scoff at any role for forgiveness, mercy, or kindness in criminal justice on the grounds that it is merely "permissiveness" or will diminish justice. As DeMarco (1995) argued, they do not understand that repentance on the part of the offender is necessary and is an understood prerequisite to the conferring of mercy: "To pardon the unrepentant is not to offer mercy, but to negate justice. Mercy follows justice and perfects it; but it does not replace it. Mercy's name is not license" (p. 168).

Those who propose the "charitable virtues," myself among them, are absolute in their insistence that the license of permissiveness be avoided. For this reason, every effort should be made to detect as many offenses as possible at the "front end of the system" and not to overlook any for "convenience's sake." Consequences for all law-violating behavior should be as certain as possible, and all persons should be held accountable for their actions. It is never merciful or kind to permit someone to do wrong without correction.

However, early interventions and consequences should be positive and "forward looking" and not be "punishment for punishment's sake" that is administered out of hatred for the offender. Just as love is often required to be "tough," so actions undertaken in a spirit of forgiveness, mercy, and kindness must often be "tough" also. For example, dangerous persons can be locked up, privileges can be restricted, and rules can be energetically enforced for "virtuous" and caring reasons. Even an action as distasteful as performing a body cavity search in a maximum-security facility can be undertaken, when necessary, with sensitivity to the feelings of the inmate, so as to counter any possible conclusion that the person conducting the search is doing so simply from punitive or sadistic motives.

Mercy adds the important ingredient of humanity to justice. It enables us to act with real compassion, even in the most difficult circumstances, and when required to do very difficult things. DeMarco (1995) argued that it is an addition to or a "crowning of" justice, never the diminution of it: "Mercy is humane not only because it crowns justice, but importantly, because it acknowledges the infirmities of human nature. . . . Mercy never stands alone. It is a virtue that presupposes another virtue, namely justice. . . . It is the light that hovers above the judgement seat" (p. 168). Similarly, the great Thomas Aquinas (1952) said centuries ago in *Summa Theologica* that mercy "does not destroy justice, but is a certain kind of fulfillment of justice" (I, XXI, III, Ad II).

Following this line of moral reasoning, I have consistently admonished my graduate criminal justice classes for many years that mercy without justice tends to be simply soppy sentimentalism and that justice without mercy leads to overbearing rigidity and cruelty.

One of the outstanding advocates for kindness in the criminal justice system, especially in corrections, is Bo Lozoff (1995), Director of the Human Kindness Foundation in Durham, N.C. He continually points out that hatred in the justice system is counterproductive:

> Over the past twenty years, we have increasingly legitimized cruelty and callousness in response to the cruelty and callousness of criminals. And with the recent elections and new crime bills, we are rushing even further down this low road. In a number of prisons across the country, we have reduced or eliminated the opportunity for inmates to earn college degrees, clamp down on family visits, restricted access to books and magazines. And now there is even a growing public sentiment to strip prisons of televisions and exercise facilities. It says that we want to make sure inmates are miserable every second of the day. We no longer want them to get their lives together. We just want them to suffer.

> Taking the "high road" does not mean being lenient toward criminals. I am certainly not advocating that we open the prison doors and let everybody out. In fact, I feel that there are many types of behavior that can cause a person to yield his or her right to stay in free society. But we need to work intensively with people who break the law; we have to structure our responses in ways that show them that they have value, that we believe in them, and that we need them. We must relegate prison to the status of last resort after all other measures have failed. (p. 158)

Again, in a recent recorded radio statement, he stated:

> Kindness does not mean letting people get away with crime; neither does it mean that we should strip persons of everything that we know makes life tolerable. The choice is not pampering versus running death camps. There is no profit in brutalizing people and then releasing them back into society. (Lozoff, 1996b)

People who work with victims, especially victims of violent crimes that have caused personal loss, cite more and more cases in which victims reveal that, after a period of hatred of the offender, they came to realize that this destructive emotion was taking a terrible toll on them and producing no positive result for the offender, the justice system, or society as a whole.

Our society is rightly very frightened and angered by violent offenses and violent offenders. However, simply to deal with all of this after the fact by hating and inflicting as much hurt as possible on the offender seems to be unproductive in most cases and harmful, in many instances, to the goals of a safe society. It is also unworthy of a society that prides itself on its humanitarian achievements in medicine and philanthropy.

THE NEED FOR POSITIVE INTERVENTION AND A PROACTIVE JUSTICE SYSTEM

The recent National Research Council report *Understanding and Preventing Violence* (1993) stated that every violent offense is an occurrence that no human characteristic, set of circumstances, or chain of events makes inevitable. There is a "chain of causality," sometimes beginning at birth through genetics, or in early childhood experiences, but all disposing causes are then triggered by various proximate causes, forming a chain that gives our society numerous opportunities to intervene positively to prevent violent acts. The authors identify well-documented risk factors that increase the odds that violence will occur in some child's life. Some of these risk factors can be modified very easily to reduce the odds of a violent event taking place. Therefore, it is incumbent on society to identify and intervene in the various stages in the chain of causality.

Community policing; community initiatives in prosecution, sentencing, and public defense; community-based corrections; and the entire mind-set, principles, and practices of restorative justice provide us with "tailor-made" programs to intervene at all these crucial points in the causal chain.

To accomplish such interventions, we must depart from stereotypical thinking and visualize a much larger philosophy under which all of these programs are to be understood. This is especially important in relation to restorative justice, which is often seen as simply embracing programs of mediation, restitution and community service. Properly conceptualized restorative justice is the all-encompassing philosophy under which all of the community and system interventions can be included without any loss of concern for community safety.

We need to emphasize the proactive thrust of all of the potential intervention elements. Community policing must be seen as presenting a wonderful opportunity to do major prevention and to begin the initial stages of community fabric repair. Community justice initiatives and corrections must be viewed imaginatively as providing a hitherto almost inconceivable array of sentencing options that are sensitive to cultural diversity and the needs of individual neighborhoods and offenders, and restorative justice must be seen as providing the basic ethical and functional concepts necessary for a complete departure from the pure punishment and hatred response of the traditional system.

Somewhere in the legal annals of this country, a great jurist observed that where we stand is not nearly so important as the direction in which we are moving. A philosophical framework of restorative justice, combined with enlightened approaches to community policing, community justice initiatives, and community corrections, provides the conceptual framework for a move in the right direction in justice planning in this country.

We have come to a stage of self-knowledge about crime control efforts in this country at which we are able to realize certain basic truths. We know, for example, that the reactive position is not effectively dealing with today's demands on the justice system. Similarly, we have become acutely aware that the informal social processes within neighborhoods control crime much more effectively than formal processes from outside. Above all, events of the recent past have emphatically reminded us that, as the inscription over the entrance to the U.S. Department of Justice building in our capitol reads, "Justice in the life and conduct of the state is possible only as it first resides in the hearts and souls of the citizens."

Effective community-oriented justice programs reach deep, all the way into the hearts and souls of individual citizens, to address the multitude of unmet needs, many for things so basic that we who are more fortunate often have difficulty imagining anyone's lacking them. Lack of food, clothing, and shelter often signal the even greater poverty of illiteracy, lack of self-esteem, and hopelessness. To recognize and attempt to meet these needs, and to bring the "left out" into full community participation, is at the very heart of a proactive justice system.

When this approach is successful, the children of the community will be able to develop those qualities that have been said to be essential for any good life. According to Lozoff (1996a), these include the classic spiritual and moral values that are common to any civilization (justice, mercy, kindness, courage, etc.), the practical skills to obtain the necessities of life and gain self-reliance, and the self-discipline and adaptability that keep one from falling apart in hard times or letting oneself be pampered or seen as needy because of not being able to provide for oneself.

When we speak of these qualities, we are speaking of moral and spiritual development "inside" the offender. Such development depends on a whole host of factors in families and communities. Early moral training and spiritual encouragement, especially effective role models, are essential. When most of the important persons in a child's life convey the direct message that "we just don't act like that," law-abiding behavior is quickly internalized by the child. This opportunity to acculturate children into "virtuous," law-abiding behavior never presents itself again in their lifetime to the same degree. I have consistently told my graduate school classes in corrections that "more law-abiding behavior is learned at one's mother's knee than will ever be learned on any hangman's scaffold."

Law-abiding family and neighborhood norms quite often flow from, and are always supported by, religious faith. I stated this in an early text on juvenile delinquency (Hahn, 1978), and I believe that it is just as valid today:

> If the term religion is understood in its strictest sense, as a bond or relationship between a creature and Creator who brought him into being out of love, and remains vitally concerned about his happiness, then religion can provide a basis of security, a source of hope, and a motivating force for real achievement in life that can be stronger than any other influence in the life

> of a human being. . . . History is replete with the evidence of religious persons who have behaved in a heroic manner under the most difficult of circumstances, motivated by a strong belief in a personal God and the relevance of their religion. . . . All the most sophisticated efforts have failed in their attempt to show that God is not the Great Motivator in the lives of untold thousands who without Him would be tempted to live lives of delinquency. (p. 227)

The important role of religion was confirmed recently in a study conducted by Charles Colson's Prison Fellowship in cooperation with the Federal Bureau of Prisons, which found that religious former inmates had a significantly lower recidivism rate than nonreligious former inmates (Johnson, Larson, & Pitts, 1997; see also Maginnis, 1996a). Todd Clear, a scholar in the field of criminal justice, concluded recently that "religion helps inmates deal with personal problems, leads to dealing with guilt, and helps them to accept personal responsibility for crimes" (quoted in Maginnis, 1996b, p. 6).

These are just reaffirmations of the accepted wisdom of most of the American population since the founding of this country—that if the principles embodied in the "golden rule" and the "Ten Commandments" were really internalized and applied in any society, crime would not present much of a problem.

Besides developing and supporting internal controls in individuals, the church and its affiliated agencies provide an enormous resource for the development of social support systems within communities. The long tradition of the church in founding orphanages, hospitals, disaster relief, and other responses to human crises is an eloquent statement of the importance of religious organizations in community initiatives.

With the dual goal of establishing a system that provides safety along with true justice, should we not recognize that this goal is impossible as long as we maintain the hostile mentality of the "war on crime" and see punishment alone as the program of choice in crime control? Is it not time that we redefine crime as injury to victims and community, as well as an affront to government? Should we not consider the proper response to crime to be community building or the restoration of the torn fabric of the community and the restoration to wholeness of all those affected by the crime, including victims, families of victims and offenders, and offenders themselves?

In such a program, we would make full provision for early prevention and for the solving of community problems and provision of necessary services. We would also arrange for plentiful participation of the community in every level of the justice process. Finally, we would make a maximum effort to reintegrate offenders, after shaming and punishment were completed, to the extent possible within the demands of community safety.

If we build prisons for a useful life of 30 to 50 years (and some have been in use for over 100 years), then we are building secure cells in which to put our grandchildren who are not even born yet. This is an exorbitantly expensive and ineffective program that is morally offensive and unworthy of a free society—yet the architects of past failure in criminal justice planning continue to urge it upon us.

Instead, should we not be building some fences at the top of the cliff rather than just paying for more ambulances at the bottom? Should we not start planning to reverse the development of asocial children before the new "baby boom" hits in a few short years? Children need homes in which they can grow in their attachment to nurturing families. They need the all-important "discipline with love" that cultivates conscience development and the social values necessary to withstand the moral pollution that surrounds them. Families and neighborhood communities need the services that will enable them to live more fully human lives, in keeping with the age-old saying that there can be no human morality in subhuman living conditions.

Agencies of the justice system need to embrace new rules, to develop new techniques of evaluating and rewarding performance. They need to receive the resource support necessary to adopt a proactive rather than simply a reactive stance. Across the board, in families, neighborhoods, and the justice system, we need to remember that goodness starts within each individual and is still required at the professional level, where professionality without goodness is cold and dangerous.

In short, we need to make a maximum effort to really live many of the principles that we have glibly espoused in our own lives and in the criminal justice system. From the Ten Commandments to the professional principle of *primum non nocere* ("above, all, do no harm") and the proud national slogan of "equal justice for all," the principles are in place and well proclaimed. A new proactive model for the criminal justice system, based on the three pillars of community policing, community corrections, and restorative justice, can give us the opportunity to put them into practice.

To plan for such a system demands that we cease responding to problems of crime control in the heat of emotion and start to focus the cool light of reason on our effort. Into this light we can perhaps bring not just the safety, but the feeling of safety, to all of our fellow citizens who suffer so much without it in our country, which continues to promise "justice for all."

References

Abate, C. M. (1996). *Dollars and cells: An analysis of Governor Pataki's sentencing reforms and proposals.* Unpublished report available from Senator Abate's office, U.S. Senate Office Building, Washington, DC 20515.

ACA calls for closer look at sentencing policy. (1994). *Criminal Justice Newsletter, 25*(24), 3-4.

A.C.I.R. urges revamping of U.S. criminal justice policies. (1993). *Corrections Digest, 24*(14), 1-4.

Adams v. Mathis, U.S. District Court, Middle District of Alabama, 458 Fed Supp. 302, affirmed 614 Red 2nd 42 (1978).

American Correctional Association. (1984). *Policy statements and resolutions.* Laurel, MD: Author.

American Correctional Association. (1994, August 10). Public correctional policy on sentencing. In American Correctional Association, *Policy and resolutions handbook* (pp. 30-31). Laurel, MD: Author.

Anderson, E. (1994, May). The code of the streets: How the inner-city environment fosters a need for self-respect and self-image based on violence. *Atlantic Monthly, 273,* 81-94.

Anti-Drug Abuse Act of 1986, 21 U.S.C.S. 801; amended, 21 U.S.C.S. 801 nt. (1988).

Aquinas, T. (1952). *Summa Theologica* (P. Caramello, Ed.). Turin, Italy: Marietta.

Austin, J. (1994). *The case for shorter prison terms: The Illinois experience.* Paper presented at the National Council on Crime and Delinquency, San Francisco.

Barajas, E., Jr. (1996, Spring). Moving toward community justice. *Perspectives* [American Pardon and Parole Association], pp. 32-35.

Bayley, D. H. (1988). Community policing: A report from the devil's advocate. In J. R. Greene & S. D. Mastrofski (Eds.), *Community policing: Rhetoric or reality?* New York: Praeger.

Bazemore, G. (1992). On mission statements and reform in juvenile justice: The case for the balanced approach. *Federal Probation, 56,* 64-70.

Bazemore, G. (1995, January). *Beyond rehabilitation and retribution: A new framework for juvenile justice.* Paper presented at the conference of the Campaign for an Effective Crime Policy, Washington, DC.

Bazemore, G., & Day, S. (1997). Restoring the balance: Juvenile and community justice. *Juvenile Justice, 3*(1), 1-14.

Bazemore, G., & Maloney, D. (1994). Rehabilitating community service: Toward restorative service sanctions in a balanced justice system. *Federal Probation, 58,* 24-34.

Bazemore, G., & Umbreit, M. S. (1994a, October). *Balanced and restorative justice: Program summary.* Washington, DC: Office of Juvenile Justice and Delinquency Prevention.

Bazemore, G., & Umbreit, M. (1994b). *Rethinking the sanctioning function in juvenile court: Retributive or restorative responses to youth crime.* Unpublished manuscript.

Bedau, H. A. (1971). Deterrence and the death penalty: A reconsideration. *Journal of Criminal Law, Criminology and Police Science, 61,* 539-545.

Blumstein, A. (1978). *Research on deterrent and incapacitative effects: Summary report.* Washington, DC: National Academy of Sciences Panel, U.S. Congress, House Committee on Science and Technology.

Blumstein, A. (1994, December). *Measurement of crime and punishment in the United States.* Paper presented at the conference of the Campaign for an Effective Crime Control Policy, Washington, DC.

Blumstein, A. (1995). *Youth violence, guns, and illicit drug markets* (Research Preview). Washington, DC: National Institute of Justice.

Blumstein, A., Cohen, J., & Nagin, D. (1978). *Deterrence and incapacitation: Estimating the effects of criminal sanctions on crime rates.* Washington, DC: National Academy of Sciences.

Boland, B. (1996, August). What is community prosecution? *Journal of the National Institute of Justice,* No. 231, pp. 35-40.

Boston mayor's panel blasts police department leadership. (1992). *Criminal Justice Newsletter, 23*(1), 5-6.

Branham, L. (1992, May). *Use of incarceration in the U.S.: A look at the present and the future.* Paper presented at the meeting of the American Bar Association, Chicago.

Breivik, K. (1995, Spring). Mamma knows best. *Justice Report: Newsletter of the Justice Fellowship,* p. 8.

Bureau of Justice Statistics. (1992). *Drugs, crime and the justice system.* Washington, DC: U.S. Department of Justice.

Bureau of Justice Statistics. (1996). *Prisoners at mid-year 1995.* Washington, DC: U.S. Department of Justice.

Campaign for an Effective Crime Policy. (Ed.). (1996a). *Crime and politics in the 1990's: Three perspectives.* Washington, DC: Editor.

Campaign for an Effective Crime Policy. (1996b). *Impact of three strikes and you're out laws: What have we learned?* Washington, DC: Author.

Carey, M. (1996, August). Restorative justice in community corrections. *Corrections Today, 58,* 152-155.

Carlson, K., & Mullen, J. (1980). *American prisons and jails: Vol. 2. Population trends and projections.* Washington, DC: Government Printing Office.

Carter, D. L., Sapp, A. D., & Stephens, D. W. (Eds.). (1989). *The state of police education: Policy directions for the 21st century.* Washington, DC: Police Executive Research Forum.

Chaiken, J. M., & Chaiken, M. R. (1982). *Varieties of criminal behavior.* Santa Monica, CA: RAND Corporation.

Chiricos, T., & Waldo, J. (1970-1971). Punishment and crime: An examination of some empirical evidence. *Social Problems, 18,* 20.

Clark, J. R. (1993, April 15). L.E.N. interview with Chief Tom Potter of Portland, Oregon. *Law Enforcement News,* pp. 6, 7, 10.

Clark, R. (1970). *Crime in America.* New York: Simon & Schuster.

Clear, T. R., & Cole, G. F. (1990). *American corrections.* Pacific Grove, CA: Brooks/Cole.

Clear, T. R., & O'Leary, V. (1982). *Controlling the offender in the community.* Lexington, MA: Lexington.

The Commish's dream system. (1993, Fall). *Justice Report: Newsletter of the Justice Fellowship,* p. 8.

Comprehensive Crime Control Act of 1984, 18 U.S.C.S. 1 nt.

Compromise is needed in juvenile justice reform. (1986). *Juvenile Justice Digest, 19*(2), 1-7.

Construction Policy and Services/National Implementation Committee, Correctional Services of Canada. (1992, July). *Regional facilities for federally sentenced women, Draft No. 4, operational plan.* Unpublished report.

Corrections Task Force of the President's Commission on Law Enforcement and Administration of Justice. (1967). *The challenge of crime in a free society.* Washington, DC: Author.

Crime down, media crime coverage up. (1994). *Media Monitor, 8*(1), 7.

Cullen, F. T. (1994). Social support as an organizing concept for criminology: Presidential address to the Academy of Criminal Justice Sciences. *Justice Quarterly, 11*(4), 531-550.

Cullen, F. T., & Gilbert, K. E. (1982). *Reaffirming rehabilitation.* Cincinnati, OH: Anderson.

Dahl, J., Banks, J., Carlson, E., Debro, J., Varnon, L., Kirkpatrick, K. (1980). *Improved probation strategies-manual.* Washington, D.C. University Research Corporation, U.S. Department of Justice, Law Enforcement Assistance Administration, National Institute of Justice.

Daly, M., & Wilson, M. (1988). *Homicide.* New York: Aldine de Gruyter.

Decker, S., & Pennell, S. (1995). *Arrestees and guns: Monitoring the illegal firearms market.* Washington, DC: National Institute of Justice.

DeMarco, D. (1995, November/December). The virtue corner: Mercy. *Social Justice Review,* No. 168, p. 168.

Deming, W. E. (1986). *Out of the crisis.* Cambridge, MA: Center for Advanced Engineering Study.

DiIulio, J. (1993). *Rethinking the criminal justice system: Toward a new paradigm* (Performance Measures for the Criminal Justice System). Washington, DC: National Institute of Justice.

Edna McConnell Clark Foundation. (1993). *Americans behind bars.* New York: Author.

Ehrlich, I. (1993, May). Participation in illegitimate activities: A theoretical and empirical investigation. *Journal of Political Economy,* pp. 531-567.

Endres, M. E. (1985). *The morality of capital punishment: Equal justice under the law?* Mystic, CT: Twenty-Third.

Ewing, C. P. (1990). *Kids who kill.* Lexington, MA: Lexington.

Fabian, J. (1995). *Towards a more effective paradigm in criminal justice.* Unpublished paper.

Fahlberg, V. (1979). *Attachment and separation: Putting the pieces together.* Lansing: Michigan Department of Social Services.

Farrington, D. P. (1989). Early predictors of adolescent aggression and adult violence. *Violence and victims, 4,* 79-100.

First federal convention for CURE set for next month. (1996, July 12). *Corrections Digest, 27*(28), 8.

Fogel, D. (1975). *We are the living proof: The justice model for corrections.* Cincinnati, OH: Anderson.

Ford, G. (1975). To insure domestic tranquility through the use of mandatory sentence for convicted felons. *Vital Speeches of the Day, 41,* 450-452.

Forum. (1984, June 11). *Law Enforcement News, 6*(1), 10, 16.

Friday, J. C. (1994, January). Violence prevention from a public health perspective: The U.S. experience. *Miami Medicine, 64,* 15.

Friedman, A., Granick, S., Kreisher, C., & Terras, A. (1993). *Miami's drug court: A different approach* (Fact Sheet). Washington, DC: National Institute of Justice.

Friedman, W. (1994). The community role in community policing. In D. P. Rosenbaum (Ed.), *The challenge of community policing* (pp. 263-269). Thousand Oaks, CA: Sage.

Gale, M. E. (1985). Retribution, punishment, and death. *U.C. Davis Law Review, 18,* 973-1035.

Geismar, L. L., & Wood, K. M. (1986). *Family and delinquency: Resocializing the young offender.* New York: Human Sciences Press.

Gendreau, P. (1996). What we know and what needs to be done. *Criminal Justice and Behavior, 23,* 144-161.

Genesee County Sheriff's Office. (1994, December). *Genesee justice.* Batavia, NY: Author.

Gibbs, J. P. (1975). *Crime, punishment, and deterrence.* New York: Elsevier.

Gibbs, J. P. (1978). The death penalty, retribution and penal policy. *Journal of Criminal Law and Criminology, 69,* 291-299.

Goldstein, H. (1993, December). *The new policing: Confronting complexity* (Research in Brief, NCJ145157). Washington, DC: National Institute of Justice.

Goldstein, H. (1994). Foreword. In D. P. Rosenbaum (Ed.), *The challenge of community policing* (pp. viii-x). Thousand Oaks, CA: Sage.

Goldstein, A., & Kalant, H. (1991). From theory to practice: The planned treatment of drug users. *International Journal of the Addictions, 25,* 307-343.

Goodwin, F. (1995). The biology of violence. *New Yorker, 70*(3), 68-77.

Greene, J. (1992, April). Designing and implementing a day-fine system for tne Staten Island Court. In C. M. McDonald (Ed.), *Day fines in American courts: The Staten Island and Milwaukee experiments* (Issues and Practices). Washington, DC: National Institute of Justice.

Greenwood, P. W., Model, K. E., Rydell, C. P., & Chiesa, J. (1996). *Diverting children from a life of crime.* Santa Monica, CA: RAND Corporation.

Gregoire, C. O. (1996). Crime, politics and the public debate. In Campaign for an Effective Crime Policy (Ed.), *Crime and politics in the 1990's: Three perspectives.* Washington, DC: Campaign for an Effective Crime Policy.

Haas, K., & Alpert, G. (1986). *The dilemmas of punishment: Readings in contemporary corrections.* Prospect Heights, IL: Waveland.

Hahn, P. H. (1971). *The juvenile offender and the law* (1st ed.). Cincinnati, OH: Anderson.

Hahn, P. H. (1975). *Community-based corrections and the criminal justice system.* Santa Cruz, CA: Davis.

Hahn, P. H. (1978). *The juvenile offender and the law* (2nd ed.). Cincinnati, OH: Anderson.

Hahn, P. H. (1991, December 29). An open letter to the next drug czar. *Chicago Tribune,* p. 19.

Hahn, P. H. (1994, August). *A standardized curriculum for correctional officers: History and rationale.* Paper presented at the American Congress on Corrections, St. Louis, MO.

Hamilton, L. H. (1971). Criminal rehabilitation should be our top priority. *Criminal Law Bulletin, 7*(3), 225-241.

Hamparian, D. M., Davis, J. M., Jacobson, J. M., & McGraw, R. E. (1985). *The young criminal years of the violent few.* Washington, DC: National Institute for Juvenile Justice and Delinquency Prevention.

Harland, A. (1992, Summer). Toward the rational assessment of economic sanctions. *Topics in Community Corrections,* pp. 2-9.

Harmelin v. Michigan, 501, U.S. Supreme Court, 957 (June 27, 1991).

Hartmann, F. X. (1988, November). *Debating the evolution of American policing* (Perspectives on Policing, No. 5). Washington, DC: National Institute of Justice.

Heymann, P. (1995, January). *A serious law enforcement program to deal with violence.* Paper presented at Crime and Politics in the 1990's: A National Leadership Conference of the Campaign for an Effective Crime Policy, Washington, DC.

Independent Commission on the Los Angeles Police Department. (1991). *Report of the Independent Commission on the Los Angeles Police Department (summary).* Unpublished mimeograph.

International City Management Association. (1989). *Management information service report* (Vol. 21, No. 9) [Looseleaf report]. Washington, DC: Author.

Johnson, B., Larson, D., & Pitts, T. (1997). Religious programs, institutional adjustment and recidivism. *Justice Quarterly, 14,* 145-163.

Justice for all: A new approach to criminal justice [Brochure for the VORP National Conference, Pennsylvania State Correctional Institution at Graterford]. (1993, October).

Kelling, G. L., & Moore, M. H. (1988, November). *The evolving strategy of policing* (Perspectives on Policing, No. 4). Washington, DC: National Institute of Justice.

Kennedy, D. (1993, January). *The strategic management of police resources* (Perspectives on Policing, No. 14, NCJ139565). Washington, DC: National Institute of Justice.

Kennedy, D. (1997). *Juvenile gun violence* (Research Preview). Washington, DC: National Institute of Justice.

Kennell, J., & Klaus, M. (1976). Parent-infant bonding. In R. Helfer & C. H. Kempe (Eds.), *Child abuse and neglect.* Cambridge, MA: Ballinger.

Kracke, K. (1996, June). *Safe futures: Partnerships to reduce youth and delinquency* (Fact Sheet No. 38). Washington, DC: Office of Juvenile Justice and Delinquency Prevention.

Langen, P. A., & Brown, J. M. (1994). *Felony sentences in state courts* (NCJ163391). Washington, DC: Bureau of Justice Statistics.

Latessa, E. J., & Allen, H. E. (1997). *Corrections in the community.* Cincinnati, OH: Anderson.

Lindenman, L. (1995, January 22). Between bars. *Chicago Tribune Magazine,* pp. 19-22.

Lipton, D., Wilks, J., & Martinson, R. (1975). *The effectiveness of correctional treatment: A survey of treatment evaluation studies.* New York: Praeger.

Loeber, R., & Stouthamer-Loeber, M. (1986). Family factors as correlates and predictors of juvenile conduct problems and delinquency. *Crime and Justice, 7,* 29-149.

Logan, C. H., & McGriff, B. W. (1989). *Comparing costs of public and private prisons: A case study* (Research in Action Fact Sheet). Washington, DC: National Institute of Justice.

Lozoff, B. (1995, September/October). Seven ways to fix the criminal justice system. *New Age Journal,* pp. 86, 87, 158, 159.

Lozoff, B. (1996a, Fall). *A little good news* (Kindness Foundation Newsletter), pp. 1-7.

Lozoff, B. (1996b, March 12). A touch of human kindness [Radio address]. *Interconnect* program, WVXU.

Luger, M. (1973, June). *Noninstitutional corrections: Alternatives to incarceration.* Paper presented at the Seven State Conference of Youth Administrators, Xavier University, Cincinnati, OH.

Maginnis, R. (1996a, October 17). *Faith-based prison programs cut costs and recidivism* (Insight Occasional Paper). Washington, DC: Family Research Council.

Maginnis, R. (1996b, August 29). A little faith works wonders. *Cincinnati Enquirer,* p. 6.

Marans, S. (1995). *Police-mental health partnership: A community-based response to urban violence.* New Haven, CT: Yale University Press.

Martinson, R. (1974, Spring). What works? Questions and answers about prison reform. *In the Public Interest,* pp. 22-54.

Martinson, R. (1979). New findings, new views: A note of caution regarding sentencing reform. *Hofstra Law Review, 7,* 243-258.

Martinson attacks his own earlier work. (1978, December 4). *Criminal Justice Newsletter,* p. 4.

Mauer, M. (1996). Punishing more wisely. *Legal Times, 19*(16), 24.

McCord, R., & Wicker, E. (1990). Tomorrow's America: Law enforcement's coming challenge. *FBI Law Enforcement Bulletin, 59*(1), 28-32.

McGlothian-Taylor, F. (1992). Community policing and minorities: Constant contact helps break down barriers. *Footprints: The Community Policing Newsletter, 4*(2), 4-7.

McKelvey, M., & McKelvey, K. (1987). *High risk.* Golden, CO: M&M Publishing.

Mendelsohn, B. (1996). Crime crackdown straining corrections professionals. *Corrections Alert, 2*(21), 1-3.

Montgomery County [Dayton, Ohio] Juvenile Court. (1995). *Annual report of Building Bridges Inc.* [Mimeographed].

Moore, M. H., & Trojanowicz, R. C. (1988, November). *Corporate strategies for policing* (Perspectives on Policing). Washington, DC: National Institute of Justice.

Morrison, W. D. (1915). *Juvenile offenders.* New York: D. Appleton.

Murphy, G. (1986). *Special care: Improving the police response to the mentally disabled.* Washington, DC: National Institute of Justice.

Murphy, P. (1989). Foreword. In D. L. Carter, A. D. Sapp, & D. W. Stephens (Eds.), *The state of police education: Policy direction for the twenty-first century.* Washington, DC: Police Executive Research Forum.

Nagel, W. (1980, June). *Institutional corrections.* Lecture given at Xavier University, Cincinnati, OH.

National Center for Education Statistics, School Safety and Discipline Component. (1994). *National household education survey of 1993* [Machine-readable data file]. Washington, DC: Author.

National Conference on Forgiveness. (1995, March-April). [Conference bulletin]. University of Wisconsin-Madison.

National Consortium on Alternatives for Youths At-Risk Inc. (1995). *Fact sheet.* Sarasota, FL: Author.

National Institute of Justice. (1995a, October). *Community policing in Chicago: Year 2* (Research Preview). Washington, DC: Author.

National Institute of Justice. (1995b, November). *Community policing strategies* (Research Preview Fact Sheet 00126). Washington, DC: Author.

National Institute of Justice. (1995c). *Managing innovation in policing: The untapped potential of the middle manager* (Research Preview Fact Sheet 00130). Washington, DC: Author.

National Institute of Justice. (1996). *Communities mobilizing against crime: Making partnerships work.* Washington, DC: Author.

National Research Council. (1993). *Understanding and preventing violence.* Washington, DC: National Academy Press.

National Task Force on Correctional Substance Abuse Strategies. (1991). *Intervening with substance abusing offenders: A framework for action.* Washington, DC: U.S. Department of Justice.

NCJJ study links restitution to lower recidivism. (1992). *Criminal Justice Newsletter, 23*(20), 5-6.

Newman, G. (1978). *The punishment response.* Philadelphia: J. B. Lippincott.

No plea bargains result in jammed California court systems. (1995). *Corrections Digest, 26*(14), 6-7.

O'Leary, V., & Duffee, D. (1971). Correctional policy: A classification of goals designed for change. *Crime and Delinquency, 17,* 373-386.

Pease, K., & McWilliams, W. (Eds.). (1980). *Community service by order.* Edinburgh: Scottish Academic Press.

Petersilia, J. (1990). Conditions that permit intensive supervision programs to survive. *Crime and Delinquency, 36,* 126-145.

Petersilia, J., & Turner, S. (1993, May). *Evaluating intensive supervision probation/parole: Results of a nationwide experiment* (Research in Brief). Washington, DC: National Institute of Justice.

Police, civil rights and corrections experts join to challenge Barr's corrections summit. (1992). *Corrections Digest, 23*(10), 1-2.

Pranis, K. (1996). Restorative justice: The next stage in responding to crime? *Corrections Alert, 3*(5), 6.

Proband, S. C. (1995, October). Corrections leads state appropriation increases for 1996. *Overcrowded Times, 6,* 4.

Programs in action. (1992, Summer). *Topics in Community Corrections,* pp. 10-15.

Reed, C. B. (1994). The next generation. In Campaign for an Effective Crime Policy (Ed.), *Prisons and colleges competing for state dollars* (pp. 1-9). Washington, DC: Campaign for an Effective Crime Policy.

Reise, H. (1962). *Heal the hurt child.* Chicago: University of Chicago Press.

Rhodes v. Chapman, 452 U.S. Supreme Court 337 (1981).

Rondeau, G. P. (1995, January 5). The brutal reality of crime in America [Guest editorial]. *Atlanta Journal-Constitution,* p. A19.

Rondeau, G., & Rondeau, E. (1996, November 1). Fighting crime upfront [Guest editorial]. *Atlanta Journal-Constitution,* p. A21.

Rosen, M. S. (1992). Interview with Police Chief Lee Brown. *Law Enforcement News, 18*(358), 10, 11, 14.

Rosenbaum, D. P. (1994). Preface. In D. P. Rosenbaum (Ed.), *The challenge of community policing* (pp. xi-xvi). Thousand Oaks, CA: Sage.

Rosenbaum, D. P., & Wilkinson, D. L. (1993). *Aurora Joliet neighborhood oriented policing and problem solving demonstration project: Impact on police personnel and community residents* (Vol. 2). Chicago: Center for Research in Law and Justice.

Rowan, J. (1978, May). *Self-help for the abusing parent.* Lecture given at Xavier University, Cincinnati, OH.

Rubin, T. H. (1986). Community service restitution by juveniles: Also in need of guidance. *Juvenile and Family Court Journal, 37*(1), 3-8.

Sadd, S., & Grinc, R. (1993). *Issues in community policing: Lessons learned in the implementation of eight innovative neighborhood-oriented policing programs.* New York: Vera Institute of Justice.

Sadd, S., & Grinc, R. (1996, February). *Implementation challenges in community policing: Innovative neighborhood oriented policing in eight cities* (Research in Brief). Washington, DC: Author.

Sampson, R. J., Raudenbush, S. W., & Earls, F. (1997). Neighborhoods and violent crime: A multi-level study of collective efficacy. *Science, 277*(5328), 918-927.

Scholtes, P. R. (1991, June). *Thinking about predictability and quality.* Lecture presented at George Washington University, Washington, DC.

Seavey Award to create new law enforcement/public understanding. (1993, March). *Police Chief,* p. 13.

Sechrest, D., & Josi, D. (1992). *Substance abuse programs for incarcerated offenders in four settings* (Report of Research). Riverside, CA: Robert Presley Institute of Corrections Research in Training.

Sentencing Reform Act of 1984, 18 U.S.C.S. 3551 *et seq.*; amended, 18 U.S.C.S. 3551 nt. (1985).

Sickmund, M., Snyder, H. N., Poe-Yamagata, E. (1997). *Juvenile offenders: 1997 update on violence.* Washington, DC: Department of Justice, Office of Juvenile Justice and Delinquency Prevention.

Silberman, C. (1978). *Criminal violence, criminal justice.* New York: Random House.

Skogan, W. G. (1990). *Disorder and decline: Crime and the spiral of decay in American neighborhoods.* New York: Free Press.

Skolnick, J. H., & Bayley, D. H. (1986). *The new blue line: Police innovations in six American cities.* New York: Free Press.

Skolnick, J. H., & Bayley, D. H. (1988). *Community policing: Issues and practices around the world.* Washington, DC: National Institute of Justice.

Smith, M. E. (1996a). Notes on public safety and the criminal justice system. In Campaign for an Effective Crime Policy (Comp.), *Crime and politics in the 1990's: Creating demand for new policies.* Unpublished compilation of conference materials for use at the Campaign's February conference, Washington, DC.

Smith, M. E. (1996b). *Who wants an effective crime policy and can deliver one?* In Campaign for an Effective Crime Policy (Ed.), *Crime and politics in the 1990's: Three perspectives.* Washington, DC: Campaign for an Effective Crime Policy.

Snyder, J., & Patterson, G. (1987). Family interaction and delinquent behavior. In H. C. Quay (Ed.), *Handbook of juvenile delinquency* (pp. 216-243). New York: John Wiley.

Snyder, H., Sickmund, M., & Poe-Yamagata, E. (1996). *Juvenile offenders and victims: 1996 update on violence.* Washington, DC: Office of Juvenile Justice and Delinquency Prevention.

Souryal, S. (1994, August). *Looking at yourself in the mirror: Everyday ethics for the correctional professional.* Paper presented at the American Congress on Corrections, St. Louis, MO.

Sparrow, M. K. (1988). *Implementing community policing* (Perspectives on Policing, No. 9, NCJ114217). Washington, DC: National Institute of Justice.

Sparrow, M. K., Moore, M. H., & Kennedy, D. M. (1990). *Beyond 911: A new era for policing.* New York: Basic Books.

Stone, C. (1996, August). Community defense and the challenge of community justice. *Communities as Criminal Justice Partners Journal, 231,* 41-45.

Straus, M. A., Gelles, R. J., & Steinmetz, S. K. (1980). *Behind closed doors: Violence in the American family.* Garden City, NY: Doubleday.

Stuart, B. D. (1995). *Circles into square systems: Can community processes be partnered with the formal justice system?* Unpublished paper.

Stuart, B. (1996a, January). *Circle sentencing.* Paper presented at the conference of the Campaign for an Effective Crime Policy, Washington, DC.

Stuart, B. D. (1996b). *Sentencing circles: Making real differences.* Unpublished paper.

Study criticizes community policing. (1991, August 8). *New York Times,* p. B2.

Tafoya, W. L. (1990). The future of policing. *FBI Law Enforcement Bulletin, 59*(1), 13-17.

ten Bensel, R. (1980). Lecture presented at Xavier University, Cincinnati, OH.

Theoret, J. L. (1994, August). *Higher education in corrections: A debate.* Paper presented at the American Congress on Corrections, Nashville, TN.

Thornburgh, R. (1989, May). *Opening remarks.* Presented at the National Drug Conference, Washington, DC.

Tien, J. M., & Rich, T. F. (1994). The Hartford COMPASS program: Experiences with a Weed and Seed program. In D. P. Rosenbaum (Ed.), *The challenge of community policing* (pp. 192-208). Thousand Oaks, CA: Sage.

Travis, J. (1996). Lessons in criminal justice from 20 years of policing reform. In Campaign for an Effective Crime Policy (Ed.), *Crime and politics in the 1990's: Three perspectives.* Washington, DC: Campaign for an Effective Crime Policy.

Travisono, A. (1990, May). Executive director of American Correctional Association cries out. *On the Line,* p. 1.

Trojanowicz, R. (1991). Community policing curbs police brutality. *Footprints: The Community Policing Newsletter, 3*(1 & 2), 1-5.

Trojanowicz, R. C. (1994). The future of community policing. In D. P. Rosenbaum (Ed.), *The challenge of community policing* (pp. 258-262). Thousand Oaks, CA: Sage.

Trojanowicz, R., & Bucqueroux, B. (1991). *Community policing and the challenge of diversity.* East Lansing, MI: National Center for Community Policing.

Trojanowicz, R., & Bucqueroux, B. (1992a). *Basics of community policing.* East Lansing: Michigan State University, National Center for Community Policing.

Trojanowicz, R., & Bucqueroux, B. (1992b). *Toward development of meaningful and effective performance evaluations.* East Lansing: Michigan State University, National Center for Community Policing.

Trojanowicz, R., & Bucqueroux, B. (1992c). What community policing can do to help. *Community Policing Newsletter, 2*(2), 1-8.

Umbreit, M. S. (1994). The effects of victim offender mediation. *Overcrowded Times, 5*(1), 5-6.

Umbreit, M. S. (1996). Restorative justice through mediation. *Overcrowded Times, 7*(3), 9-11.

Umbreit, M., & Coates, R. (1993). Cross-site analysis of victim offender mediation in four states. *Crime and Delinquency, 39,* 15-25.

U.S. Department of Justice. (1990). *A survey of intermediate sanctions.* Washington, DC: Government Printing Office.

Urschel, J. (1995, April 11). Expert seeks classroom of millions. *U.S.A. Today,* pp. 1A-2A.

Vachss, A. H., & Bakal, Y. (1979). *The life-style violent juvenile.* Lexington, MA: Lexington.

Van den Haag, E., & Conrad, J. (1983). *The death penalty: A debate.* New York: Plenum.

Vermont Department of Corrections. (1995a). *Restructuring corrections: A continuum of intermediate sanctions.* Unpublished executive summary.

Vermont Department of Corrections. (1995b). *Sentencing options: Restructuring corrections for the 21st century.* Waterbury, VT: Author.

Wadman, R. C., & Bailey, S. E. (1993). *Community policing and crime prevention in America and England.* Chicago: University of Illinois at Chicago, Office of International Criminal Justice.

Walters, P. M. (1993, November). Community-oriented policing: A blend of strategies. *FBI Law Enforcement Bulletin,* pp. 20-23.

Ward, R. (1991). Community policing comes of age. *CJ: The Americas, 4*(2), 1, 19.

Wardens reject mandatory terms for drug offenders. (1994). *Corrections Digest, 25*(26), 1-2.

Weaver, S. (1992, Fall/Winter). Neighborhood network center concept at work. *Footprints: The Community Policing Newsletter, 5*(2), 2-3.

Webster's New World Dictionary (college ed.). (1957). New York: World.

Widom, C. S. (1989a). The cycle of violence. *Science, 244,* 160-166.

Widom, C. S. (1989b). Does violence beget violence: A critical examination of the literature. *Psychological Bulletin, 106,* 3-28.

Williams, H., & Murphy, P. V. (1990). *The evolving strategy of policing: A minority view* (Perspectives on Policing, No. 13). Washington, DC: National Institute of Justice.

Wilson, J. Q. (1994). *Essays on character.* Washington, DC: American Enterprise Institute for Public Policy Research.

Wilson, J. Q., & Kelling, G. (1982, March). Broken windows. *Atlantic Monthly,* pp. 31-37.

Wood, F. W. (1996). Cost effective ideas in penology: The Minnesota approach. *Corrections Today, 58*(1), 52-56.

Wright, K. N., & Wright, K. E. (1994). *Summary: Family life, delinquency and crime: A policy maker's guide.* Washington, DC: Office of Juvenile Justice and Delinquency Prevention.

Wycoff, M., & Oettmeier, T. (1994). *Evaluating patrol officer performance under community policing: The Houston experience* (Research Report). Washington, DC: National Institute of Justice.

Wycoff, M. A., & Skogan, W. G. (1993). *Community policing in Madison: Quality from the inside out. An evaluation of implementation and impact* (NCJ144390). Washington, DC: National Institute of Justice.

Youth offer advice on juvenile crime to governors' meeting. (1994). *Juvenile Justice Digest, 22*(4), 5-8.

Zehr, H. (1990). *Changing lenses.* Scottsdale, PA: Herald.

Additional Selected Readings

Emerging Criminal Justice

Aaronson, D. E., Hof, B. H., Jaszi, P., Kittrie, N., & Sarri, D. (1977). *The new justice: Alternatives to conventional criminal adjudication.* Washington, DC: Government Printing Office.

Alper, B. S. (1974). *Prisons inside-out.* Cambridge, MA: Ballinger.

American Correctional Association. (1993). *Community partnerships in action.* Laurel, MD: Author.

American Friends Service Committee. (1971). *Struggle for justice.* New York: Hill & Wang.

Atkins, B., & Pogrebin, M. (1982). *Invisible justice system: Discretion and the law* (2nd ed.). Cincinnati, OH: Anderson.

Baker, R., & Meyer, F. A., Jr. (1980). *The criminal justice game.* Belmont, CA: Duxbury.

Baldus, D. C., Woodworth, G., & Pulaski, C. A., Jr. (1990). *Equal justice and the death penalty: A legal and empirical analysis.* Boston: Northeastern University Press.

Beccaria, C. (1963). *On crimes and punishments* (H. Paulucci, Trans.). Indianapolis: Bobbs-Merrill. (Original work published 1764)

Beck, A., & Bonczar, T. (1994). *State and federal prison population tops one million.* Washington, DC: U.S. Department of Justice.

Benekos, P., & Merlo, A. (Eds.). (1992). *Corrections: Dilemmas and directions.* Cincinnati, OH: Anderson.

Bentham, J. (1973). *An introduction to the principles of morals and legislation.* Garden City, NY: Anchor. (Original work published 1789)

Black, D., & Mileski, M. (1973). *The social organization of law.* New York: Seminar.

Blumstein, A., Cohen, J., Roth, J. A., & Visher, C. A. (Eds.). (1986). *Criminal careers and "career criminals."* Washington, DC: National Academy Press.

Bohm, R. M. (1991). *The death penalty in America: Current research.* Cincinnati, OH: Anderson.

Bouza, A. V. (1990). *The police mystique: An insider's look at cops, crime, and the criminal justice system.* New York: Plenum.

Bowman, G. W., Hakim, S., & Seidenstat, P. (Eds.). (1993). *Privatizing correctional institutions.* Laurel, MD: American Correctional Association.

Braithwaite, J. (1989). *Crime, shame and reintegration.* New York: Cambridge University Press.

Braswell, M., Fletcher, T., & Miller, L. (1994). *Human relations and corrections.* Prospect Heights, IL: Waveland.

Braswell, M., McCarthy, B., & McCarthy, B. (1991). *Justice, crime and ethics.* Cincinnati, OH: Anderson.

Bureau of Justice Statistics. (1995). *Correctional populations in the United States.* Washington, DC: U.S. Department of Justice.

Camp, C., & Camp, G. (1995). *The corrections yearbook, 1994: Adult corrections.* South Salem, NY: Criminal Justice Institute.

Castle, M. (1989). *Alternative sentencing: Selling it to the public.* Washington, DC: U.S. Department of Justice.

Champion, D. J. (Ed.). (1989). *The U.S. sentencing guidelines: Implications for criminal justice.* Westport, CT: Praeger.

Clear, T. R. (1994). *Harm in American penology.* Albany: State University of New York Press.

Close, D., & Meier, N. (1995). *Morality in criminal justice: An introduction to ethics.* Belmont, CA: Wadsworth.

Cole, G. F. (1984). *Criminal justice: Law and politics.* Monterey, CA: Brooks/Cole.

Coleman, S., & Guthrie, K. (1988). *Sentencing effectiveness in preventing crime.* St. Paul, MN: Criminal Justice Statistical Analysis Center.

Colvin, M. (1994). *The penitentiary in crisis.* Albany: State University of New York Press.

Culbertson, R. G., & Weisheit, R. (1994). *Order under law: Readings in criminal justice* (5th ed.). Prospect Heights, IL: Waveland.

Darrow, C. (1991). *Clarence Darrow on the death penalty.* Evanston, IL: Chicago Historical Bookworks.

DiIulio, J. J., Jr. (1991). *No escape: The future of American corrections.* New York: Basic Books.

DiIulio, J. (1992). *Courts, corrections and the Constitution.* New York: Oxford University Press.

Dodge, C. (1979). *A world without prisons.* Lexington, MA: Lexington.

Earley, P. (1992). *The hot house: Life inside Leavenworth Prison.* New York: Bantam.

Ferdico, J. (1992). *Ferdico's criminal law and justice directory.* St. Paul, MN: West.

Flowers, R. (1989). *Demographics and criminality: The characteristics of crime in America.* Westport, CT: Greenwood.

Flowers, R. (1990). *Minorities and criminality.* New York: Praeger.

Fogel, D. (1988). *On doing less harm.* Chicago: University of Chicago Press.

Fogel, D., & Hudson, J. (1981). *Justice as fairness.* Cincinnati, OH: Anderson.

Frankel, M. (1973). *Criminal sentences: Law without order.* New York: Hill & Wang.

Gibbons, D. C. (1988). *The limits of punishments as social policy.* New York: Edna McConnell Clark Foundation.

Glaser, D. (1969). *The effectiveness of a prison and parole system.* Indianapolis: Bobbs-Merrill.

Goldstein, H. (1990). *Problem oriented policing.* Philadelphia: Temple University Press.

Gottfredson, M. R., & Gottfredson, D. M. (1980). *Decision making in criminal justice: Toward the rational exercise of discretion.* Cambridge, MA: Ballinger.

Gottfredson, S., & Gottfredson, D. (1992). *Incapacitation strategies and the criminal career.* Sacramento, CA: California Division of Law Enforcement.

Gottfredson, S. D., & McConville, S. (1987). *America's correctional crisis.* New York: Greenwood.

Gottfredson, S. D., & Taylor, R. B. (1983). *The correctional crisis: Prison populations and public policy.* Washington, DC: U.S. Department of Justice.

Greene, J. R., & Mastrofski, S. (Eds.). (1988). *Community policing: Rhetoric or reality.* New York: Praeger.

Greenwood, P. (1983). *Selective incapacitation.* Santa Monica, CA: RAND Corporation.

Greenwood, P. W., & Zimring, F. E. (1985). *One more chance: The pursuit of promising intervention strategies for chronic juvenile offenders.* Santa Monica, CA: Rand Corporation.

Gross, H., & Von Hirsch, A. (1981). *Sentencing.* New York: Oxford University Press.

Guyot, D. (1991). *Policing as though people matter.* Philadelphia: Temple University Press.

Haas, K. C., & Alpert, G. P. (Eds.). (1992). *The dilemmas of corrections: Contemporary readings.* Prospect Heights, IL: Waveland.

Hahn, P. H. (1976). *Crimes against the elderly: A study of victimology.* Santa Cruz, CA: Davis.

Hahn, P. H. (1984). *The juvenile offender and the law* (3rd ed.). Cincinnati, OH: Anderson.

Holten, N. G., & Jones, M. E. (1982). *The system of criminal justice* (2nd ed.). Boston: Little, Brown.

Horwitz, A. V. (1990). *The logic of social control.* New York: Plenum.

Huff, C. R., Rattner, A., & Sagarin, E. (1996). *Convicted but innocent: Wrongful conviction and public policy.* Thousand Oaks, CA: Sage.

Irwin, J., & Austin, J. (1994). *It's about time: America's imprisonment binge.* Belmont, CA: Wadsworth.

Israel, J. H., Kamisae, Y., & LaFave, W. R. (1989). *Criminal procedure and the Constitution.* St. Paul, MN: West.

Johnson, R. (1987). *Hard time.* Monterey, CA: Brooks/Cole.

Johnson, R., & Toch, H. (1994). *The pains of imprisonment.* Prospect Heights, IL: Waveland.

Katzmann, G. (1991). *Inside the criminal process.* New York: Norton.

Keller, O. J., & Alpert, B. (1970). *Halfway houses.* Lexington, MA: Lexington.

Klein, A. (1988). *Alternative sentencing: A practitioner's guide.* Cincinnati, OH: Anderson.

Klofas, J., & Stojkovic, S. (1995). *Crime and justice in the year 2010.* Belmont, CA: Wadsworth.

Kress, J., Wilkins, L., Gottfredson, D., Calpin, J., & Gelman, A. (1978). *Developing sentencing guidelines: Trainer's handbook.* Washington, DC: U.S. Department of Justice.

Lauen, R. L. (1988). *Community-managed corrections.* College Park, MD: American Correctional Association.

Logan, C. H. (1990). *Private prisons: Cons and pros.* New York: Oxford University Press.

Lozoff, B., & Braswell, M. (1989). *Inner corrections.* Cincinnati, OH: Anderson.

Mair, G. (1997). *Evaluating the effectiveness of community penalties.* Brookfield, VT: Ashgate.

Martinson, R. M., & Wilks, J. (1971). *Treatment evaluation survey.* Unpublished study, New York Division of Criminal Justice Services.

McDonald, D. (Ed.). (1992). *Private prisons and the public interest.* New Brunswick, NJ: Rutgers University Press.

McLaughlin, E. (1994). *Community policing and accountability: The politics of policing in the 1980's.* Brookfield, VT: Aldershot.

Meier, R. F., & Miethe, T. D. (1994). *Crime and its social context.* Albany: State University of New York Press.

Miller, K., & Radelet, M. (1993). *Executing the mentally ill.* Newbury Park, CA: Sage.

Mitford, J. (1973). *Kind and usual punishment.* New York: Knopf.

Morris, N. (1974). *The future of imprisonment.* Chicago: University of Chicago Press.

Morris, N., & Tonry, M. (1989). *Between prison and probation.* New York: Oxford University Press.

Munro, J. (1976). *Classes, conflict and control.* Cincinnati, OH: Anderson.

Nagel, W. (1973). *The new red barn: A critical look at the modern American prison.* New York: Walker.

Neely, R. (1982). *Why courts don't work.* New York: McGraw-Hill.

Newman, G. (1983). *Just and painful: The case for the corporal punishment of criminals.* New York: Free Press.

O'Leary, V., & Clear, T. (1984). *Directions for community corrections in the 1990's.* Washington, DC: U.S. Department of Justice.

Packer, H. (1968). *The limits of the criminal sanction.* Stanford, CA: Stanford University Press.

Pate, A. M., Wycoff, M. A., Skogan, W. G., & Sherman, L. W. (1986). *Reducing fear of crime in Houston and Newark: A summary report.* Washington, DC: Police Foundation.

Paternoster, R. (1992). *Capital punishment in America.* Lexington, MA: Lexington.

Pepinsky, H. E., & Quinney, R. (Eds.). (1991). *Criminology as peacemaking.* Bloomington: Indiana University Press.

Petersilia, J. M. (1983). *Racial disparities in the criminal justice system.* Santa Monica, CA: RAND Corporation.

Petersilia, J., & Wilson, J. Q. (Eds.). (1995). *Crime.* San Francisco: ICS.

Pollock, J. M. (1994). *Ethics in crime and justice* (2nd ed.). Belmont, CA: Wadsworth.

Practicing Law Institute and the Sentencing Project. (Eds.). (1991). *1991 National Conference on Sentencing Advocacy, Practicing Law Institute and the Sentencing Project.* New York: Practicing Law Institute.

Radelet, M. L., Bedau, H. A., & Putnam, C. E. (1992). *In spite of innocence.* Boston: Northeastern University Press.

Reiman, J. (1995). *The rich get richer and the poor get prison* (4th ed.). Boston: Allyn & Bacon.

Roberts, A. (1994). *Critical issues in crime and justice.* Thousand Oaks, CA: Sage.

Rollo, N., & Adams, L. (1993). *A map through the maze: A guide to surviving the criminal justice system.* Laurel, MD: American Correctional Association.

Rosenbaum, D. P. (Ed.). (1987). *Community crisis prevention: Does it work?* Beverly Hills, CA: Sage.

Rosenbaum, D. P. (Ed.). (1994). *The challenge of community policing.* Thousand Oaks, CA: Sage.

Sanders, W. B., & Dandistell, H. C. (1976). *The criminal justice process: A reader.* New York: Praeger.

Schwartz, I. M. (1992). *Juvenile justice and public policy.* New York: Lexington.

Scott, J. E., & Hirschi, T. (Ed.). (1988). *Controversial issues in crime and justice.* Newbury Park, CA: Sage.

Shusta, R. M., Levine, D. R., Harris, P. R., & Wong, H. Z. (1995). *Multicultural law enforcement.* Englewood Cliffs, NJ: Prentice Hall.

Silberman, M. (1995). *A world of violence: Corrections in America.* Belmont, CA: Wadsworth.

Stojkovic, S., Klofas, J., & Kalinich, D. (Eds.). (1994). *The administration and management of criminal justice organizations.* Prospect Heights, IL: Waveland.

Taylor, R. (1994). *Research methods in criminal justice: Exploring alternate pathways.* New York: McGraw-Hill.

Thompson, J. A., & Mays, G. L. (1991). *American jails: Public policy issues.* Chicago: Nelson-Hall.

Tomasic, R., & Dobinson, I. (1979). *The failure of imprisonment.* Sydney, Australia: Law Foundation.

Tonry, M., & Will, R. (1989). *Intermediate sanctions.* Washington, DC: Government Printing Office.

Umbreit, M. (1994). *Victim meets offender: The impact of restorative justice and mediation.* Monsey, NY: Criminal Justice Press.

van den Haag, E. (1975). *Punishing criminals: Concerning a very old and painful question.* New York: Basic Books.

Van Ness, D. W., Carlson, D. R., Jr., Crawford, T., & Strong, K. (1989). *Restorative justice: Theory.* Washington, DC: Justice Fellowship.

von Hirsch, A. (1985). *Past or future crimes: Deservedness and dangerousness in the sentencing of criminals.* New Brunswick, NJ: Rutgers University Press.

von Hirsch, A. (1986). *Doing justice: The choice of punishments.* Boston: Northeastern University Press. (Original work published 1976).

Wadman, R. C., & Olson, R. K. (1990). *Community wellness: A new theory of policing.* Washington, DC: Police Executive Research Forum.

Weisheit, R. A. (1990). *Drugs, crime and the criminal justice system.* Cincinnati, OH: Anderson.

Whitehead, J., Miller, L., & Myers, L. (1995). The diversionary effectiveness of intensive supervision in a community corrections program. In J. Smykla & W. Selke

(Eds.), *Intermediate sanctions: Sentencing in the 1990s* (pp. 135-151). Cincinnati, OH: Anderson.

Wilkins, L. (1969). *Evaluation of penal measures.* Berkeley: University of California Press.

Wilson, J. Q. (Ed.). (1983). *Crime and public policy.* San Francisco: ICS.

Wilson, J. Q. (1983). *Thinking about crime.* New York: Basic Books.

Wolfgang, M. (1979). *Prisons: Present and possible.* Lexington, MA: Lexington.

Wright, M. (1991). *Justice for victims and offenders: A restorative response to crime.* Philadelphia: Open University Press.

Zimmerman, S. E., & Miller, H. D. (1981). *Corrections at the crossroads.* Beverly Hills, CA: Sage.

Zimring, F., & Hawkins, G. (1995). *Incapacitation: Penal confinement and the restraint of crime.* New York: Oxford University Press.

Zupan, L. (1991). *Jails: Reform and the new generation philosophy.* Cincinnati, OH: Anderson.

Zvekic, U. (1994). *Alternatives to imprisonment in comparative perspective.* Chicago: Nelson-Hall.

Violence

Adler, P. A. (1985). *Wheeling and dealing: An ethnography of an upper-level dealing and smuggling community.* New York: Columbia University Press.

Anderson, E. (1990). *Streetwise: Race, class, and change in an urban community.* Chicago: University of Chicago Press.

Bandura, A. (1973). *Aggression: A social learning analysis.* Englewood Cliffs, NJ: Prentice Hall.

Bandura, A., & Walters, R. H. (1959). *Adolescent aggression.* New York: Ronald.

Baron, L., & Straus, M. A. (1989). *Four theories of rape in American society.* New Haven, CT: Yale University Press.

Beasley, R. W., & Antunes, G. (1974). The etiology of urban crime: An ecological analysis. *Criminology, 11,* 439-461.

Bolton, F., Morris, L., & MacEachron, A. (1989). *Males at risk: The other side of child sexual abuse.* Newbury Park, CA: Sage.

Brodsky, S. L. (1975). *Families and friends of men in prison.* Lexington, MA: D. C. Heath.

Browne, A., & Finkelhor, D. (1986). Impact of child sexual abuse: A review of the research. *Psychological Bulletin, 99,* 66-77.

Bureau of the Census. (1990). *Statistical abstract of the United States: 1990.* Washington, DC: Government Printing Office.

Bureau of Justice Statistics. (1986). *The use of weapons in committing crimes.* Washington, DC: Government Printing Office.

Bureau of Justice Statistics. (1989). *Criminal victimization in the United States, 1987.* Washington, DC: Government Printing Office.

Bureau of Justice Statistics. (1989). *Injuries from crime: Special report.* Washington, DC: Government Printing Office.

Bureau of Justice Statistics. (1990). *Criminal victimization in the United States, 1988* (NCJ-122024). Washington, DC: Government Printing Office.

Bureau of Justice Statistics. (1992). *Criminal victimization in the United States, 1990.* Washington, DC: Government Printing Office.

Byrne, J., & Sampson, R. (Eds.). *The social ecology of crime.* New York: Springer-Verlag.

Carson, R. C., Butcher, J. N., & Coleman, J. C. (1988). *Abnormal psychology and modern life* (8th ed.). New York: HarperCollins.

Centers for Disease Control. (1991). "Forum on Youth Violence in Minority Communities: Setting the Agenda for Prevention," December 10-12, 1990, summary of the proceedings. *Public Health Reports, 106,* 225-277.

Cloward, R. A., & Ohlin, L. E. (1960). *Delinquency and opportunity.* Glencoe, IL: Free Press.

Comstock, G., & Paik, H. (1990). *The effects of television violence on aggressive behavior: A meta-analysis.* Unpublished report to the National Academy of Sciences Panel on the Understanding and Control of Violent Behavior, Washington, DC.

Coser, R. L. (1982). The American family: Changing patterns of social control. In J. Gibbs (Ed.), *Social control: Views from the social sciences.* Beverly Hills, CA: Sage.

Crawford, D., & Bodine, R. (1996). *Conflict resolution education.* Washington, DC: Office of Juvenile Justice and Delinquency Prevention.

Curtis, L. A. (1974). *Criminal violence: National patterns and behavior.* Lexington, MA: D. C. Heath.

Curtis, L. (1975). *Violence, race, and culture.* Lexington, MA: D. C. Heath.

Damon, W. (1988). *The moral child: Nurturing children's natural moral growth.* New York: Free Press.

Elliott, D. S., Huizinga, D., & Menard, S. (1989). *Multiple problem youth: Delinquency, substance use, and mental health problems.* New York: Springer-Verlag.

Elliott, D. S., Huizinga, D., & Morse, B. J. (1985). *The dynamics of deviant behavior: A national survey progress report.* Boulder, CO: Behavioral Research Institute.

Fagan, J. (1990). Social processes of drug use and delinquency among gang and non-gang youths. In C. R. Huff (Ed.), *Gangs in America.* Newbury Park, CA: Sage.

Farrington, D. P. (1979). Environmental stress, delinquent behavior, and convictions. In J. G. Sarason & C. D. Spielberger (Eds.), *Stress and Anxiety.* Washington, DC: Hemisphere.

Farrington, D. P. (1986). Stepping stones to adult criminal careers. In D. Olweus, J. Block, & M. Radke-Yarrow (Eds.), *Development of antisocial and prosocial behavior: Research, theories, and issues* (pp. 359-384). Orlando, FL: Harcourt Brace Jovanovich.

Farrington, D. P. (1989). Later adult life outcomes of offenders and nonoffenders. In M. Brambring, F. Losel, & H. Skowronek (Eds.), *Children at risk: Assessment, longitudinal research and intervention* (pp. 220-244). New York: Walter de Gruyter.

Farrington, D. P. (1991). Childhood aggression and adult violence: Early precursors and later-life outcomes. In D. J. Pepler & K. H. Rubin (Eds.), *The development and treatment of childhood aggression* (pp. 5-29). Hillsdale, NJ: Lawrence Erlbaum.

Farrington, D. P., Ohlin, L. E., & Wilson, J. Q. (1986). *Understanding and controlling crime: Toward a new research strategy.* New York: Springer-Verlag.

Federal Bureau of Investigation. (1968-1992). *Uniform crime reports: Crime in the United States.* Washington, DC: Government Printing Office.

Finkelhor, D. (1984). *Child sexual abuse: New theory and research.* New York: Free Press.

Finkelhor, D., Hotaling, G., & Sedlak, A. (1990). *Missing, abducted, runaway, and throwaway children in America, first report.* Washington, DC: Office of Juvenile Justice and Delinquency Prevention.

Freedman, J. L. (1986). Television violence and aggression: A rejoinder. *Psychological Bulletin, 100,* 372-378.

Friedrich-Cofer, L., & Huston, A. C. (1986). Television violence and aggression: The debate continues. *Psychological Bulletin, 100,* 364-371.

Furstenberg, F. (1990, August). *How families manage risk and opportunity in dangerous neighborhoods.* Paper presented at the annual meeting of the American Sociological Association, Washington, DC.

Gandossy, R. P., Williams, J., Cohen, J., & Hardwood, H. (1980). *Drugs and crime: A survey and analysis of the literature.* Washington, DC: National Institute of Justice.

Garfinkel, I., & McLanahan, S. S. (1986). *Single mothers and their children: A new American dilemma.* Washington, DC: Urban Institute Press.

Garofalo, J., Siegel, L., & Laub, J. (1987). School-related victimizations among adolescents: An analysis of National Crime Survey narratives. *Journal of Quantitative Criminology, 3,* 321-338.

Gibbs, J. (1987). The need to facilitate empathy as well as sociomoral reasoning. In W. Kurtines & J. Gewirtz (Eds.), *Moral development through social interaction.* New York: John Wiley.

Glueck, S., & Glueck, E. (1950). *Unraveling juvenile delinquency.* Cambridge: Harvard University Press.

Goldstein, P. J. (1989). Drugs and violent crime. In N. A. Weiner & M. E. Wolfgang (Eds.), *Pathways to criminal violence* (pp. 16-48). Newbury Park, CA: Sage.

Gordon, L. (1988). *Heroes of their own lives: The politics and history of family violence, Boston 1880-1960.* New York: Viking.

Gottfredson, D. M., Wilkins, L. T., & Hoffman, P. B. (1978). *Guidelines for parole and sentencing decisions.* Lexington, MA: Lexington.

Guarino, S. (1985). *Delinquent youth and family violence* (Pub. No. 14, 020-100-74-4-85-CR). Boston: Commonwealth of Massachusetts, Department of Youth Services.

Gurr, T. R. (1989). Historical trends in violent crime: Europe and the United States. In T. R. Gurr (Ed.), *Violence in America: Vol. 1. The history of crime.* Newbury Park, CA: Sage.

Hagedorn, J. (1988). *People and folks: Gangs, crime, and the underclass in a Rustbelt city.* Chicago: Lakeview.

Hamparian, D. M., Schuster, R., Dinitz, S., & Conrad, J. P. (1978). *The violent few.* Lexington, MA: D. C. Heath.

Harries, K. D. (1990). *Serious violence: Patterns of homicide and assault in America.* Springfield, IL: Charles C Thomas.

Hartstone, E., & Hansen, K. V. (1984). The violent juvenile offender: An empirical portrait. In R. A. Mathias (Ed.), *Violent juvenile offenders: An anthology* (pp. 83-112). San Francisco: National Council on Crime and Delinquency.

Heath, L., Bresolin, L. B., & Rinaldi, R. C. (1989). Effects of media violence on children. *Archives of General Psychiatry, 46,* 376-379.

Herzog, E., & Sudia, C. E. (1970). *Boys in fatherless families.* Washington, DC: Office of Child Development.

Hindelang, M., Gottfredson, M., & Garofalo, J. (1978). *Victims of personal crime: An empirical foundation for a theory of personal victimization.* Cambridge, MA: Ballinger.

Holinger, P. C. (1987). *Violent deaths in the United States: An epidemiologic study of suicide, homicide, and accidents.* New York: Guilford.

Huesmann, L. R., & Miller, L. S. (in press). Long term effects of repeated exposure to media violence in childhood. In G. Comstock (Ed.), *Public communication and behavior* (Vol. 3). Orlando, FL: Academic Press.

Inciardi, J. A. (1980). Youth, drugs, and street crime. In F. Scarpitti & S. K. Datesman (Eds.), *Drugs and the youth culture* (pp. 175-204). Beverly Hills, CA: Sage.

Inciardi, J. A. (1989, September). *The crack/violence connection within a population of hard-core adolescent offenders.* Paper presented at the National Institute of Drug Abuse Technical Review on Drugs and Violence, Rockville, MD.

Jankowski, M. S. (1991). *Islands in the street: Gangs and American urban society.* Berkeley: University of California Press.

Jencks, C., & Mayer, S. E. (1990). The social consequences of growing up in a poor neighborhood. In L. E. Lynn, Jr., & M. G. H. McGeary (Eds.), *Inner-city poverty in the United States* (pp. 111-186). Washington, DC: National Academy Press.

Kazdin, A. E. (1985). *Treatment of antisocial behavior in children and adolescents.* Homewood, IL: Dorsey.

Keith, C. R. (Ed.). (1984). *The aggressive adolescent.* New York: Free Press.

Kleck, G. (1991). *Point blank: Guns and violence in America.* New York: Aldine de Gruyter.

Klein, M., & Maxson, C. (1989). Street gang violence. In N. A. Weiner & M. E. Wolfgang (Eds.), *Violent crime, violent criminals* (pp. 198-234). Newbury Park, CA: Sage.

Kornhauser, R. R. (1978). *Social sources of delinquency: An appraisal of analytic models.* Chicago: University of Chicago Press.

Lane, T. W., & Davis, G. E. (1987). Child maltreatment and juvenile delinquency: Does a relationship exist? In J. D. Burchard & S. N. Burchard (Eds.), *Prevention of delinquent behavior* (pp. 122-138). Newbury Park, CA: Sage.

Lockwood, D. (1980). *Prison sexual violence.* New York: Elsevier.

Loeber, R., & Stouthamer-Loeber, M. (1987). Prediction. In H. C. Quay (Ed.), *Handbook of juvenile delinquency* (pp. 325-382). New York: John Wiley.

Loeber, R., Stouthamer-Loeber, M., Van Kammen, W., & Farrington, D. P. (1991). Initiation, escalation and desistance in juvenile offending and their correlates. *Journal of Criminal Law and Criminology, 82,* 36-82.

Loeber, R., Weissman, W., & Reid, J. B. (1983). Family interactions of assaultive adolescents, stealers, and non-delinquents. *Journal of Abnormal Child Psychology, 11,* 1-14.

Long, N., & Forehand, R. (1987). The effects of parental divorce and parental conflict on children: An overview. *Developmental and Behavioral Pediatrics, 8,* 292-296.

MacLeod, J. (1987). *Ain't no makin' it: Leveled aspirations in a low-income neighborhood.* Boulder, CO: Westview.

Matsueda, R. L., & Heimer, K. (1987). Race, family structure, and delinquency: A test of differential association and social control theories. *American Sociological Review, 52,* 826-840.

McCord, J. (1986). Instigation and insulation: How families affect antisocial aggression. In J. Block, D. Olweus, & M. R. Yarrow (Eds.), *Development of antisocial and pro-social behavior.* New York: Academic Press.

McCord, J. (1990). Long-term perspectives on parental absence. In L. N. Robins & M. Rutter (Eds.), *Straight and devious pathways from childhood to adulthood* (pp. 116-134). Cambridge, MA: Cambridge University Press.

McCord, W., & McCord, J. (1956). *Psychopathy and delinquency.* New York: Grune & Stratton.

Miller, S. J., Dinitz, S. D., & Conrad, J. P. (1982). *Careers of the violent.* Lexington, MA: Lexington.

Miller, W. B. (1975). *Violence by youth gangs and youth groups as a crime problem in major American cities.* Washington, DC: Government Printing Office.

Miller, W. B. (1980). Gangs, groups, and serious youth crime. In D. Shichor & D. Kelly (Eds.), *Critical issues in juvenile delinquency* (pp. 115-138). Lexington, MA: D. C. Heath.

Monahan, J. (1988). Risk assessment of violence among the mentally disordered: Generating useful knowledge. *International Journal of Law and Psychiatry, 11,* 249-257.

Moore, J. W. (1978). *Homeboys: Gangs, drugs, and prisons in the barrios of Los Angeles.* Philadelphia: Temple University Press.

Mouzakitis, C. M. (1981). An inquiry into the problem of child abuse and juvenile delinquency. In R. J. Hunner & Y. E. Walker (Eds.), *Exploring the relationship between child abuse and delinquency* (pp. 220-231). Montclair, NJ: Allanheld, Osmun.

National Center for Health Statistics. (1991). *Vital statistics of the United States 1988: Vol. 2. Mortality.* Washington, DC: Government Printing Office.

National Health/Education Consortium. (1991). *Healthy brain development: Precursor to learning.* Washington, DC: National Commission to Prevent Infant Mortality.

Nye, F. I. (1958). *Family relationships and delinquent behavior.* New York: John Wiley.

Office of National Drug Control Policy, Executive Office of the President. *The National Drug Control Strategy, 1997.* Washington, DC: Author.

Olweus, D. (1987). Bully/victim problems among school children. In S. A. Mednick, T. E. Moffitt, & S. A. Stack (Eds.), *The causes of crime: New biological approaches.* Cambridge, UK: Cambridge University Press.

Olweus, D. (1991). Bully/victim problems among schoolchildren: Basic facts and effects of a school based intervention program. In D. J. Pepler & K. H. Rubin (Eds.), *The development and treatment of childhood aggression* (pp. 411-448). Hillsdale, NJ: Lawrence Erlbaum.

Paternoster, R., & Triplett, R. (1988). Disaggregating self-reported delinquency and its implications for theory. *Criminology, 26,* 591-647.

Patterson, G. R. (1980). Children who steal. In T. Hirschi & M. Gottfredson (Eds.), *Understanding crime: Current theory and research* (pp. 73-90). Beverly Hills, CA: Sage.

Pfouts, J. H., Scholper, J. H., & Henley, H. C., Jr. (1981). Deviant behaviors of child victims and bystanders in violent families. In R. J. Hunter & Y. E. Walker (Eds.), *Exploring the relationship between child abuse and delinquency* (pp. 79-99). Montclair, NJ: Allanheld, Osmun.

Polk, K., Alder, C., Bazemore, G., Black, G., Cordray, S., Coventry, J., Galvin, J., & Temple, M. (1981). *Becoming adult: An analysis of maturational development from age 16 to 30 of a cohort of young men.* Eugene, OR: University of Oregon Department of Sociology.

Prothrow-Stith, D. (1987). *Violence prevention curriculum for adolescents.* Newton, MA: Education Development Center.

Pulkkinen, L. (1983). Search for alternatives to aggression in Finland. In A. P. Goldstein & M. Segall (Eds.), *Aggression in global perspective.* New York: Pergamon.

Reiss, A. J., Jr. (1986). Why are communities important in understanding crime? In A. Reiss, Jr., & J. A. Roth (Eds.), *Communities and crime* (pp. 1-33). Chicago: University of Chicago Press.

Rhoads, P. W., & Parker, S. L. (1981). *The connections between youth problems and violence in the home.* Portland, OR: Oregon Coalition Against Domestic and Sexual Violence.

Robins, L. N. (1966). *Deviant children grown up: A sociological and psychiatric study of sociopathic personality.* New York: Russell Sage Foundation.

Rutter, M. (1978). Family, area and school influences in the genesis of conduct disorders. In L. A. Hersov, M. Berger, & D. Schaffer (Eds.), *Aggression and antisocial behavior in childhood and adolescence.* New York: Pergamon.

Sampson, R. J. (1986). Crime in cities: The effects of formal and informal social control. In A. J. Reiss, Jr., & M. Tonry (Eds.), *Communities and crime* (pp. 271-311). Chicago: University of Chicago Press.

Sampson, R. J. (1987). Urban black violence: The effect of male joblessness and family disruption. *American Journal of Sociology, 93,* 348-382.

Schwartz, G. (1987). *Beyond conformity or rebellion: Youth and authority in America.* Chicago: University of Chicago Press.

Sedlak, A. J. (1991). *National incidence and prevalence of child abuse and neglect: 1988.* Washington, DC: Westat, Inc.

Sedlak, A. J. (1991). *Supplementary analyses of data on the national incidence of child abuse and neglect.* Washington, DC: Westat, Inc.

Shaw, C. R., & McKay, H. D. (1942). *Juvenile delinquency and urban areas.* Chicago: University of Chicago Press.

Short, J. F., & Strodtbeck, F. L. (1965). *Group process and gang delinquency.* Chicago: University of Chicago Press.

Simcha-Fagan, O., Langer, T. S., Gersten, J. C., & Eisenberg, J. G. (1975). *Violent and antisocial behavior: A longitudinal study of urban youth.* Unpublished report, Office of Child Development.

Singer, J. L., & Singer, D. G. (1981). *Television, imagination, and aggression: A study of pre-schoolers.* Hillsdale, NJ: Lawrence Erlbaum.

Smith, C., Weiher, A. W., & Van Kammen, W. B. (1991). Family attachment and delinquency. In D. Huizinga, R. Loeber, & T. P. Thornberry (Eds.), *Urban delinquency and substance abuse: Technical report* (Vol. 1). Washington, DC: Office of Juvenile Justice and Delinquency Prevention.

Solway, K. S., Richardson, L., Hays, J. R., & Elcon, V. H. (1981). Adolescent murderers. In J. R. Hayes, T. K. Roberts, & K. S. Solway (Eds.), *Violence and the violent individual* (pp. 193-209). Jamaica, NY: Spectrum.

Sorrells, J. M. (1977). Kids who kill. *Crime and Delinquency, 23,* 312-320.

Stouthamer-Loeber, M., Schmaleng, K. B., & Loeber, R. (1984). *The relationship of single-parent family status and marital discord to antisocial child behavior.* Unpublished manuscript, University of Pittsburgh.

Straus, M. A. (1981, November). *Family violence and non-family crime and violence.* Paper presented at the annual meeting of the American Society of Criminology, Washington, DC.

Sullivan, M. (1989). *Getting paid: Youth crime and work in the inner city.* Ithaca, NY: Cornell University Press.

Taylor, C. S. (1990). *Dangerous society.* East Lansing: Michigan State University Press.

Thrasher, F. M. (1963). *The gang: A study of 1,313 gangs in Chicago* (Abridged ed.). Chicago: University of Chicago Press. (Original work published 1927)

Toby, J. (1983). Violence in school. *Crime and Justice, 4,* 1-47.

Toby, J. (1983). *Violence in school* (Research in Brief Fact Sheet). Washington, DC: National Institute of Justice.

Toch, H. (1992). *Violent men.* Washington, DC: American Psychological Association.

Toch, H., & Adams, K. (1989). *The disturbed violent offender.* New Haven, CT: Yale University Press.

U.S. Department of Health and Human Services. (1990). *Child abuse and neglect: Critical first steps in response to a national emergency.* Washington, DC: Government Printing Office.

Van Dine, S., Conrad, J. P., & Dimitz, S. (1979). *Restraining the wicked: The violent offender program.* Lexington, MA: Lexington.

Van Voorhis, P., Cullen, F. T., Mathers, R. A., & Garner, C. C. (1988). The impact of family structure and quality on delinquency: A comparative assessment of structural and functional factors. *Criminology, 26,* 235-261.

Wadsworth, M. (1979). *Roots of delinquency, infancy, adolescence and crime.* Oxford, UK: Robertson.

Weis, J. G. (1986). Issues in the measurement of criminal career. In A. Blumstein, J. Cohen, J. A. Roth, & C. Visher (Eds.), *Criminal careers and "career criminals"* (Vol. 2, pp. 1-51). Washington, DC: National Academy Press.

West, D. J. (1982). *Delinquency: Its roots, careers and prospects.* London: Heinemann.

West, D. J., & Farrington, D. P. (1973). *Who becomes delinquent?* London: Heinemann.

Widom, C. S. (1990, March). *Research, clinical, and policy issues: Childhood victimization, parent alcohol problems, and long term consequences.* Paper presented at the National Forum on the Future of Children, Workshop on Children and Parental Illegal Drug Abuse, National Research Council, Institute of Medicine, Washington, DC.

Wilkinson, K. (1980). The broken home and delinquent behavior: An alternative interpretation of contradictory findings. In T. Hirschi & M. Gottfredson (Eds.), *Understanding crime: Current theory and research* (pp. 21-42). Beverly Hills, CA: Sage.

Williams, T. (1989). *The cocaine kids: The inside story of a teenage drug ring.* Menlo Park, CA: Addison-Wesley.

Wilson, W. J. (1987). *The truly disadvantaged: The inner city, the underclass, and public policy.* Chicago: University of Chicago Press.

Wolfgang, M., & Ferracuti, F. (1967). *The subculture of violence.* London: Tavistock.

Wolfgang, M. E., Figlio, R. M., & Sellin, T. (1972). *Delinquency in a birth cohort.* Chicago: University of Chicago Press.

Wolfgang, M. E., & Tracy, P. E. (1982, February). *The 1945 and 1958 birth cohorts: A comparison of the prevalence, incidence, and severity of delinquent behavior.* Paper presented at the Conference on Public Danger, Dangerous Offenders, and the Criminal Justice System, New Haven, CT.

Wright, J. D., & Rossi, P. H. (1985). *The armed criminal in America: A survey of incarcerated felons.* Washington, DC: National Institute of Justice.

Wright, J. D., Rossi, P. H., & Daly, K. (1983). *Under the gun: Weapons, crime and violence in America.* Hawthorne, NY: Aldine.

Zimring, F. E., & Hawkins, G. (1987). *The citizen's guide to gun control.* New York: Macmillan.

Community Policing

Bayley, D. H. (1989). *A model of community policing: The Singapore story.* Washington, DC: National Institute of Justice.

Bayley, D. H. (1991). *Forces of order.* Berkeley: University of California Press.

Bennett, T. (Ed.). (1983). *The future of policing.* Cambridge, MA: Cambridge Institute of Criminology.

Bowers, W. J., & Hirsch, J. H. (1986). *The impact of foot patrol staffing on crime and disorder in Boston: An unmet promise.* Boston: Northeastern University, Center for Applied Social Research.

Bursik, R. J., & Grasmick, H. G. (1993). *Neighborhoods and crime: The dimensions of effective community control.* New York: Lexington.

DePew, R. (1986). *Native policing in Canada: A review of current issues.* Ottawa, Canada: Ministry of the Solicitor General.

De Witt, C. B. (1992). *Community policing in Seattle: A model partnership between citizens and police.* Washington, DC: National Institute of Justice.

Dunn, C. S., & Steadman, H. J. (1982). *Mental health services in local jails.* Rockville, MD: U.S. Department of Health and Human Services.

Eck, J., & Spelman, W. (1987). *Problem solving: Problem oriented policing in Newport News.* Washington, DC: Police Executive Research Forum.

Ericson, R. V. (1982). *Reproducing order: A study of police patrol work.* Toronto, Canada: Toronto University Press.

Esbensen, F. (1987). Foot patrols: Of what value? *American Journal of Police, 6*(1), 45-65.

Goldstein, H. (1977). *Policing a free society.* Cambridge, MA: Ballinger.

Goldstein, H. (1979). Improving policing: A problem oriented approach. *Crime and Delinquency, 25,* 236-258.

Goldstein, H. (1990). *Problem oriented policing.* Philadelphia: Temple University Press.

Goldstein, H., & Susmlich, C. E. (1981). *Project on development of a problem oriented approach to improving police service.* Madison, University of Wisconsin Law School.

Goldstein, J. (1960). Decisions not to invoke the criminal process: Low visibility decisions in the administration of justice. *Yale Law Journal, 69,* 543-594.

Greene, J. R., & Mastrofski, S. (Eds.). (1988). *Community policing: Rhetoric or reality?* New York: Praeger.

Guyot, D. (1991). *Policing as though people matter.* Philadelphia: Temple University Press.

Hartmann, F. X. (1988). *Community policing: Would you know it if you saw it?* East Lansing: Michigan State University Press.

Hayeslip, D. W., Jr., & Cordner, G. W. (1995). The effects of community oriented patrol on police officer attitudes. *American Journal of Police, 4*(1), 95-119.

Heal, K., & Laycock, G. (Eds.). (1986). *Situational crime prevention: From theory into practice.* London: HMSO.

Hoff, L. A. (1984). *People in crisis: Understanding and helping* (2nd ed.). Menlo Park, CA: Addison-Wesley.

Kelling, G. L., & Bratton, W. J. (1993). *Implementing community policing: The administrative problem* (NCJ141236). Washington, DC: National Institute of Justice.

Kelling, G. L., Pate, T., Dieckman, D., & Brown, C. E. (1974). *The Kansas City Prevention Patrol experience: A summary report.* Washington, DC: Police Foundation.

Kelling, G. L., & Stewart, J. K. (1989). Neighborhoods and police: The maintenance of civil authority (NCJ115950). Washington, DC: National Institute of Justice.

Kennedy, D. (1986). *Neighborhood policing in Los Angeles.* Cambridge, MA: Harvard University, John F. Kennedy School of Government.

Mair, G. (1997). *Evaluating the effectiveness of community penalties.* Brookfield, VT: Ashgate.

Mattei, D. A. (1983). *The order maintenance function of the police.* Philadelphia: Temple University School of Law.

McLaughlin, E. (1994). *Community policing and accountability: The politics of policing in the 1980's.* Brookfield, VT: Aldershot.

Miller, L. S., & Hess, K. M. (1993). *Community policing: Theory and practice.* Minneapolis: West.

Monahan, J. (Ed.). (1976). *Community mental health and the criminal justice system.* Elmsford, NY: Pergamon.

Moore, M. H., & Stephens, D. W. (1991). *Beyond command and control: The management of police departments.* Washington, DC: Police Executive Research Forum.

Murphy, G. (1989). *Managing persons with mental disabilities: A Curriculum guide for trainers.* Washington, DC: Police Executive Research Forum.

Murphy, P. V. (1977). *Commissioner: A view from the top of American law enforcement.* New York: Simon & Schuster.

National Coalition for Jail Reform. (1983). *Jail: The new mental institution* [Pamphlet summary of the conference "The Mentally Ill in Jail: Public Policy Recommendations"]. Washington, DC: Author.

National Coalition for Jail Reform. (1984). *Removing the mentally ill from jail: Case studies of collaboration between local criminal justice and mental health systems.* Washington, DC: Author.

National Institute of Justice. (1984). *Informal citizen action and crime prevention at neighborhood level: Synthesis and assessment of the research* (NCJ094221). Washington, DC: Author.

National Institute of Justice. (1984). *Police and communities: The quiet solution* (NCJ109955). Washington, DC: Author.

National Institute of Justice. (1985). *Guardian Angels: An assessment of citizen response to crime* (NCJ100911). Washington, DC: Author.

National Institute of Justice. (1986). *Crime Stoppers: A national evaluation* (NCJ102292). Washington, DC: Author.

National Institute of Justice. (1987). *Crime Stoppers: A national evaluation of program operations and effects* (NCJ104343). Washington, DC: Author.

National Institute of Justice. (1987). *Problem oriented policing* (NCJ102371). Washington, DC: Author.

National Institute of Justice. (1988). *Community policing: Issues and practices around the world* (NCJ111428). Washington, DC: Author.

National Institute of Justice. (1988). *Crime and policing* (NCJ111460). Washington, DC: Author.

National Institute of Justice. (1988). *Improving the use and effectiveness of neighborhood watch programs* (NCJ108618). Washington, DC: Author.

National Institute of Justice. (1988). *Police accountability and community policing* (NCJ114211). Washington, DC: Author.

National Institute of Justice. (1988). *Policing and the fear of crime* (NCJ111459). Washington, DC: Author.

National Institute of Justice. (1988). *Street level drug enforcement: Examining the issues* (NCJ115403). Washington, DC: Author.

National Institute of Justice. (1989). *Community policing: A practical guide for police officials* (NCJ118001). Washington, DC: Author.

National Institute of Justice. (1992). *Community policing in Seattle: A model partnership between citizens and police* (NCJ136608). Washington, DC: Author.

National Institute of Justice. (1992). *Controlling street level drug trafficking: Evidence from Oakland and Birmingham* (NCJ136165). Washington, DC: Author.

National Institute of Justice. (1992). *Modern policing and the control of illegal drugs: Testing new strategies in two American cities* (NCJ133785). Washington, DC: Author.

National Institute of Justice. (1992). *Police, drugs and public housing* (NCJ136316). Washington, DC: Author.

National Institute of Justice. (1995). *Policing a city's central district: The Oakland story* (NCJ096708). Washington, DC: Author.

Pate, A. M., Skogan, W. G., Wycoff, M. A., & Sherman, L. W. (1985). *Reducing the signs of crime: The Newark experience— executive summary.* Washington, DC: Police Foundation.

Pate, A. M., Wycoff, M. A., Skogan, W. G., & Sherman, L. W. (1986). *Reducing fear of crime in Houston and Newark: A summary report.* Washington, DC: Police Foundation.

Police Foundation. (1981). *The Newark foot patrol experiment.* Washington, DC: Author.

Rosenbaum, D. P. (Ed.). (1987). *Community crisis prevention: Does it work?* Beverly Hills, CA: Sage.

Rosenbaum, D. P. (Ed.). (1994). *The challenge of community policing.* Thousand Oaks, CA: Sage.

Rosenbluh, E. S. (1974). *Techniques of crisis intervention.* Louisville, KY: Rosenbluh & Associates.

Schwartz, A. I., & Clarren, S. N. (1977). *The Cincinnati team policing experiment: A summary report.* Washington, DC: Urban Institute of Police Foundation.

Sherman, L. W. (1995). *Reducing gun violence: Community policing against gun crime* (NCJ 153730) [Videotape]. Washington, DC: National Institute of Justice.

Sherman, L. W., Milton, C. H., & Kelly, T. V. (1973). *Team policing: Seven case studies.* Washington, DC: Police Foundation.

Skogan, W. *Community policing in Chicago: Fact or fiction?* (NCJ153273) [Videotape]. Washington, DC: National Institute of Justice.

Skogan, W. G., & Maxfield, M. (1981). *Coping with crime: Individual and neighborhood reactions.* Beverly Hills, CA: Sage.

Snibbe, J. R., & Snibbe, H. M. (Eds.). (1973). *The urban policeman in transition.* Springfield, IL: Charles C Thomas.

Spelman, W., & Eck, J. (1989). *Newport News tests problem oriented policing* (NCJ104314). Washington, DC: National Institute of Justice.

Trojanowicz, R. C. (1982). *An evaluation of the Neighborhood Foot Patrol Program in Flint, Michigan.* East Lansing: Michigan State University Press.

Trojanowicz, R. C., & Bucqueroux, B. (1993). *Community policing: How to get started.* Cincinnati, OH: Anderson.

Wadman, R. C., & Olson, R. K. (1990). *Community wellness: A new theory of policing.* Washington, DC: Police Executive Research Forum.

Walker, S. (1977). *A critical history of police reform.* Lexington, MA: D. C. Heath.

Walker, S. (1992). *The police in America.* New York: McGraw-Hill.

Wasson, D. K. (1977). *Community based preventive policing: A review.* Ottawa, Canada: Solicitor Generals Office.

Willmott, P. (Ed.). (1987). *Policing and the community.* London: Policing Studies Institute.

Wilson, J. Q. (1986). Foreword. In Police Foundation, *Reducing fear of crime in Houston and New York: Summary report.* Washington, DC: Police Foundation.

Wycoff, M., & Oettmeier, T. N. (1994). *Evaluating patrol officer performance under community policing: The Houston experiment* (NCJ 142462). Washington, DC: National Institute of Justice.

Wycoff, M. A., Skogan, W., Pate, A., & Sherman, L. W. (1985). *Citizen contact patrol: Executive summary.* Washington, DC: Police Foundation.

Wycoff, M. A., Skogan, W., Pate, A., & Sherman, L. W. (1985). *Citizen contract patrol: The Houston field test.* Washington, DC: Police Foundation.

Wycoff, M. A., Skogan, W., Pate, A., & Sherman, L. W. (1985). *Police community stations: The Houston field test.* Washington, DC: Police Foundation.

Yin, R. K. (1994). Community crime prevention: A synthesis of eleven evaluations. In D. P. Rosenbaum (Ed.), *Community crime prevention: Does it work?* (pp. 294-308). Beverly Hills, CA: Sage.

Community-Based Corrections

Aaronson, D. E., Hof, B. H., Jaszi, P., Kittrie, N., & Sarri, D. (1977). *The new justice: Alternatives to conventional criminal adjudication.* Washington, DC: Government Printing Office.

Adams, S. (1977). *Evaluative research in corrections: A practical guide.* Washington, DC: U.S. Department of Justice, Law Enforcement Assistance Administration, National Institute of Law Enforcement and Criminal Justice.

Allen, H. E., Carlson, E. W., Parks, E. C., & Latessa, E. J. (1980). *Parole effectiveness in the United States: An assessment.* San Jose, CA: San Jose State University Research Foundation.

Allen, H. E., & Simonsen, C. (1995). *Corrections in America.* Englewood Cliffs, NJ: Prentice Hall.

American Correctional Association. (1993). *Community partnerships in action.* Laurel, MD: Author.

Beccaria, C. (1963). *On crimes and punishments* (H. Paulucci, Trans.). Indianapolis: Bobbs-Merrill. (Original work published 1764)

Beck, A., & Bonczar, T. (1994). *State and federal prison population tops one million.* Washington, DC: U.S. Department of Justice.

Bentham, J. (1973). *An introduction to the principles of morals and legislation.* Garden City, NY: Anchor. (Original work published 1789)

Blumstein, A., Cohen, J., Roth, J. A., & Visher, C. A. (Eds.). (1986). *Criminal careers and "career criminals."* Washington, DC: National Academy Press.

Braithwaite, J. (1989). *Crime, shame and reintegration.* New York: Cambridge University Press.

Bureau of Justice Statistics. (1995). *Correctional populations in the United States.* Washington, DC: U.S. Department of Justice.

Camp, C., & Camp, G. (1995). *The corrections yearbook, 1994: Adult corrections.* South Salem, NY: Criminal Justice Institute.

Castle, M. (1989). *Alternative sentencing: Selling it to the public.* Washington, DC: U.S. Department of Justice.

Champion, D. (1994). *Measuring offender risk: A criminal justice sourcebook.* Westport, CT: Greenwood.

Clear, T. R. (1978). *A model for supervising the offender in the community.* Washington, DC: National Institute of Corrections.

Clear, T. (1987). *The new intensive supervision movement* [Mimeographed paper, Rutgers University.

Coleman, S., & Guthrie, K. (1988). *Sentencing effectiveness in preventing crime.* St. Paul, MN: Criminal Justice Statistical Analysis Center.

Crawford, D., & Bodine, R. (1996). *Conflict resolution education.* Washington, DC: Office of Juvenile Justice and Delinquency Prevention.

Cullen, F., Van Voorhis, P., & Sundt, J. (1996). Prisons in crisis: The American experience. In R. Matthews & F. Francis (Eds.), *Prisons 2000: An international perspective on the current state and future of imprisonment* (pp. 21-52). New York: Macmillan.

Duffee, D. (1989). *Corrections: Practice and policy.* New York: Random House.

Duffee, D. E., & McGarrell, E. F. (1990). *Community corrections.* Cincinnati, OH: Anderson.

Ellsworth, T. (Ed.). (1992). *Contemporary community corrections.* Prospect Heights, IL: Waveland.

Erwin, B. (1984). *Georgia's intensive supervision program: First year evaluation.* Atlanta: Department of Offender Rehabilitation.

Farrington, D., & Tarling, R. (Eds.). *Prediction in criminology* (pp. 78-94). Albany: State University of New York Press.

Garland, D. (1990). *Punishment and modern society: A study in social theory.* Chicago: University of Chicago Press.

Gendreau, P. (1995). The principles of effective intervention with offenders. In A. Harland (Ed.), *Choosing correctional options that work: Defining the demand and evaluating the supply.* Thousand Oaks, CA: Sage.

Gendreau, P., & Paparozzi, M. (1995). Examining what works in community corrections. *Corrections Today, 56*(8), 28-30.

Gendreau, P., & Ross, R. R. (1987). Revivification of rehabilitation: Evidence from the 1980s. *Justice Quarterly, 4,* 349-408.

Gibbons, D. C. (1988). *The limits of punishments as social policy.* New York: Edna McConnell Clark Foundation.

Glaser, D. (1969). *The effectiveness of a prison and parole system.* Indianapolis: Bobbs-Merrill.

Greenfield, L., & Minor-Harper, S. *Women in prison.* Washington, DC: U.S. Department of Justice.

Greenwood, P. W., & Zimring, F. E. (1985). *One more chance: The pursuit of promising intervention strategies for chronic juvenile offenders.* Santa Monica, CA: RAND Corporation.

Gottfredson, S., & Gottfredson, D. (1992). *Incapacitation strategies and the criminal career.* Sacramento, CA: California Division of Law Enforcement.

Gottfredson, S. D., & Taylor, R. B. (1983). *The correctional crisis: Prison populations and public policy.* Washington, DC: U.S. Department of Justice.

Gowdy, V. (1993). *Intermediate sanctions.* Washington, DC: U.S. Department of Justice.

Greenwood, P. (1983). *Selective incapacitation.* Santa Monica, CA: RAND Corporation.

Hahn, P. (1984). *The juvenile offender and the law* (3rd ed.). Cincinnati, OH: Anderson.

Huff, C. R., Rattner, A., & Sagarin, E. (1996). *Convicted but innocent: Wrongful conviction and public policy.* Thousand Oaks, CA: Sage.

Janowski, L. (1990). *Probation and parole 1989* (Bureau of Justice Statistics Bulletin). Washington, DC: U.S. Department of Justice.

Irwin, J., & Austin, J. (1994). *It's about time: America's imprisonment binge.* Belmont, CA: Wadsworth.

Klofas, J., & Stojkovic, S. (1995). *Crime and justice in the year 2010.* Belmont, CA: Wadsworth.

Krisberg, B., Austin, J., & Steele, P. A. (1989). *Unlocking juvenile corrections: Evaluating the Massachusetts Department of Youth Services.* San Francisco: National Council on Crime and Delinquency.

Lauen, R. L. (1988). *Community-managed corrections.* Washington, DC: American Correctional Association.

Lemert, E. M. (1970). *Social action and legal change.* Chicago: Aldine.

Lozoff, B., & Braswell, M. (1989). *Inner corrections.* Cincinnati, OH: Anderson.

Mair, G. (1997). *Evaluating the effectiveness of community penalties.* Brookfield, VT: Ashgate.

Martinson, R. M., & Wilks, J. (1971). *Treatment evaluation survey.* Unpublished study, New York Division of Criminal Justice Services.

McCleary, R. (1978). *Dangerous men: The sociology of parole.* Beverly Hills, CA: Sage.

McDonald, D., Greene, J., & Worzella, C. (1995). *Day fines in American courts.* Washington, DC: U.S. Department of Justice.

Miller, A. D., & Ohlin, L. E. (1983). *Final report of research on correctional reforms in the Massachusetts Department of Youth Services.* Boston: Harvard Law School, Center for Criminal Justice.

Miller, A. D., & Ohlin, L. E. (1985). *Delinquency and community.* Beverly Hills, CA: Sage.

Miller, J. G. (1991). *Last one over the wall.* Columbus: Ohio State University Press.

Mitford, J. (1973). *Kind and usual punishment.* New York: Knopf.

Morris, N. (1974). *The future of imprisonment.* Chicago: University of Chicago Press.

Morris, N., & Tonry, M. (1990). *Between prison and probation.* New York: Oxford Press.

Nagel, W. (1973). *The new red barn.* New York: Walker.

National Advisory Commission on Criminal Justice Standards and Goals. (1973). *Corrections.* Washington, DC: Government Printing Office.

National Institute of Corrections. (1989). *1989 directory of residential community corrections facilities in the United States.* Longmont, CO: National Institute of Corrections.

Newman, G. (1983). *Just and painful: The case for the corporal punishment of criminals.* New York: Free Press.

Office of National Drug Control Policy, Executive Office of the President. (1997). *The National drug control strategy, 1997.* Washington, DC: Author.

O'Leary, V., & Clear, T. (1984). *Directions for community corrections in the 1990's.* Washington, DC: U.S. Department of Justice.

Packer, H. (1968). *The limits of the criminal sanction.* Stanford, CA: Stanford University Press.

Petersilia, J. M. (1983). *Racial disparities in the criminal justice system.* Santa Monica, CA: RAND Corporation.

Petersilia, J. (1987). *Expanding options for criminal sentencing.* Santa Monica, CA: RAND Corporation.

Petersilia, J. (1988). *Conditions for implementing successful intensive supervision programs.* Santa Monica, CA: RAND Corporation.

Pollock, J. M. (1994). *Ethics in crime and justice* (2nd ed.). Belmont, CA: Wadsworth.

President's Commission on Law Enforcement and Administration of Justice. (1967). *Task force report: Corrections.* Washington, DC: Government Printing Office.

Reiman, J. (1995). *The rich get richer and the poor get prison* (4th ed.). Boston: Allyn & Bacon.

Rubin, H. T. (1985). *Juvenile justice: Policy, practice and law* (2nd ed.). New York: Random House.

Schwartz, I. M. (1992). *Juvenile justice and public policy.* New York: Lexington.

Shusta, R. M., Levine, D. R., Harris, P. R., & Wong, H. Z. (1995). *Multicultural law enforcement.* Englewood Cliffs, NJ: Prentice Hall.

Silberman, M. (1995). *A world of violence: Corrections in America.* Belmont, CA: Wadsworth.

Simon, J. (1993). *Poor discipline: Parole and social control of the underclass, 1890-1990.* Chicago: University of Chicago Press.

Skogan, W. G., & Maxfield, M. G. (1981). *Coping with crime: Individual and neighborhood reactions.* Newbury Park, CA: Sage.

Smykla, J., & Selke, W. (Eds.). (1976). *Intermediate sanctions: Sentencing in the 1990s.* Cincinnati, OH: Anderson.

Stanley, D. (1976). *Prisoners among us.* Washington, DC: Brookings Institute.

Toch, H. (1977). *Living in prison: The ecology of survival.* New York: Free Press.

Toch, H. (1981). *Therapeutic communities.* New York: Praeger.

Tonry, M., & Will, R. (1989). *Intermediate sanctions.* Washington, DC: Government Printing Office.

Tunis, S., Morris, M., Hardyman, P., & Bolyard, M. (1996). *Evaluation of drug treatment in local corrections.* Washington, DC: U.S. Department of Justice.

Umbreit, M. (1994). *Victim meets offender: The impact of restorative justice and mediation.* Monsey, NY: Criminal Justice Press.

van den Haag, E. (1975). *Punishing criminals: Concerning a very old and painful question.* New York: Basic Books.

von Hirsch, A. (1985). *Past or future crimes: Deservedness and dangerousness in the sentencing of criminals.* New Brunswick, NJ: Rutgers University Press.

von Hirsch, A. (1986). *Doing justice: The choice of punishments.* Boston: Northeastern University Press. (Original work published 1976)

von Hirsch, A., & Hanrahan, K. (1978). *Abolish parole?* Washington, DC: Government Printing Office.

von Hirsch, A., & Hanrahan, K. (1979). *The question of parole: Retention, reform, or abolition.* Cambridge, MA: Ballinger.

von Hirsch, A., Knapp, K. A., & Tonry, M. (1987). *The sentencing commission and its guidelines.* Boston: Northeastern University Press.

Wagner, D., & Baird, C. (1993). *Evaluation of the Florida community control program.* Washington, DC: U.S. Department of Justice.

Wilson, J. Q. (1983). *Thinking about crime.* New York: Basic Books.

Winterfield, L., & Hillsman, S. (1993). *The Staten Island day-fine project.* Washington, DC: U.S. Department of Justice.

Zimring, F., & Hawkins, G. (1995). *Incapacitation: Penal confinement and the restraint of crime.* New York: Oxford University Press.

Restorative Justice

Armstrong, T., Maloney, D., & Romig, D. (1990, Winter). The balanced approach in juvenile probation. *Perspectives,* pp. 8-13.

Bazemore, G. (1991). New concepts in alternative practice in community supervision of juvenile offenders. *Journal of Crime and Justice, 14,* 27-35.

Berman, H. (1983). *Law and resolution: The formation of Western legal tradition.* Cambridge, MA: Harvard University Press.

Clarke, S. (1993, October). *Community justice and victim offender mediation programs.* Working paper prepared for the National Symposium on Court Connected Dispute Resolution Research, Alexandria, VA.

Day, F., & Gallati, R. (1978). *Introduction to law enforcement in criminal justice.* Springfield, IL: Charles C Thomas.

Doble, J., Immerwahr, S., & Richardson, A. (1991). *Punishing criminals: The people of Delaware consider the options.* New York: Edna McConnell Clark Foundation.

Eglash, A. (1977). Beyond restitution: Creative restitution. In J. Hudson & B. Galaway (Eds.), *Restitution in criminal justice.* Lexington, MA: Lexington.

Galaway, B., & Hudson, J. (Eds.). (1990). *Criminal justice, restitution and reconciliation.* Monsey, NY: Criminal Justice Press.

Goldstein, A., & Huff, R. (Eds.). (1992). *The gang intervention handbook.* Champaign, IL: Research Press.

Hahn, P. H. (1984). *The juvenile offender and the law* (3rd ed.). Cincinnati, OH: Anderson.

Hughes, S. P., & Schneider, A. C. (1989). Victim offender mediation: A survey of program characteristics and perceptions of effectiveness. *Crime and Delinquency, 35,* 217-238.

Kelling, G. L., & Coles, C. M. (1996). *Fixing broken windows: Restoring order and reducing crime in our communities.* New York: Free Press.

Klein, A. (1988). *Alternative sentencing: A practitioner's guide.* Cincinnati, OH: Anderson.

Lawrence, R. (1991). Re-examining community corrections models. *Crime and Delinquency, 37,* 436-449.

Lozoff, B., & Braswell, M. (1989). *Inner corrections.* Cincinnati, OH: Anderson.

Maloney, D., Romig, D., & Armstrong, T. (1988). Juvenile probation: The balanced approach. *Juvenile and Family Court Journal, 39*(3), 1-63.

Morris, N., & Tonry, M. (1989). *Between prison and probation.* New York: Oxford University Press.

Pact Institute of Justice. (n.d.). *Restorative justice resources* [Brochure].

Pittman, K., & Fleming, W. (1991). *A new vision: Promoting youth development.* Testimony to House Select Committee on Children, Youth and Families, Washington, DC.

Pranis, K., & Umbreit, M. (1992). *Public opinion research challenges perception of widespread public demand for harsher punishment.* Minneapolis: Minnesota Citizens Council.

Rosenberry, M. (1986). *Urban conservation and Service Corps programs: A series of research reports.* Washington, DC: Washington Human Environment Center.

Schneider, A. (1986). Restitution and recidivism rates of juvenile offenders: Results from four experimental studies. *Criminology, 24,* 533-552.

Schneider, A. (1985). *Deterrence in juvenile crime: Results from a national policy experiment.* New York: Springer-Verlag.

Souryal, S. (1992). *Ethics in criminal justice.* Cincinnati, OH: Anderson.

Stoneman, D., & Calvert, J. (1990). *Youth build: A manual for the implementation of the Housing Related Enhanced Work Experience Program.* New York: Coalition for $20 Million.

Umbreit, M. (1989). Victims seeking fairness, not revenge: Toward restorative justice. *Federal Probation, 53*(3), 52-57.

Umbreit, M. (1993). *How to increase referrals to victim offender mediation programs.* Ontario, Canada: Funds for Dispute Resolution.

Van Ness, D. W. (1990). Restorative justice. In B. Galaway & J. Hudson (Eds.), *Criminal justice, restitution and reconciliation.* Monsey, NJ: Willowtree.

Van Ness, D. W., Carlson, D. R., Jr., Crawford, T., & Strong, K. (1989). *Restorative justice: Theory.* Washington, DC: Justice Fellowship.

Zehr, H. (1985). *Retributive justice, restorative justice.* Office of Criminal Justice, Canada Victim Offender Ministries Program.

Index

About the Author

Paul H. Hahn is an author, lecturer, and consultant. He founded the Department of Criminal Justice at Xavier University in Cincinnati, Ohio, and served as Department Chair until his retirement in 1997. Before that he was Chief Probation Officer and Director of Court Services for a large metropolitan area juvenile court and was cofounder and Director of one of the earliest halfway houses for delinquent boys in the United States. He served on the faculty of the National College of Juvenile and Family Court Judges (Reno, Nevada) for several years and at the National Conference on Corrections Policy (Williamsburg II). He is the author of five books and numerous articles. He has been an expert witness in federal courts in several states on such topics as jail conditions and classification of risk factors. He has received many awards, including the Peter Lejins Award from the American Correctional Association and the President's Award from the International Association of Correctional Officers. He has testified before committees of the U.S. Senate and House of Representatives and has provided staff training and technical assistance in numerous jurisdictions throughout the country.